PRAYER: A GUIDE FOR THE PERPLEXED

BLOOMSBURY GUIDES FOR THE PERPLEXED

Bloomsbury's Guides for the Perplexed are clear, concise and accessible introductions to thinkers, writers and subjects that students and readers can find especially challenging. Concentrating specifically on what it is that makes the subject difficult to grasp, these books explain and explore key themes and ideas, guiding the reader towards a thorough understanding of demanding material.

Guides for the Perplexed available from Bloomsbury include:

Atonement: A Guide for the Perplexed, Adam Johnson
Balthasar: A Guide for the Perplexed, Rodney Howsare
Barth: A Guide for the Perplexed, Paul Nimmo
Benedict XVI: A Guide for the Perplexed, Tracey Rowland
Bonhoeffer: A Guide for the Perplexed, Joel Lawrence
Calvin: A Guide for the Perplexed, Paul Helm
De Lubac: A Guide for the Perplexed, David Grummett
Luther: A Guide for the Perplexed, David M. Whitford
Pannenberg: A Guide for the Perplexed, Timothy Bradshaw
Pneumatology: A Guide for the Perplexed, Daniel Castelo
Political Theology: A Guide for the Perplexed, Elizabeth Philips
Postliberal Theology: A Guide for the Perplexed, Ronald T. Michener
Schleiermacher: A Guide for the Perplexed, Theodore Vial
Scripture: A Guide for the Perplexed, William Lamb
Tillich: A Guide for the Perplexed, Andrew O' Neil
Wesley: A Guide for the Perplexed, Jason A. Vickers
Žižek: A Guide for the Perplexed, Sean Sheehan

Forthcoming Guides for the Perplexed available from Bloomsbury include:

Catholic Social Teaching: A Guide for the Perplexed, Anna Rowlands
God-Talk: A Guide for the Perplexed, Aaron B. James and Ryan S. Peterson
Resurrection: A Guide for the Perplexed, Lidija Novakovic
Salvation: A Guide for the Perplexed, Ivor J. Davidson
Schillebeeckx: A Guide for the Perplexed, Stephan van Erp

PRAYER: A GUIDE FOR THE PERPLEXED

Ashley Cocksworth

LONDON • NEW YORK • OXFORD • NEW DELHI • SYDNEY

T&T CLARK

Bloomsbury Publishing Plc

50 Bedford Square, London, WC1B 3DP, UK

BLOOMSBURY, T&T CLARK and the T&T Clark logo are trademarks of Bloomsbury
Publishing Plc

First published in Great Britain 2018

A catalogue record for this book is available from the British Library.

A catalog record for this book is available from the Library of Congress.

ISBN: HB: 978-0-5671-9872-3
PB: 978-0-5672-2667-9
ePDF: 978-0-5676-8222-2
eBook: 978-0-5676-8221-5

Typeset by Deanta Global Publishing Services, Chennai, India
Printed and bound in Great Britain

To find out more about our authors and books visit www.bloomsbury.com and
sign up for our newsletters.

CONTENTS

ACKNOWLEDGEMENTS

The thinking expressed in this book has been shaped over several years of teaching Christian doctrine at the Queen's Foundation, Birmingham. Many of the ideas developed in what follows saw the light of day in the lecture room and have been gratefully refined in dialogue with students and colleagues. To my colleagues, I owe further debt of gratitude for their assistance in crafting the annotated bibliography and for their unfailing support and encouragement through the highs and lows of writing this book. Those who have been available to step in on the many occasions when my curiosity extended beyond my proficiency are numerous and deserving of my thanks: David Allen, Eunice Attwood, Al Barrett, Ann Conway-Jones, Jonathan Dean, Mark Earey, Samuel Ewell, David F. Ford, Matthias Grebe, David Grumett, Gary Hall, Andrew Hayes, Mike Higton, Robert Leigh, Andrea Russell, Nicola Slee, Rachel Starr, Richard Sudworth and Simon Sutcliffe – many of whom endured the unenviable job of reading and commenting on the first drafts of individual chapters. The book is better for their labour, and all remaining errors are mine. Ampleforth Abbey in North Yorkshire provided a place of prayer, study and Benedictine hospitality during the final stages of writing this book, for which I am grateful. The Society for the Study of Theology remains a place of support and friendship. I owe thanks to Gillian Lever for conversations about prayer and for her kind permission to feature one of her splendid paintings on the cover of this book. Anna Turton and her team at T&T Clark have been patient and discerning in bringing the work to print. It is always a pleasure to work with them.

The debts of gratitude to my family continue to mount. I am grateful to Hannah, my wife, for her love, companionship and expertise on the theme of prayer in the Gospel of Luke and the Book of Acts that formed much of the thinking behind Chapter 4 of this book. Then there is Gatsby, who is to be acknowledged for his feline interjections. My brothers and sisters-in-law, mostly unknowingly, have been pillars of support, as have my nieces and goddaughters – Ruby, Ivy, Ciara Brigit, Annabelle and Piper – all of whom arrived over the course of writing this book. Finally, to my parents and parents-in-law, Charlotte and Christopher, and Elaine and Graham, to whom this book is dedicated, I am always indebted. My thanks especially to Graham for the conversations and companionship we shared on the Camino de Santiago during which the final draft of this book was finished. Each in their own way has taught me more than I could express in writing about the theology of prayer.

COPYRIGHT ACKNOWLEDGEMENTS

LIST OF ABBREVIATIONS

ACW	Ancient Christian Writers
ANF	The Ante-Nicene Fathers: Translations of the Writings of the Fathers down to A.D. 325
CD	Karl Barth, *Church Dogmatics*, 4 volumes in 13 parts (Edinburgh: T&T Clark, 1956-75)
ChrL	Karl Barth, *The Christian Life: Church Dogmatics IV/4 – Lecture Fragments* (Edinburgh: T&T Clark, 1981)
CWS	Classics of Western Spirituality
De oratione	Origen, 'On Prayer', in *Origen: An Exhortation to Martyrdom, Prayer and Selected Works*, trans. by Rowan E. Greer, CWS (New York: Paulist Press, 1979), 41–79
Inst.	John Calvin, *Institutes of the Christian Religion*, The Library of Christian Classics (Louisville: Westminster John Knox Press, 1960)
On Prayer	Evagrius of Ponticus, 'On Prayer', in *Evagrius Ponticus*, trans. by Augustine Casiday (London: Routledge, 2006), 185–201
NPNF	A Select Library of the Nicene and Post-Nicene Fathers of the Christian Church
SCG	Thomas Aquinas, *Summa contra Gentiles* (Notre Dame: University of Notre Dame Press, 1975)
ST	Thomas Aquinas, *Summa Theologiae*, 61 volumes (London: Blackfriars, 1964–81).

INTRODUCTION

This book stands in a long tradition of giving guidance on that most perplexing of subjects: the practice of Christian prayer. The tradition of teaching about Christian prayer is as old as prayer itself. The disciples sought guidance from Jesus on the topic of prayer (Mt. 6.9-13; Lk. 11.2-4). The first theological engagements with the subject usually took form as letters written in response to those seeking guidance on prayer and as pastoral homilies providing instruction on prayer to congregations. Down the ages there have been countless treatises on prayer distilling and communicating centuries of wisdom from one generation to the next. Guides on prayer have been written from nearly every conceivable angle. There are prayer manuals, resources, courses, even 'pray-as-you-go' apps for smartphones. Some of these guides recover classical ways of praying that have been lost in history. Others tackle some of the trickier issues prayer presents. How can we make theological sense of the litany of prayers that go unanswered? How can we deepen through prayer in relationship with God? How do we discern what we should pray for in the first place? Others still target particular demographics – women, men, children, Anglicans, Methodists, Pentecostals, Roman Catholics, new Christians, old Christians. That prayer has so often required teaching, explanation and accompaniment makes one thing clear: prayer is not always self-explanatory. Prayer requires a guide. My hope is that this book might contribute in a small way to the rich body of wisdom that gives guidance on the topic of Christian prayer.

In another sense, this book attempts something a little different. The contribution of this book is to pursue the everyday practice of prayer on a more 'doctrinal' level than is sometimes customary. These days, books on prayer are more likely to populate the shelves of Christian bookstores than the Christian doctrine stacks of academic libraries. Courses on prayer are more likely to be offered by churches than by universities. Prayer is very often confined to the 'devotional realm'. But this has not always been the case. Once prayer was seen to be utterly central to the intellectual task of theology. While Chapter 2 will attempt to address some of the factors that led to the pulling apart of 'prayer' and 'theology', the general aim in each of the chapters is to showcase prayer as indispensable to the nature and task of Christian theology. Some of the key questions this book asks include: What is the theological significance of prayer? What are we doing theologically when we pray? How can a focus on prayer reveal new depths to our theological understanding of God, the world and the self? And, what, theologically speaking, *is* prayer?

Working very deliberately at what we will soon discover to be the fertile intersection of prayer and theology, this book assumes and agrees with what Mark A. McIntosh has called the 'integrity' of spirituality and theology.[1] To explain what he means by this integrity, McIntosh refers to the twentieth-century contemplative Thomas Merton and his oft-cited description of the relation between theology and contemplation, which is worth citing again:

> Contemplation, far from being opposed to theology, is in fact the normal perfection of theology. We must not separate intellectual study of divinely revealed truth and contemplative experience of that truth as if they could never have anything to do with one another. On the contrary, they are simply two aspects of the same thing. Dogmatic and mystical theology, or theology and 'spirituality', are not to be set apart in mutually exclusive categories, as if mysticism were for saintly women and theological study were for practical but, alas, unsaintly men. This fallacious division perhaps explains much that is actually lacking in theology and spirituality. But the two belong together. Unless they are united there is no fervour, no life and no spiritual value in theology, no substance, no meaning and no sure orientation in the contemplative life.[2]

Following Merton, we will also treat theology and prayer as rightly 'belonging together'. This book seeks to describe a porous relation between theology and prayer with each osmotically flowing into the other, interpreting the other, revealing new perspectives on each other. In prayer, the theologian learns to use the word 'God' with more wisdom and a bit less muddle; and doctrine provides the practice of prayer with articulation, shape and definition. Central doctrines of the church, as we shall see, develop out

---

[1] See Mark A. McIntosh, *Mystical Theology: The Integrity of Spirituality and Theology* (Oxford: Wiley-Blackwell, 1998), 3–38.
[2] Thomas Merton, *New Seeds of Contemplation* (New York: New Directions Publishing, 1972), 254–5.

of a context and community of prayer; and prayer enacts, embodies and renders visible these doctrines in the life of the community. The things Christians believe and the things Christians practice in prayer should 'hang together' and make sense of each other. The practice of prayer also holds the theological task to account. It keeps the study of theology focused on its subject matter: God, and on its doxological telos. Theology, classically understood, does not seek merely to speak about God but its ultimate end is to delight in the glorification of God.[3] In constant dialogue with prayer, the study of theology becomes more obviously formative: it becomes itself a sort of prayer, a spiritual practice.

One of this book's primary dialogue partners is the fourth-century desert mystic Evagrius of Ponticus. He dominates Chapter 1, which provides a close reading of his zany treatise *On Prayer*, and he looms large over many of the chapters thereafter. Although guidance on prayer is the presenting issue in his treatise – it is the reason Evagrius is writing in the first place – the subject of prayer is not his exclusive concern. His broader concern is not so much the one praying but the unavoidably related question of the One addressed in prayer. In other words, the subject of *On Prayer* is not simply prayer, but also God. As Karl Rahner writes, 'The question of God and the question of prayer are not properly two questions that must be answered consecutively, but *one* question.'[4] Similarly, in thinking about prayer in this book, we cannot avoid thinking about God. Who is the God experienced in prayer? How does God's action in the world relate to the human activity of prayer? How can our understandings of God be invigorated and challenged by prayer?

The kind of commitment to the theological shape of prayer and the doxological shape of theology that this book is attempting to explicate reaches back to the ancient understanding of the union of prayer and theology that is typical of Evagrius and summarized by others as the *lex orandi, lex credendi* (which can be translated as 'the law of prayer is the law of belief'). Although doing theology according to the *lex orandi* appears somewhat unfashionable in some of the intellectual trends of modern theology, there are other contemporary theological discourses, important

---

[3]For a brilliant example of theology culminating in praise, see Daniel W. Hardy and David Ford, *Jubilate: Theology in Praise* (London: Darton, Longman and Todd, 1984).
[4]Karl Rahner, *Christian at the Crossroads* (New York: Seabury Press, 1975), 52.

to mention from the outset, that are already well underway in reclaiming what was anciently held together.

In particular, an analogous Christian wisdom about the theological importance of the experience of prayer emanates from feminist theologies, liberation theologies and the field of practical theology more generally. The influence of these discourses can be felt on a subterranean level throughout this book and surface in Chapter 6 when we come to consider the politics of prayer in the Christian life. These discourses began in critical dialogue with many of the conventional assumptions and criteria by which modern theology was seen to operate. Especially relevant to the present discussion is the way these discourses called into question what David Tracy named the 'fatal split' between theory and practice (and the assertion of the former over the latter) that unhelpfully crept into modern ways of doing theology.[5] Practical theology, according to Elaine Graham, therefore seeks 'to recognize that theory and practice do not exist independently'.[6] The methodological point of departure within practical theology tends to be the practising of practices rather than the thinking of belief. Much of feminist theology has similarly questioned the modern habit of holding the practice of prayer and the theory of theology apart. Tina Beattie, for example, seeks a way of weaving 'together spirituality and theology that might take us beyond modernity'.[7] Feminist theology also pre-empts a further methodological move this book makes concerning what 'counts' as sources for theological reflection. While much of modern systematic theology has been dominated by a rather narrowly conceived canon of literature, feminist theology widens the field to include the silenced voices of women and the genres of theological writing in which those voices are historically held – such as poetry, devotional writing, hymn writing and lived experience. Following feminist theology, this book likewise aims to listen to the occluded voices and genres of theological writing that are sometimes marginalized by the theological canon. A focus on

---

[5]David Tracy, 'On Theological Education: A Reflection', in *Theological Literacy for the Twenty-First Century*, ed. by Rodney L. Petersen and Nancy M. Rourke (Grand Rapids: William B. Eerdmans, 2002), 15.

[6]Elaine L. Graham, *Transforming Practice: Pastoral Theology in an Age of Uncertainty* (London: Mowbray, 1996), 7. For an account of the relation of prayer and theology in the field of practical theology, see Andre van Oudtshoorn, 'Prayer and Practical Theology', *International Journal of Practical Theology*, 16.2 (2012), 285–303.

[7]Tina Beattie, *New Catholic Feminism: Theology and Theory* (London: Routledge, 2006), 82. https://www.amazon.co.uk/New-Catholic-Feminism-Theology-Theory/dp/0415301483

prayer makes attending to marginalized figures (such as Evagrius), sidelined writings of mainline thinkers and neglected genres of writing unavoidable for it is here that discussions on prayer tend to take place. Finally, as we will see in Chapter 6, Latin American liberation theologies also assume the same integrity of prayer and theology. 'When it is said and done, then, all authentic theology is spiritual theology', says Gustavo Gutiérrez.[8] Rerouting the theological task through the practice of prayer, as liberation theologians and others have done, means that the question of what it means to live wisely in this world, as well as what it means to think theologically, finds its answer in prayer.[9]

Another noticeable development in contemporary systematic theology informing this book's approach is the current 'turn' to the practices of the Christian life as sources of theology. The reasons for the theological turn to practices are complex. They include, as Reinhard Hütter explains, 'a recovery of Aristotelian practical theology, mainly through the words of Alasdair MacIntyre; a re-emergence of the never completely extinguished interest in the practical aspect of the Christian faith in the Wesleyan, Holiness and Pentecostal strands of American theology; and an overall renewal of interest in various forms of pragmatism after the alleged demise of metaphysical thinking'.[10] The renewed theological interest in practices manifests itself visibly in the influential strand of Christian ethics known as 'ecclesial ethics' (also discussed in Chapter 6) and by those interested in explicating

---

[8]Gustavo Gutiérrez, *We Drink from Our Own Wells: The Spiritual Journey of a People* (London: SCM Press, 2005), 37.

[9]The following list, incomplete as it is, should give an indication of the rich potential of prayer as a dialogue partner elsewhere in contemporary theological discussion: Francesca Bugliani Knox and John Took (eds), *Poetry and Prayer: The Power of the Word II* (London: Routledge, 2015); Giuseppe Giordan and Linda Woodhead (eds), *A Sociology of Prayer* (London: Routledge, 2015); Bernard Spilka and Kevin L. Ladd, *The Psychology of Prayer: A Scientific Approach* (London: The Guildford Press, 2013); David Marshall and Lucinda Mosher (eds), *Prayer: Christian and Muslim Perspectives* (Washington: Georgetown University Press, 2013); Bruce Ellis Benson and Norman Wirzba (eds), *The Phenomenology of Prayer* (New York: Fordham University Press, 2005); and Andrew Prevot, *Thinking Prayer: Theology and Spirituality amid the Crisis of Modernity* (Notre Dame: University of Notre Dame Press, 2015).

[10]Reinhard Hütter, 'The Christian Life', in *The Oxford Handbook of Systematic Theology*, ed. by John Webster, Kathryn Tanner and Iain Torrance (Oxford: Oxford University Press, 2007), 285–305 (296–7). See also, Colin M. McGuigan and Brad J. Kallenberg, 'Ecclesial Practices', in *The Oxford Handbook of the Epistemology of Theology*, ed. by William J. Abraham and Frederick D. Aquino (Oxford: Oxford University Press, 2017), 141–56.

the theological significance of 'everyday practices' of the Christian life.[11] In any case, the result is roughly the same: practices become the primary subject matter of theological discourse. The meanings of the word 'God' are discovered in what the community of God *does*. Christianity practises what it believes. Caught up in the sustained interest in Christian practices are the more specific turns to the practice of prayer currently underway within systematic theology.[12] This book rides off the back of these 'turns to prayer' that discover anew (often helped along by a recovery of the mystical traditions of spirituality) theology's inextricable relation to prayer. Systematic theology, we shall see, is thus most systematic when it attends to prayer and loses some of its edge when prayer is neglected. But before going any further, there is a more fundamental question to ask: what do we mean by 'prayer'?

A note on Christian 'prayer'

In the Christian tradition prayer accommodates multiple meanings and definitions. Prayer can mean the individual practices of petition, contemplation, thanksgiving, lament, meditation, praise and much more. It can mean praying in tongues and in silence. It can mean praying privately and corporately. Prayer can take place through sacred objects – prayer beads, prayer ropes – and through sacred art such as icons. It can be accompanied by fasting and feasting. Prayer can involve methods such as the Prayer of the Heart, the Jesus Prayer and Hesychasm.[13] For some prayer means kneeling, for others it can also mean using the body in other ways such as signing the body, clasping hands, lifting hands, closing eyes, keeping eyes open. And any one of the individual practices of prayer, some of which derive directly from Paul's letter to Timothy (1 Tim. 2.1) and others do not, may well accommodate multiple meanings. Individual practices of prayer

---

[11]Dorothy C. Bass and Miroslav Volf (eds), *Practicing Theology: Beliefs and Practices in Christian Life* (Grand Rapids: William B. Eerdmans, 2001).

[12]Systematic theology, as a discipline, is currently experiencing something of a revival. Interestingly, in the new wave of systematic theology, practices of prayer are embraced with renewed theological seriousness. Examples of contemporary theologians (referenced in Chapter 2) undertaking their systematic theology with explicit reference to prayer include the large-scale, ongoing systematic projects of Sarah Coakley, Graham Ward, Katherine Sonderegger and Paul R. Hinlicky.

[13]On these methods, see John Anthony McGuckin, *The Orthodox Church: An Introduction to its History, Doctrine, and Spiritual Culture* (Oxford: Wiley-Blackwell, 2010), 347–54.

are embedded theologically, historically and culturally; and thus the same practice of prayer takes on different meanings in different contexts.[14]

It is this multifaceted, endlessly generative, interestingly elastic nature of prayer that makes prayer such a fascinating topic of study. But it also makes prayer rather tricky to pin down. In equal measure, prayer is strikingly ordinary and vastly complicated. On the one hand, prayer comes as naturally to us as breathing. Hence in his lengthy engagement with prayer in the *Summa Theologiae* (2a2æ, q.83), Aquinas offers surprisingly little instruction on actually how to pray. Of course, he is interested in what is going on theologically when we pray but not once does he assume that prayer is not a very ordinary thing to do. Just as breathing does not require much of a guide, neither does prayer. For Aquinas, prayer is so simple it demands from us little expertise, skill or technique. Prayer is a given; better, it is God's given – it is the gift of grace (*ST* 2a2æ, q.83, art.15). If nothing else, as Karl Barth says, prayer is the release from all anxiety, including the anxiety of worrying about how to pray (*CD* IV/3, 673). Yet, on the other hand, Aquinas devotes sizable chunks of his *Summa* to think through the perceived simplicity of prayer. It becomes quickly apparent that this everyday practice, when broken open, does not end up being quite as simple as first expected. It is no wonder, then, that the question on prayer is the longest in the *Summa*, as is the chapter on prayer in John Calvin's *Institutes of the Christian Religion*, as are the sections on prayer in Barth's *Church Dogmatics*. Although very ordinary, prayer is not straightforward. It is vastly complicated.

Some of the inner tensions that lie at the heart of the theology of prayer can be felt in one of George Herbert's well-known poems on prayer:

> Prayer the Churches banquet, Angels age,
>   Gods breath in man returning to his birth,
>   The soul in paraphrase, heart in pilgrimage,
> The Christian plummet sounding heav'n and earth;
>
> Engine against th'Almightie, sinners towre,
>   Reversed thunder, Christ-side-piercing spear,
>   The six-daies world transposing in an houre,
> A kinde of tune, which all things heare and fear;

---

[14]More generally, as with all things theological, every theology of prayer is contextually conditioned; and the account of prayer described in this book is no exception.

Softnesse, and peace, and joy, and love, and blisse,
   Exalted Manna, gladnesse of the best,
   Heaven in ordinarie, man well drest,
The Milkie way, the bird of Paradise,

     Church-bels beyond the starres heard, the souls bloud,
     The land of spices; something understood.[15]

As Herbert captures in this famous cascade of images, prayer is extraordinarily complex, multiple and resistant to single definition. 'In fourteen lines he heaps up twenty-seven different images of the experience of prayer.'[16] The images he uses are contradictory. Prayer is as loud as earth shattering 'Reversed thunder', as powerful as an 'Engine against' God, yet something of 'Softnesse, and peace'. It is as cosmic as the Milky Way and as corporate as the 'Churches banquet', yet as intimate as 'souls bloud'. As strange as an exotic 'land of spices', prayer is as familiar as a well sung 'kinde of tune'. Prayer is full of these tensions, paradoxes and contradictions.

Moreover, there is something *inherently* perplexing about prayer. Prayer is the most fundamental characteristic of our humanity. We are 'praying animals', Robert W. Jenson says.[17] We are most fully human, fully alive when at prayer. 'Man well drest,' as Herbert puts it. Prayer is part of what helps us to become 'us'. We must pray without ceasing, give thanks in all circumstances (1 Thess. 5.17), live life by the breath and rhythm of prayer. As the 'Churches banquet', there is something exquisite about the life of prayer. It is the feast in foretaste of the banquet of heaven. 'Prayer is the actualization of our eschatological reality that is possible in the here and now,' says Barth.[18] It is the stuff of heaven practised on earth. And yet, Paul also says that 'we do not know how to pray as we ought' (Rom. 8.26). This could mean that with more practice and with the right training we can get better at praying. If only I do this or that I can be

---

[15]George Herbert, 'Prayer (I)', in *The Temple* (Cambridge: Printed by Thomas Buck and Roger Daniel, 1633). Public Domain. https://www.ccel.org/h/herbert/temple/Prayer1.html [accessed 17 October 2017].

[16]Malcolm Guite, *Faith, Hope and Poetry: Theology and the Poetic Imagination* (Farnham: Ashgate, 2012), 21–5 (21).

[17]Robert W. Jenson, 'The Praying Animal', *Zygon*, 28.3 (1983), 311–25.

[18]Karl Barth, *Ethics* (New York: Seabury Press, 1981), 472–73.

more 'successful' at prayer – gaining a more successful, more satisfying, more instant experience of God. And the Christian market is already well saturated with guides promising some kind of success or another in prayer. However, for Paul, when it comes to prayer, practice does not seem to make perfect. Here we come up against the deep paradox of prayer: we are called to pray without ceasing and yet we cannot pray as we ought.

Paul is raising a question in his letter to the Romans about the 'ontology' of prayer. What is the 'stuff' of prayer? In the preface to one of the earliest feature-length guides on prayer, picking up on Paul's question raised in Romans 8, Origen comments that we cannot be good at prayer because prayer is not, strictly speaking, a thing that we 'do' in the first place (*De oratione* 2.3-4). Prayer is not any old human practice. Instead, for Origen and many others after him, prayer is the vastly complicated practice of *God's* into which we are drawn. It is much more than the thing that I do, though it is that too; it is also God's 'breath in man', to cite Herbert once more. It is perplexingly fully human and fully divine. Perhaps this is why Paul is unfazed at the prospect of being unable to do the very thing he asked the Thessalonian church to do unceasingly: prayer is not his alone to do in the first place.[19]

Despite its title, this book tries hard to avoid ironing out the perplexity of prayer. Its hope, quite conversely, is to see prayer for what it is: inherently complicated. As we will explore in this book, prayer is both much 'bigger' than simply a human practice and much broader than any one thing. It means at least twenty-seven things to Herbert and many more to others. Suggestively, when trying to pinpoint prayer, like Herbert, the early church did not look to one of the individual practices of prayer – petition, invocation, thanksgiving. Time and again the earliest engagements with prayer appealed instead to a metaphor to speak of prayer. One of the most important metaphors for prayer in the early church is that of 'conversation'. Prayer is like dialoguing with God as one converses with a loved one – sometimes in words, sometimes in silence, sometimes together, sometimes alone. But as we will see in Chapter 1, in this context 'conversation' meant much more than daring to dialogue with God. It meant relationship,

---

[19] As Denys Turner explains in a sermon on Romans 8, 'he [Paul] meant that not being good at it was in the nature of prayer, and in our nature too: that given what prayer is, we could not, in the nature of things, be any good at it'. See Denys Turner, *Faith Seeking* (London: SCM Press, 2002), 93.

participation, even 'union' with God. Prayer is about the 'conversing' of the divine and the human, the catching up of humanity into the life of the trinitarian God and the invitation to share in God's ways in the world. It is about being given 'a share in the Divine Power, bringing them as it were to kinship with the Divine Nature', as Gregory of Nyssa explains in his commentary on the Lord's Prayer.[20] Much more than a discretely human practice that comes and goes, prayer is more akin to what has been called 'practicing the presence of God'. As the 'soul in paraphrase', the momentary act of prayer starts to become a lifelong habit. 'Now when we think of habits we tend to think of things like smoking or repeating yourself, but the ancient sense of the term – while it does not exclude these – is much more profound. A habit is a pattern that you *inhabit*, and it is not so much something you see as something through which you see everything else.'[21] To the extent that we become habituated in prayer and see all things through it, prayer no longer has much of a 'point'. Prayer is not a means to an end (such as having this or that petition answered by God). It is the end. Hence later we will hear how Evagrius finds the 'place of prayer' at the summit of human existence, which for him is communion with God.

The aim of this book, then, is to think as expansively as possible about the theme of prayer. Prayer is not one thing among many but the thing through which all things gain their meaning: God, the world and the self. Take, for example, the front cover of this book which is a detail from a painting entitled 'Embrace' by the Birmingham-based artist Gillian Lever. For Lever, the cover image is not simply a work of art but a work of prayer that in her terms does not describe or resolve mystery but 'evokes' it.[22] The practice of art is the practice through which one can be drawn into the mysterious presence of God, into the 'embrace' of God, and therefore into conversation with God. It is both the vehicle into prayer and prayer itself. The same can be said of poetry and of spiritual reading, and indeed of thinking about prayer: theological thinking about prayer is itself an exercise in prayer. Thus, drawing on the Benedictine tradition of 'prayer and work'

---

[20]Gregory of Nyssa, *The Lord's Prayer, The Beatitudes*, ACW, vol. 18 (London: Longman, 1954), 21–84 (35).

[21]Michael Hanby, 'Interceding: Giving Grief to Management', in *The Blackwell Companion to Christian Ethics*, ed. by Stanley Hauerwas and Samuel Wells (Oxford: Blackwell, 2011; 2nd edn), 251–63 (262).

[22]In private correspondence with Gillian Lever.

(*orare et laborare*), where the *orare* is found in the *lab-orare*, this is a book on prayer, but also very much a work of prayer.

Yet books, including this one, can only go so far in guiding through the perplexity of prayer. Origen begins his *De oratione* with these telling words. 'There are realities that are so great that they find a rank superior to humanity and our moral nature; they are impossible for our rational and moral race to understand' (*De oratione* 1.1). Prayer is one of these impossible realities. But he continues: 'This impossibility has become a possibility by the boundless excellence of the grace of God' (*De oratione* 1.1). Prayer, by the grace of God, interprets prayer. 'Therefore, the discussion of prayer is so great a task that it requires the Father to reveal it, His Firstborn Word to teach it, and the Spirit to enable us to think and speak rightly of so great a subject' (*De oratione* 2.6). The best guidance for those seeking teaching on prayer is simply, then, to pray. Ben Myers reaches a similar conclusion when he says this of Herbert's poem:

> The real purpose of all the conflicting images was simply to clear this space – not, in fact, a space for understanding (as though the poem were trying to 'explain' prayer), but a space for prayer itself. As talk-about-prayer passes over into praying, something is understood that language can never capture. In fourteen lines we have plumbed heaven and earth, feasted and made war, spanned all the farthest reaches of time and space. But now – as so often in Herbert – we find ourselves kneeling alone in the dusky light of a little country church, listening softly to that profound yet homely silence. Here at last, where understanding ceases, prayer is understood.[23]

The fullest definition of prayer comes in prayer itself.

The plan of this book

It will become apparent that this book is not structured around the particular practices that have come to define Christian understandings

---

[23]Ben Myers, 'George Herbert: Prayer, Language, Silence', on *Faith and Theology*, 7 July 2010, http://www.faith-theology.com/2010/07/george-herbert-prayer-language-silence.html [accessed 28 June 2017], and used by kind permission.

of prayer. This is not only because of the broader definition of prayer this book is pursuing – prayer as beyond any one individual practice – but also because the meaning of individual practices of prayer are shaped within actual communities of prayer. They are, in a word, 'traditioned', and their specificities are defined as they are carried out within the context of those traditions. As Roy Hammerling explains,

> For as soon as one tries to analyze prayer, the complexity of the notion manifests itself, because prayers are not only as diverse as the people who utter them, but they exist in a myriad of contexts, forms, and practices, which if ignored will cause confusion and lead to erroneous scholarly analysis. The content of prayer requires that it be analyzed in its own habitat; whether the context is a cathedral or a cloister, a mountain top or cavern, or an arena filled with deadly animals or a closet – the context clearly matters.[24]

There are many more able guides than can be offered here that are structured around individual practices and provide the deep attention to the dense particularity of the traditioned nature of prayer, and I would encourage the reader to consult the annotated bibliography in the appendix for some cherry-picked examples from across the tradition. This is not to say that we will not encounter many of the specific practices of prayer along the way. But they tend not to take on structural significance in this particular guide to prayer. Instead, this book unfolds doctrinally.

After exploring Evagrius's writings on prayer (Chapter 1) and then some contemporary expressions of the relation between theology and prayer (Chapter 2), we set about examining some of the major loci of Christian doctrine through the lens of prayer: the Trinity (Chapter 3), Christology (Chapter 4), providence and creation (Chapter 5) and the Christian life (Chapter 6). In each case, we consider how prayer provides unique insights into the nature of Christian doctrine, its formation and purpose. Some of the chapters draw liberally on the broad tradition of Christian spirituality, including contemporary writers who have made important headway in explicating the doctrinal significance of prayer. Other chapters are more

---

[24]Roy Hammerling, 'Introduction: Prayer – A Simply Complicated Scholarly Problem', in *A History of Prayer: The First to the Fifteenth Century*, ed. by Roy Hammerling (Leiden: Brill, 2008), 1–27 (3).

circumscribed in focus and offer close engagements with key texts and thinkers. Chapter 1, as we have said, attends to a single document by Evagrius of Ponticus. Chapter 3 includes detailed case studies of two contemporary expressions of the doctrine of the Trinity in which prayer is critical – Sarah Coakley's 'prayer-based' model of the Trinity and the 'doxological trinitarianism' of Jürgen Moltmann, Catherine Mowry LaCugna and Alan J. Torrance. Chapter 4 devotes attention to Cyril of Alexandria's commentary on Christ's prayer in chapter seventeen of the Gospel of John. Similarly, most of Chapter 5 sticks closely to the writings of Thomas Aquinas and Karl Barth. And the final chapter focuses on the role of prayer in the Christian life as worked out in the strand of Christian ethics known as 'ecclesial ethics' (as represented by figures such as Stanley Hauerwas and Samuel Wells), Latin American liberation theology (chiefly but not exclusively via a discussion of Leonardo Boff's theology of prayer) and in some feminist and post-colonial treatments of the intersection of the political and the praying body. We begin, though, in the deserts of the early Christian world and with the sometimes strange, often odd and always compelling treatise on prayer by Evagrius of Ponticus.

CHAPTER 1
'KNEELING THEOLOGY': EVAGRIUS
OF PONTICUS ON PRAYER

Once there was little difference between theology and prayer. As Evagrius of Ponticus says, 'If you are a theologian, you will pray truly, and if you pray truly, you will be a theologian' (*On Prayer* 61). For much of the history of Christianity this short statement, which has an importance disproportionate to its length, would have been taken for granted. In Evagrius's day, theology and prayer even shared the same word: *theologia*.[1] It would have been presumed in the early Christian world that speech about God, if to be counted as truly theological, should be undertaken in the context of prayer; and it would have gone without saying that the experience of God in prayer is necessarily connected to the pursuit of theological truth. Prayer and theology were not two distinct activities that might sometimes collide but just as there is no smoke without fire, there could be no theology without prayer. As such, it has often been said that Christianity does its theology 'on the knees'.

And yet, as A. N. Williams explains, the 'unwritten conventional wisdom of contemporary Christianity is that one must choose between these varieties of knowledge, either speaking theologically or in adoration, but not both, lest one contaminate the other'.[2] The chapter following this one considers some of the knotty factors that contributed to the percieved breakdown of the 'integrity' of prayer and theology. The aim that lies before us now is to explore what it might mean to do theology in a very explicit, unashamed way 'on the knees'. Charting a way back to a kneeling kind of theology requires, therefore, something of a *ressourcement* (which means

---

[1] Andrew Louth, *Discerning the Mystery: An Essay on the Nature of Theology* (Oxford: Clarendon Press, 1983), 3.

[2] A. N. Williams, 'Contemplation: Knowledge of God in Augustine's *De Trinitate*', in *Knowing the Triune God: The Work of the Spirit in the Practices of the Church*, ed. by James J. Buckley and David S. Yeago (Grand Rapids: William B. Eerdmans, 2001), 121–46 (124).

'return to biblical and patristic sources'). It requires returning to some of the key sources in the Christian tradition to recover patterns of theological reasoning in which the integrity of prayer and theology fares better than it appears to under the 'conventional wisdom' of contemporary Christianity. To that end, this chapter provides a close reading of an early Christian document: *On Prayer* by Evagrius of Ponticus.

The first of the four sections that structure this chapter introduces Evagrius and his writings. The second explores the ways that reading a text in the curious style of *On Prayer* can be understood as 'spiritual practice' and how, therefore, the integrity of theology and prayer is maintained by Evagrius in the formal arrangement of the text as well as in its content. The third section says something about the text's pedagogical trajectory, that is, how Evagrius organizes his writing to lead the pray-er through a process of purgation, purification and ascent into its ultimate destination: transformative union with God, which Evagrius uniquely styles 'imageless prayer'. And the final section investigates his use of the metaphor of 'conversation', which is the way Evagrius, and others throughout the history of Christianity, comes to parse the union with the divine experienced in prayer.

Introducing Evagrius

Classical examples of the foregrounding of the integrity of prayer and theology are thick on the ground. Augustine's *Confessions*, for instance, is justly celebrated for working very subtly at the juncture of doctrine and autobiography, philosophy and spirituality, theology and prayer. Speech about God and speech to God are interwoven so elegantly in the *Confessions* that it is never quite clear where prayer ends and theology begins. Hence in his handbook on the Christian faith (the *Enchiridion*), the Lord's Prayer and the Apostles' Creed are discussed together in the same context – piety and belief go hand in hand.[3] The same slipping from theology to prayer and back again with barely a pause for breath can be observed in the writings of the medieval theologian and abbot Anselm of Canterbury. Like Augustine, Anselm worked prayer deeply into the structure of his theology. He composed his theology as prayer and 'prayed his theology till there was

---

[3]Augustine, 'Enchiridion', in *St Augustine: On the Holy Trinity, Doctrinal Treatises, Moral Treatises*, NPNF, series 1, vol. 3 (Edinburgh: T&T Clark, 1998), 237–76.

no difference between theology and prayer', Benedicta Ward writes.[4] One of Anselm's most important works, the *Proslogion*, is prayer at its heart. It begins and ends with lines of direct doxological speech to God. Moreover, the argument itself was received in prayer during Matins and the point of the text, Anselm reminds his reader, is not to prove the existence of God but 'to rouse the mind for the contemplation of God'.[5] In addition to working prayer into the heart of his theological works, Anselm also produced 'prayed versions' of key doctrinal treatises. For example, his classic expression of the doctrine of the atonement, articulated doctrinally in *Cur Deus Homo*, was set to prayer in his fantastically interesting *The Meditation on Human Redemption*. The alternative Anselm of the redemption prayer adds curious twists to what is commonly thought to be the 'Anselmian theory' of the atonement.[6]

It is tempting to think that the intellectual climate for a happy relation between theology and prayer existed exclusively in the premodern period. But there are significant exceptions from the modern period for this metanarrative of decline to be wholly adequate. Good examples from the twentieth century in which prayer and theology interestingly interact include the writings of Hans Urs von Balthasar – from whom we borrow the term 'kneeling theology' – who is well known for emphasizing the inherent connection between contemplation and theology.[7] As mentioned in the introduction, another fine example of someone committed to overcoming

---

[4]Benedicta Ward, 'The Prayers and Meditations', in *The Prayers and Meditations of St Anselm with the Proslogion*, ed. by Benedicta Ward (London: Penguin, 1973), 51–86 (77).

[5]Anselm, *Pros*. 1. Read from *Pros*. 1, and therefore as 'prayer', the *Proslogion* behaves differently than it would if the reader began at *Pros*. 2 and skipped over the opening prayer. I am following the likes of John Caputo's interpretation of Anselm by stating that it is prayer that gives Anselm's 'proof' its coherence. 'In a sense he was saying that it is not an argument (in the modern sense) but an effort at conceptualizing or clarifying something that is intuitively obvious to all those who experience God in their daily lives. In fact, when Anselm said this, he wasn't standing, he was kneeling, and this bit of reasoning was meant to clarify the God of his faith, the God given to him in the life of prayer.' See John D. Caputo, *Philosophy and Theology* (Nashville: Abingdon Press, 2006), 15.

[6]Approaching Anselm's atonement theology via the comparably neglected *Meditation* problematizes in interesting ways the Anselm as rehearsed in history of dogma textbooks. I have explored this 'alternative Anselm' in Ashley Cocksworth, 'Prayer', in *T&T Clark Companion to the Atonement*, ed. by Adam Johnson (London: T&T Clark, 2017), 701–5.

[7]For his influential critique of the separation of prayer and theology, see Hans Urs von Balthasar, 'Theology and Sanctity', in *Explorations in Theology – Volume 1: The Word Made Flesh* (San Francisco: Ignatius Press, 1989), 181–209; for his most dedicated treatment of prayer, see *Prayer* (San Francisco: Ignatius Press, 1986).

the distinction that comes to separate prayer and theology is the Cistercian monk Thomas Merton, who like Balthasar was an able reader of Evagrius.[8]

Similarly, in the writings of Karl Barth, the twentieth-century Swiss Reformed theologian who died on the same day as Merton, is to be found an unusual blend of prayer and theology.[9] It might come as a surprise that Barth insists on the opening pages of the first volume of his monumental *Church Dogmatics* that 'there can be no dogmatic work without prayer' (*CD* I/1, 23). Placed within Barth's broader methodological commitments, however, the claim that the context of prayer is the only context out of which the theological task is possible becomes a recognizably Barthian concern. Barth leaves no doubt that Christian dogmatics has its own distinctive language, discourse and set of rules, which are to be interpreted on their own terms without recourse into other spheres of intellectual life. And it is prayer that provides Barth with the particular epistemic conditions to enable the irreducibility of Christian language and the specificity of its self-logic to be expressed and interpreted. As Hans Frei writes, in Barth 'first-person address *to* God, speaking and acting in his presence, and talk or discourse *about* God are presumably not nearly so sharply distinguishable as they are for some other theologians'.[10] It can even be said that Barth's entire dogmatic project, pursued so rigorously and with such conviction throughout the *Church Dogmatics*, is most appropriately understood as one (long) prayer – as a contemplative stretching to the divine, undertaken in the obedience and humility of prayer.

The chief interlocutor of this chapter, however, is not Augustine, Anselm, Balthasar, Merton or Barth – though careful readings of any of these figures

---

[8]Helped along by his immersion in French scholarship and through his fondness for John Cassian, Merton was part of an early wave of English-speaking theologians who were fascinated by Evagrius. Merton's friend, for example, John Bamberger, was among the first to translate Evagrius's writings on prayer into English – published as *Evagrius Ponticus: The Praktikos and Chapters on Prayer* (Kalamazoo: Cistercian Publications, 1981). Some years earlier, Merton himself translated some of Evagrius's writings into English. I thank my colleague Gary Hall and his encyclopaedic knowledge of all things Merton for these details.

[9]I have investigated these themes in Ashley Cocksworth, *Karl Barth on Prayer* (London: T&T Clark, 2015). The key sections on prayer in Barth's writings can be found in his doctrine of providence (*CD* III/3, 265–88); his ethics of creation (*CD* III/4, 87–115); his late 1940s seminars on the Lord's Prayer in dialogue with Reformation thought (*Prayer: 50th Anniversary Edition* (Louisville: Westminster John Knox Press, 2002)); his ethics of reconciliation, which is structured around the petitions of the Lord's Prayer and unfolds under the controlling concept of invocation (*ChrL*); and Chapter 14 of *Evangelical Theology: An Introduction* (London: Collins, 1965) in which Barth discusses the relation between prayer and theology.

[10]Hans W. Frei, *Types of Christian Theology* (New Haven: Yale University Press, 1992), 39.

would reveal fascinating insights into the relation between prayer and theology. Instead, this chapter reaches further back in history, into the fourth-century deserts of Egypt to engage the writings of abba Evagrius.

There are several reasons to spend time with Evagrius of Ponticus. He was among the first to reflect at length on prayer and distil those reflections into one of the earliest treatises dedicated to the subject: *On Prayer*, written towards the end of his life. Evagrius also stands, as Balthasar comments, at the curious position of 'influencing in a decisive manner' the development of both Eastern and (largely through the mediating work of his disciple John Cassian) Western monastic teaching.[11] But despite the significant influence he had over matters spiritual, Evagrius was deemed heretical for his doctrinal association with Origen and suffered posthumous condemnation in the Origenist purges of the sixth century; a condemnation that has chequered the reception of his writings down the ages. As we mentioned in this book's introduction, the project of systematic theology, when minted in the context of prayer, is at its most 'systematic' when attending to the writers that have been neglected by the theological mainstream and to the sources that are not always considered as canonical as strictly doctrinal treatises. These might include the writings of the mystics, the lives of the saints, hymns, liturgies, poetry, sermons and the experience of prayer itself. Evagrius was a marginalized, indeed defeated and silenced voice in conciliar theology and *On Prayer*, couched in the register of devotion, contemplation and spiritual instruction, is a genre of writing that sits on the edge of the theological canon.

The primary reason, however, for selecting this desert father is that although many in the ancient world spoke about prayer, few wrote with such clarity, purpose and indeed practical conviction about the connection between praying to God and knowing about God than did Evagrius. His chief concern in the treatise is to explicate the connection between the practice of prayer and the disclosure of theological truth. For Evagrius, theology and prayer are two sides of the same coin of the mind's purification, ordering and ascent into union with God.[12] There simply cannot be one without the other. But who was Evagrius?

---

[11] Hans Urs von Balthasar, 'The Metaphysics and Mystical Theology of Evagrius', *Monastic Studies*, 3 (1965), 183–95 (183).

[12] It is worth clarifying Evagrius's use of the term 'mind'. 'In the Greek theological tradition, the mind is our intuitive side. It enables us to know and recognize the truth of things instantly, whether a friend's face or a mathematical proof. For Evagrius, the way the mind knows God is through direct intuition, not logic: "for knowledge of God, one needs not a debater's soul,

Born in 345, the son of a bishop, Evagrius grew up in Pontus, near the Black Sea. We know from Palladius of Helenopolis (sometime disciple and writer of *The Life of Evagrius*) that in 382 Evagrius migrated from the intellectual hub of the early Christian world, Constantinople, to the spiritual epicentre of the emerging monastic movement: the deserts of Lower Egypt.[13] Evagrius's time in Constantinople brought him into contact with the 'who's who' of Christian orthodoxy. He was ordained lector by Basil of Caesarea, deacon by Gregory of Nazianzus and was present at the ecumenical council held in Constantinople during which the version of the Nicene Creed still said in many churches today was formulated. A skilled orator, Evagrius was famous throughout the early Christian world for his eloquent defence of creedal orthodoxy. It is said that 'he was victorious over all the heretics' at the Second Ecumenical Council in 381.[14]

On fleeing Constantinople a year later after falling in love with a married woman he headed first to Nitria and then journeyed deeper into the Egyptian desert to settle finally in the harsh landscape of Kellia – known to the ancient world as the 'innermost desert'. The cells of Kellia were so remote that his friend Rufinus said that the monks were 'divided from one another by so great a distance' that no one could 'catch sight of another'.[15] Dying in 399 in the desert, Evagrius led a life totally immersed in prayer. Palladius records that he prayed 'one hundred prayers a day'.[16] Practising what he preached, he would spend most of his day and indeed much of the night in prayer. And when he was not in prayer, prayer accompanied his fasting and his labour, as it did his writing of theology.

Despite the toil the extreme asceticism had on his body, which probably cost him his life, the desert was a place of great intellectual productivity.

---

but a seer's soul.'" See William Harmless, *Mystics* (New York: Oxford University Press, 2008), 151–2. Prayer, then, is not simply an activity of the mind, but a condition of *being* – involving the body and soul as well as the mind.

[13]Tim Vivian (trans.), *Four Desert Fathers: Pambo, Evagrius, Macarius of Egypt, and Macarius of Alexandria – Coptic Texts Relating to the Lausiac History of Palladius* (Crestwood: St Vladimir's Seminary Press, 2004), 69–92 – hereafter, Palladius, *Life of Evagrius*.

[14]Palladius, *Life of Evagrius*, 75. In the final scene of the *Life of Evagrius*, Palladius speaks of a strange encounter with three demons 'disguised as servants of the church', each one representing a 'heretical' doctrine. Evagrius, we are told, tackled each in turn and, with the eloquence and skill for which he was famed, left each 'defeated'. See, Palladius, *Life of Evagrius*, 90.

[15]Cited in Harmless, *Mystics*, 138.

[16]Palladius, *Life of Evagrius*, 80.

During this time, as well as copying manuscripts, he hammered out in his own name a vast number of treatises, letters and commentaries on a variety of philosophical, spiritual and biblical issues. He composed his great trilogy on the ascetical life (consisting of the *Praktikos*, the *Gnostikos* and the *Kephalaia Gnostika*) and devised the classification that in the hands of Cassian would be codified into the canonical list of the seven deadly sins. The fruit of his hermetic experience, however, was his exhilarating treatise *On Prayer*.

Evagrius took up the tradition set by Origen in writing his own 'On Prayer'. As well as adopting the same title as his teacher, Evagrius utilizes a similar framework of ascent to describe theologically the stages of prayer. He reveals further indebtedness to Origen by drawing on the same Romans 8 material for textual inspiration. There is also a similar didactical tone to their texts: both are concerned with the sharing of wisdom on prayer and are writing at the request of those seeking guidance on prayer. But Evagrius breaks from Origen and indeed from patristic literature on prayer more generally at one decisive point: he says very little about the central prayer of the early church. Unlike nearly every other patristic treatise on prayer, Evagrius's *On Prayer* does not follow the 'paternoster' format. Breaking patristic conventions, he neither structures his treatise around the petitions of the Lord's Prayer nor says much about the petitions themselves. Whereas Origen places a long treatment of the Lord's Prayer right at the centre of his treatise (in *De oratione* 18–31), thereby reflecting the centrality of the Lord's Prayer in the early church, Evagrius has almost nothing to say about it, bar the passing reference to some of its petitions (in *On Prayer* 59). His concern is with other issues: the things that distract the pray-er from prayer, the things the pray-er needs to do to pray truly and the relation 'true' prayer has with 'true' theology. Evagrius breaks further from his teacher not only in the things he says about prayer, but also in how he says those things. While Origen presents his teaching in full prose, Evagrius's *On Prayer* takes a rather different form. It takes the form of 153 short 'chapters'.

As we have said, like Origen's, the reception of Evagrius's writings has been rather inconsistent. Some revere him for the 'enormous influence [he had] on Eastern Orthodox spiritual and mystical theology'.[17] Yet despite his eloquent promulgation of doctrinal orthodoxy at Constantinople, the

---

[17] Andrew Louth, *The Origins of the Christian Mystical Tradition: From Plato to Denys* (Oxford: Oxford University Press, 2007; 2nd edn), 110.

orthodox company he kept and his contribution to the formation of desert monasticism, many have thrown him out with the Origenist bathwater. Along with Origen and Didymus the Blind, he was posthumously anathematized in the Origenist purges of 553, a charge ratified at three subsequent ecumenical councils. Simon Tugwell explains that Evagrius is 'one of the greatest masters of the spiritual life and of psychology in ancient monasticism; but his theological and philosophical speculation led him into wild heresy'.[18] Sitting so awkwardly in the history of Christianity raises some pressing questions – which cannot easily be resolved now but deserve to be noted – around the tension between doctrine, prayer and orthodoxy in the early church. Here the early church was very much at odds with itself: how can it be said that Evagrius 'prayed truly' (in recognizing his contribution to the formation of desert spirituality) if his doctrine was so 'wildly' false?

It was not only his name but also many of his writings that were suppressed in the heresy hunting of the sixth century. Many of his writings disappeared without a trace. The writings that survived the bitter inquisition were those protected either in translation (Syrian mainly) or under the names of other writers. *On Prayer* is one of those texts. Surviving the purges under the name of the respected Nilus of Sinai,[19] and then translated into many languages ready to be disseminated across the ancient world, the chapters on prayer models how 'theology can be thoroughly infused by prayer in a way that is no longer immediately available to us'.[20]

Of the 153 'chapters', there was one that was destined to become Evagrius's most famous:

> 61. If you are a theologian, you will pray truly, and if you pray truly, you will be a theologian.

In this single sentence, which became associated with his name above all else, Evagrius is suggesting that prayer is the prerequisite for theology, contemplation provides the right intellectual and spiritual conditions for

---

[18]Simon Tugwell, *Prayer – Volume 2: Prayer in Practice* (Springfield: Templegate Publishers, 1974), 148.

[19]It was not until the 1930s that Evagrius was revealed as its true author.

[20]Augustine Casiday, 'Introduction', in *Evagrius Ponticus*, ed. and trans. by Augustine Casiday (London: Routledge, 2006), 38.

theological work and that the work of theology should be offered as prayer, in the context of a praying community and in penitence and praise. He is also saying that theological work should end in prayer, in gratitude and with an 'Amen'. But in the same breath Evagrius is getting at something more suggestive than the bookending of theological work in prayer. Theological work is not only nourished by prayer, 'just as bread is nourishment for the body' (*On Prayer* 101), but the very work of theology itself is a practice of prayer. Theology is a form of prayer. Under these conditions, far from a retreat into a piety that is potentially embarrassing to the intellectual venture of theology, prayer is unrepentantly celebrated as 'the highest function of the mind' (*On Prayer* 35): all theological knowing for Evagrius is disciplined by the pedagogy of prayer. Knowledge of God is never an external knowledge but is experienced through the inner work of prayer by which the pray-er is caught up in God's own knowledge of God's self. Evagrius attempted to convey the relation between prayer and theology materially in all that he said. He also worked it out in the form of the text – which as we have said and will say more now takes on a curious and distinctive style.

'Settling on the mind': Prayer and 'slow reading'

Evagrius was renowned throughout the early Christian world as a gifted spiritual teacher. Despite the isolation to which the cells of Kellia committed him for much of the week, Palladius' *Life* records that the 'brothers would gather around him on Saturday and Sunday, discussing their thoughts with him throughout the night, listening to his words of encouragement until sunrise. And they would leave rejoicing and glorifying God, for Evagrius's teaching was very sweet.'[21] So too was the teaching contained in *On Prayer*. In the prologue to the text Evagrius tells his reader that he is writing at the request of someone desiring a guide through the perplexity of prayer. His aim is to teach his patron and the Christian community at large to pray. Sure enough, as many have noted, this is a document of great practical and spiritual subtlety. It contains both practical advice about how to pray and shrewd psychological diagnoses of the things that get in the way of prayer. While some of his teaching on prayer appears to the modern reader

---

[21] Palladius, *Life of Evagrius*, 83.

quite bizarre, there is much in this text that continues to ring true today. His recommendation that it 'is not simply quantity that is praiseworthy in prayer, but rather quality' is perhaps as appropriate now as it was then (*On Prayer* 151). He offers to his reader wise teaching about how to pray more attentively, for longer periods of time, more intensely, with more focus and so on. The practical teaching offered by Evagrius helps the reader to be in better control of their prayer life: the pray-er might as a result use the psalmody more, be wary of the idolatrous tug of the 'image' (on this, more later) and be more joyous in prayer.

However, *On Prayer* is more than a repository of teaching on the practicalities of prayer. In addition to its educative work of imparting information about prayer and praying well, the text itself includes pedagogical features – in its style, form and structure – that are designed to lead the reader actually into prayer. Put differently, Evagrius wants to give 'maximal value' to the text and considers it a vehicle for prayer.[22] We will consider the style and form of the text in this section, and say something about its structure in the next.

It may sound strange to say that the way a text approaches the subject of prayer matters as much as what it says about prayer. But as Mark A. McIntosh finds in his study of the integrity of theology and spirituality, texts belonging to the tradition of Christian spirituality, and particularly those undertaken in the mystical mood, 'are – precisely as texts – events of meaning themselves, which draw their readers into a new world of understanding and perception, a world that is inherently theological in its ramification'.[23] In a similar way, in his theological account of reading, Peter M. Candler explores how texts of this kind lead the reader 'by the hand' into participation in the life of the divine. He argues that 'texts are organized as structures for the manuduction ("leading-by-the-hand") of readers along an itinerary of exit and return from creation to eschatological beatitude'.[24] For both, as in Evagrius's *On Prayer*, spiritual texts are cartographic: they map out before the reader the journey into God.

Take Augustine's *Confessions*, which we have already cited as a prime example of the integrity of prayer and theology, as characteristic of this kind

---

[22]McIntosh, *Mystical Theology*, 122.
[23]Ibid., 129.
[24]Peter M. Candler, *Theology, Rhetoric and Manuduction, or Reading Scripture Together on the Path to God* (Grand Rapids: William B. Eerdmans, 2006), 4.

of text. The *Confessions* begins in Book 1 with those famous words, 'Our heart is restless until it rests in you,' and ends in Book 13 with a meditation on the eternal rest of the Sabbath, in which Augustine says, 'We may also rest in you ... [and] you will rest in us.'[25] The ascending autobiographical structure of the *Confessions* seeks to guide the reader into the same ascent from restlessness to rest in God that the text is narrating. Augustine's story of conversion and prayer becomes the reader's story of conversion and prayer. But for Candler, in the transition from pre-modernity to modernity, this 'grammar of participation' was unilaterally displaced by a 'grammar of representation' in which texts are no longer seen as itineraries into the divine life but become reduced to containers of information to be grasped: the mystical text becomes the encyclopaedia.

Read through the 'grammar of representation', the point of reading Evagrius's *On Prayer* would be about the acquisition of information concerning, in this case, prayer. The role of the text would be to fill in the gaps in our knowledge of prayer. But read through what Candler calls the 'grammar of participation', as well as a repository of information about prayer, *On Prayer* becomes a guide into prayer itself and thus into transformative union with God. In this sense, the form of the treatise is as important in the task of leading the pray-er to prayer as the things the text says about prayer. One particularly striking feature of text's form is worth exploring further in this connection: Evagrius's trademark use of the 'kephalaiac' style of writing.

Evagrius presents *On Prayer* as a series of 'kephalaia' (or 'chapters'); 153 of them to be precise.[26] Although this is an odd literary form to the modern eye, it was popular in the early Christian world (particularly with the desert fathers and mothers and their 'sayings') and popularized further by Evagrius. It would be adopted, for example, by Maximus the Confessor, Symeon the New Theologian and Gregory Palamas. A chapter is usually a short saying, and Evagrius's chapters are shorter still. The following sample may be instructive in giving a flavour of their style and variety.

14. Prayer is the offshoot of meekness and freedom from wrath.
15. Prayer is the promontory of joy and thanksgiving.

---

[25] Augustine, *Confessions* (Oxford: Oxford University Press, 2008), 1 and 304.
[26] On the 'kephalaiac' style, see Augustine Casiday, *Reconstructing the Theology of Evagrius Ponticus* (Cambridge: Cambridge University Press, 2013), 37–42.

16. Prayer is the remedy for grief and faintheartedness.

35. Undistracted prayer is the highest function of the mind.

36. Prayer is the mind's ascent to God.

37. If you yearn to pray, abandon everything so that you can inherit everything.

Each chapter is a densely succinct numbered maxim, weighty with depth and meaning. Their brevity reflected the monastic privileging of simplicity and clarity above elaborate and convoluted prose in the task of communicating truth. They are often uncoordinated, usually obscure, always subversive of systematic coordination and short enough to be 'inwardly digested' by the monk and then recalled from memory. In the introduction to the treatise, Evagrius gives clear instruction to his reader about how to read what follows. He instructs us to read each chapter in turn, slowly, meditatively, rhythmically and until the chapter has been absorbed by the mind.

Not unlike the 'Jesus Prayer' (which involves meditating on a short sentence such as: 'Lord Jesus Christ, Son of God, have mercy on me'),[27] constant repetition would accompany the prescribed 'slow reading' of the chapters until they became woven into the fabric of the mind. Learning about prayer does not end with the acquisition of information. Much like the later Benedictine practice of *lectio divina*, Evagrius imagined a chewing over of his teaching on prayer until it was inscribed into the fibre of the monk's being – a monastic 'munching' on words. The point of the text, Evagrius tells his reader, is not to have teaching on prayer 'simply at hand in ink on paper, but also settled on your mind' (*On Prayer*, Intro.). As with *lectio*, the teaching on prayer would be learned off by heart 'in the fullest sense of this expression, that is, with one's whole being: with the body, since the mouth pronounced it, with the memory which fixes it, with the intelligence which understands its meaning, and with the will which desires to put it into practice'.[28]

The hope was that in this process of 'settling on the mind' his teaching on prayer would be so integrated into the monastic conscience that the words about prayer actually become prayer. The reader is taken beyond a 'grammar of representation', to use Candler's term again, in which the

---

[27]On this, see Kallistos Ware, *The Jesus Prayer* (London: Catholic Truth Society, 2014).

[28]Jean Leclercq, *The Love of Learning and The Desire for God: A Study of Monastic Culture* (Fordham University Press, 1982; 3rd edn), 17.

text functions as a container of information and knowledge is transmitted from text to reader in a unilateral way, and is brought into a hermeneutics of participation that would persist well beyond the life cycle of the text. Approached in prayer, the reader, as McIntosh writes, participates 'in the fundamental momentum of mystical texts towards the infinite being of God'.[29] Evagrius makes reading his text on prayer like reading a liturgy, a contemplative exercise. But as Pierre Hadot describes in his seminal essay on spiritual exercises in the philosophical tradition, 'We have forgotten *how* to read: how to pause, liberate ourselves from our worries, return into ourselves, and leave aside our search for subtlety and originality, in order to meditate calmly, ruminate, and let the texts speak to us.'[30] The kind of slow, attentive reading Evagrius is promoting (which Hadot cites with approval more than once) involves humility, patience and a refusal to rush towards a premature conclusion – qualities that are themselves training for the theological task of speaking about God.[31] In a similar vein, Thomas Merton writes that 'reading becomes *contemplative* when, instead of reasoning we abandon the sequence of the author's thoughts in order not only to follow our own thoughts (meditation), but simply to rise above thought and penetrate into the mystery of truth which is experienced intuitively as present and actual'.[32] Merton's reference to the ideal of the 'abandonment of thought', which may well have its genesis in Evagrius, is worth simply flagging now as it will become important later in our discussion of 'imageless prayer'.

The 'kephalaiac' style of the text is carefully chosen by Evagrius to function as an itinerary into the 'mystery of truth'. Words on prayer become prayer. Teaching about union with God in prayer becomes union with God in prayer. In addition to the style, the specific number of chapters is also carefully chosen by Evagrius to play a role in the text's movement towards God.

Evagrius was mesmerized by numbers. He instructs his reader to 'find delight' in the symbolism of the number of chapters featured in his treatise on prayer: 153. He was not alone in his fascination with this number. It gained

---

[29]McIntosh, *Mystical Theology*, 133.

[30]Pierre Hadot, *Philosophy as a Way of Life: Spiritual Exercises from Socrates to Foucault* (Oxford: Blackwell, 1995), 109.

[31]The reading habits implied by Evagrius are more akin to 'religious reading' as opposed to 'consumerist reading'. On this distinction, see Paul J. Griffiths, *Religious Reading: The Place of Reading in the Practice of Religion* (Oxford: Oxford University Press, 1999).

[32]William H. Shannon, *Thomas Merton's Dark Path: The Inner Experience of a Contemplative* (London: Penguin, 1982), 126.

an almost mystical significance in the early church, seizing the imagination of many patristic theologians who sought to decipher its hidden symbolism. Augustine, for example, found much significance in the fact that 153 is the sum of one through seventeen. The number seventeen comprises the seven gifts of the Holy Spirit and the Ten Commandments, and therefore combines in one grace and law. It is also a 'triangular' number, he noticed, which might have summoned to the mind the image of a mountain and with it the metaphor of prayerful ascent.[33]

Addressing his reader directly, Evagrius expends a great deal of energy offering his own reasons for dividing the text into 153 chapters.

> By dividing the book on prayer into one hundred and fifty-three chapters, we have despatched to you gospel provender so that you may find delight in the symbolic number, along with the triangular figure and the hexagonal figure (where the former exemplifies the pious knowledge of the Trinity, and the latter the parameters of the universe's orderly arrangement). … The triangular number might signify for you the knowledge of the Holy Trinity. But if you closely consider the number 153 as a triangle from many numbers, then think of ascetic practice, natural contemplation and theological contemplation, or faith, hope and love (1 Cor. 13.13), gold, silver, precious stones (1 Cor. 3.12). So much, then, for the number (*On Prayer*, Intro.).

The carefully selected number is connected, therefore, to orderly thinking, to 'the pious knowledge of the Trinity', and, above all, as Evagrius would later say, to the theme of revelation. Indeed, Evagrius takes great thrill in relaying to his reader that the number refers to the catch of fish at the Sea of Tiberius reported at the end of John's gospel. 'So Simon Peter went aboard and hauled the net ashore, full of large fish, a hundred fifty-three of them; and though there were so many, the net was not torn' (Jn 21.11). Why this verse? He is attracted to this verse, like one of the first cited in the treatise (Exod. 3.5 in *On Prayer* 4), because it speaks of theophany, revelation. It

---

[33]For more on the history of interpretation of the number, see George R. Beasley-Murray, *John*, Word Bible Commentary, 36 (Nashville: Thomas Nelson, 1998; 2nd edn), 401–4; and for a fuller explanation of the number as it relates specifically to Evagrius, see William Harmless, *Desert Christians: An Introduction to the Literature of Early Monasticism* (Oxford: Oxford University Press, 2004), 339–41.

was on the shores of Tiberius that the resurrected Christ was first revealed to the disciples; and it was on Horeb, the mountain of God, that the divine was revealed to Moses in the burning bush. To make this link to revelation unambiguous, he describes prayer as the 'perfect place of God' (*On Prayer* 58), which is again drawn from the Exodus tradition (Exod. 24.10-11). On ascending Sinai, Moses and the elders of Israel are said in Evagrius's Septuagint to arrive at the 'place of God', the site of revelation.

What is being drilled in by Evagrius is not that prayer leads to a physical place of God, of course. As Ann Conway-Jones explains, the "'place of God" is an oxymoron, implying a spatial confinement of the transcendent deity' in ways that Evagrius's doctrine of God does not allow.[34] His point instead concerns less the place of prayer itself than the journey the pray-er takes to get there; a journey animated by prayer. Prayer provides the requisite practices of attention and the 'desired conditions' for the mind to receive the revelation of the triune God, which orders and structures all knowledge of God and without which the task of theology is impossible. Before arriving at the place of prayer, the pray-er faces the treacherous path of the mind's purgation, purification and expansion.

Purgation, purification and epistemic expansion

The previous section said that the composition of *On Prayer* includes pedagogical features – in its style and form – to 'involve' the reader in the trajectory of prayer. It is in a matter not only of style and form, but also structure that *On Prayer* attends to the integrity of prayer and theology. This will become apparent again as we sketch the contours of Evagrius's account of the stages of the pray-er's spiritual ascent into union in God.

'Prayer is the mind's ascent to God,' says Evagrius (*On Prayer* 36). The metaphor of ascent is key to his entire system of the spiritual life, as it was to the mystical theology rooted in neo-Platonism more broadly.[35] Evagrius's

---

[34]Ann Conway-Jones, "'The Greatest Paradox of All": The "Place of God" in the Mystical Theologies of Gregory of Nyssa and Evagrius of Pontus', *Journal of the Bible and its Reception*, forthcoming.

[35]There is a complicated convergence in Evagrius's thinking on prayer of the neo-Platonic and the Christian that needs more work to untangle than is possible here. For example, the fifth-century philosopher Proclus's 'Fire-Song' bears striking similarities with what Evagrius would go on to describe as 'imageless prayer': 'Union with God is the result of a procedure … which

rendition of the ascent into union in God takes place in three stages: *praktikê* (asceticism), *physike* (contemplation of creation) and *theologia* (theology).[36] Although spelt out at length elsewhere,[37] these three stages of ascent are inscribed into the structure of the treatise on prayer.

Some spiritual texts structure the process of the ascent of prayer in a broadly linear way. Again, take a text like Augustine's *Confessions*. While the trajectory of a text such as the *Confessions* unfolds straightforwardly (from restlessness to rest), the process of 'manuduction' in *On Prayer* is almost absurdly obscure. Much to the frustration of his commentators, the treatise does not begin in a state of un-prayer, end in true prayer and journey through the three stages of the mind's ascent into union with God in succession. Instead, the stages appear out of order and are experienced in a more vorticular than linear way – again, this is entirely intentional and forms part of the text's *theological* performance. As McIntosh writes, the 'refusal to follow a systematic order' is characteristic of a spiritual text.[38] The text is performing what Rowan Williams might call 'dispossession'.[39] The idea of prayerful dispossession will form one of the motifs on prayer introduced in the next chapter, so details do not need to detain us at this point. In short, prayerful dispossession is about disrupting the reader's propensity to exert 'control' over God or in this case over the text and its processes of ascent. The kind of reading possible in prayer is less about 'possessing' the content of the text as being dispossessed by it; less about controlling the text as being led out of control by it; and less about reading the text as being 'read' by it. All this is because the subject matter to which the text leads – God – cannot be possessed, controlled or mastered. The arrangement of the text 'is not due to chance', as Andrew Louth puts it; 'it represents the incompleteness of the unlimited ignorance of *theologia*'.[40] The messiness of the Evagrian corpus in general, and the elusively anti-systematic structure of the prayerful ascent

---

rises, through a variety of spiritual exercises, to a direct confrontation with, and absorption into, a fiery light-source.' See John Dillon, 'The Platonic Philosopher at Prayer', in *Platonic Theories of Prayer*, ed. by John Dillon and Andrei Timotin (Leiden: Brill, 2016), 7–24 (23).

[36] These three stages provide the groundwork for threefold advance of the soul (through purgation, illumination and union) that would permeate the mystical traditions of Christian spirituality for many years to come.

[37] Chiefly in the *Praktikos*, his famed account of the monastic life – which can be found at Bamberger, *Evagrius Ponticus*, 12–42.

[38] McIntosh, *Mystical Theology*, 142.

[39] Rowan Williams, *On Christian Theology* (Oxford: Blackwell, 2000), 10–11.

[40] Louth, *The Origins of the Christian Mystical Tradition*, 106.

as described in *On Prayer* in particular, reflects textually the process of the dispossessive loss of control experienced internally. The form and the content are once again integrally matched.

Despite its intentionally unsystematic structure, the pray-er is not left rattling around the text aimlessly. As elsewhere, in *On Prayer* Evagrius is clear that the first stage (*praktikê*) of ascent (wherever it may textually appear) is about the pray-er advancing from the 'practical' life into silent contemplation by acquiring the virtues to break free from the passions (*apatheia*) of the heart and battle the demons that distract the mind. The original purity of the mind is corrupted, says Evagrius, by demons from whom the pray-er must be on constant guard.

> 91. If you are intent on praying, make yourself ready for the demons' onslaughts and boldly endure their lashes – for they will come upon you suddenly like ferocious animals and harm your whole body.

Evagrius has a great deal to say about demons in his writings on prayer. He describes in graphic detail how 'having attached' themselves 'to the area around the brain', the demons 'pluck the veins' of the mind and implant conceptual roadblocks that obstruct its ascent into communion with God (*On Prayer* 73).

For all he says about demons, his chief concern, however, is not with the demons themselves but the things demons implant into the mind to get in the way of true prayer: thoughts, passions and false images. In the hard work of prayer, the pray-er learns to let go of these weighty things to be freed to speak truly of God without distraction. Evagrius thus includes specific chapters to train the pray-er to identify and resist one threat after the other.

> 9. Stand fast, pray vigorously and deflect the success of concerns and chains of thought – for they agitate and trouble you so that they may divert your attention.

> 71. You will not be able to pray purely while being tangled up with material things and shaken by unremitting cares. For prayer is the setting aside of representations.

> 38. Pray firstly to be purified of passions.

He divides the 'passions' into eight (which eventually would be modified into the seven deadly sins), takes each in turn and displays great pastoral concern in the advice he gives to his reader about how to deal with them (*On Prayer* 6–14). Much like Jacob wrestling with the unnamed figure (Gen. 32.22-32), whom Evagrius cites in his introduction, the pray-er does not emerge from their dealings with the passions of the heart and the thoughts of the mind unscathed. As is often the case in the spirituality of the desert, prayer becomes about battle. The battleground is the mind and the enemies are the thoughts and passions that have been planted in the mind by the demon. The pray-er must thus 'fight to set your mind deaf and dumb at the hour of prayer' (*On Prayer* 11).

Free from the impulsion of the passions and now purified, purged and undistracted by the idols of the mind, the second stage (*physikê*) is about seeing the universe and the inner structure of all things in a new light: as utterly dependent on God. This gives way to the third stage of the ascent of prayer, 'theology' (*theologia*), which simply is the contemplation of God. Finally, the pray-er has reached the final resting place of prayer, when the mind delights in God – for God's sake – free from the burden of the image. This stage, in other words, is about the 'conversing' of the divine and the human that issues in what Evagrius calls 'imageless prayer'.

On reading the treatise on prayer, one cannot help but be struck by its controlling theme of 'imagelessness'. The pray-er's ascent into a prayerful knowing of God involves the 'putting aside' of all images of the divine, Evagrius says, until the pray-er advances into an experience of imagelessness (*On Prayer* 114–20). We have already said that images get a rough ride in Evagrius's theology. They come in many shapes and sizes. However they come, just as a seal imprints hot wax, images 'imprint on and shape the mind and place it far from God' (*On Prayer* 57). When images of the world are applied onto God, they 'frivolously limit the divine' (*On Prayer* 74) who is always supra-abundantly beyond the self-generated images of the mind. For this reason, Evagrius recommends 'never giving a shape to the divine' (*On Prayer* 67). The kneeling work of prayer counters, therefore, what is an ever-present danger: the mind's idolatrous longing to 'control' the divine through image, thought and concept. As Columba Stuart says, Evagrius offers a caution 'against our presuming to control the encounter with our expectations of what it and God will – or should – be like'.[41] Thus prayer

---

[41]Columba Stewart, 'Imageless Prayer and the Theological Vision of Evagrius Ponticus', in *A History of Prayer: The First to the Fifteenth Century*, ed. by Roy Hammering (Leiden: Brill, 2008), 137–66 (155).

involves the 'setting aside of representations' (*On Prayer* 71) and being released from the 'chains of thoughts' (*On Prayer* 9) to give space for the sanctifying of the mind that comes from the revelation of God.

It could be said that imageless prayer is the intellectual vertigo that comes from arriving at the 'place of God' and realizing that everything looks different. It is as if the very air the pray-er now breathes has thinned and the images that have until this point clouded the mind have finally lifted. But paradoxically, far from clarifying the image of God, as the blinding fog of the mind lifts the image of God that lays before Evagrius is complexified: the God revealed is not another image only brighter and bigger and clearer but is beyond image. God is imageless, freed from the neat confines of the image. Under the conditions of concentrated contemplation and its accompanying programme of theological formation, God is made stranger – more perplexing, and more, not less, intellectually demanding.

Having said all of this, as the pray-er moves into the final stage of contemplative ascent (*theologia*) what is found is not strictly speaking image*less*ness. The imagelessness that would occupy the space where the image once stood is surely as susceptible to becoming an idol as the image itself.[42] And Evagrius knows this, and wants to avoid this kind of unexpected idolatry at all cost. What is being purged, therefore, in the crucible of prayer is not every image but a certain kind of image.[43] Generally speaking, it would seem that Evagrius is working with two kinds of image. The first is the image that is impressed on the mind by the demons. These are 'impassioned' images, pertaining to possessions, food, materiality and other devices and desires of the heart – each woefully inadequate to represent God. The second kind of image is the image that is implanted not by the demon but 'gifted' by the divine. It is into this second kind of image that the pray-er advances. One of the key chapters clarifying Evagrius's theology of the 'image' is one that follows shortly the famous sixty-first (on the theologian who 'prays truly'):

---

[42]This is Rowan Williams's argument forwarded in *The Wound of Knowledge: Christian Spirituality from the New Testament to St John of the Cross* (London: Darton, Longman and Todd, 1990; 2nd edn), 70.

[43]Evagrius spells out a more developed typology of thoughts, some to be resisted (demonic), others to be embraced (angelic) and others still in between (human) in his other dealings with prayer: *Thoughts* and *Reflections* – which can be found respectively in Robert E. Sinkewicz, *Evagrius of Pontus: The Greek Ascetic Corpus* (Oxford: Oxford University Press, 2006), 136–82 and 210–16.

63. The Holy Spirit, sympathizing with our weakness (cf. Rom. 8.26), regularly visits us even when we are impure. And if he should find the mind praying to him alone from love of truth, he lights upon it and obliterates the whole battle-array of thoughts or representations that encircle it, advancing it in the love of spiritual prayer.

Made with suggestive reference to Romans 8, Evagrius is describing a logic of 'incorporation' that begins first with the purgative identification of the 'weakness' of the images that are already lodged in the mind. The Holy Spirit, Evagrius is adamant, 'regularly visits us' and casts revelatory light on thoughts, concepts and images to reveal the idols that lurk within. These 'thoughts or representations' need to be not only judged but 'obliterated', which again falls on the work of the Holy Spirit. However, this negative process of identification and obliteration is only one side of the pneumatological story. In the very next chapter Evagrius describes the positive process of how the epistemic stripping gives way to the opening of the mind to receive the knowledge of God as it 'descends' in Christ:

64. Whereas all the rest implant in the mind thoughts or representations or contemplations through changing the body, God does the opposite. Descending upon the same mind, he inserts in it the knowledge of such things as he wills, and through the mind he lulls the body's bad temperament.

The mind is purged and stripped but not left naked. It is made 'receptive of the desired state' (*On Prayer* 2). 'Abandon everything,' he says, 'so that you can inherit everything' (*On Prayer* 37) and the 'everything' of which Evagrius speaks is the one true image of the divine: the image of the Trinity. In broad terms, the entire spiritual project of prayer, as described by Evagrius, is the ascent from one kind of image (the demonic) to another (the divine Other). The activity of prayer is not about ascending from image into strict imagelessness but about leaving behind ready-made images of God to be 'incorporated' into a particular kind of image: an image so bright it is experienced as profound imagelessness. With this image in mind, the task of theology can truly begin.

Putting these pneumatological moves together, Evagrius presents a theory of knowing more subtle than commonly recognized and one rooted fundamentally in prayer. Knowing involves the Spirit-led purgation of false images and the revelatory gifting of the divine image that shines forth with the most radiant, brilliant light: the blinding light of 'sapphire'.[44] It is through this process of prayer that the mind is expanded into the knowledge of the Trinity. As John Bamberger writes, 'Prayer lifts man above his very nature, to set him on a level with the angels. "By true prayer, the monk becomes the equal of an angel" (*On Prayer* 113). By his contemplation he also becomes a temple of the trinitarian God. Finally, it elevates him to the knowledge of the very Trinity itself.'[45] There is to be found in Evagrius, then, a very logical connection between the practice of 'pure prayer' and true knowledge of God. It is only as the theologian 'converses' with God in prayer that the theologian can speak truly of God – a theme now to be discussed more fully.

Conversing with God

The first time the word 'prayer' appears in the main body of the treatise is within Evagrius's most succinct definition of prayer across all his writings. He writes that 'prayer is the mind's conversation with God' (*On Prayer* 3). For Evagrius, conversation with God stands at the very summit of human existence. There is nothing 'higher than conversing with God', he says (*On Prayer* 34). The overall point of the treatise is to help readers see that at the centre of all existence is deep dialogue with the divine. Evagrius was almost certainly not the originator of the term. Describing prayer in terms of 'conversation', even in his time, tapped into an established spiritual

---

[44]On the theme of sapphire, see William Harmless and Raymond R. Fitzgerald, 'The Sapphire Light of the Mind: The *Skemmata* of Evagrius Ponticus', *Theological Studies*, 62.3 (2001), 498–529.
[45]Bamberger, *Evagrius Ponticus*, 48. It is worth saying that, given the trinitarian underpinning of Evagrius's theory on prayer, it is somewhat curious that Balthasar would charge Evagrius with a deficient trinitarianism. 'Certainly he knows the Trinity,' Balthasar concludes, 'but in practice his teaching holds to an almost absolute superiority of the unity over the trinity of God, with clear traces of a subordination of Persons.' See Balthasar, 'The Metaphysics and Mystical Theology of Evagrius', 193. It might be that Balthasar struggles to place his finger on the trinitarian structure of Evagrius's theory of prayer because the rendition of the doctrine of the Trinity worked out in *On Prayer* (rooted in the experience of prayer and textually in Romans 8) has tended to be historically marginalized by theological orthodoxy. Evagrius thus falls into what Sarah Coakley has called the 'prayer-based' trinitarian tradition – membership of which includes theologians who tend to flirt at the fringes of that which is doctrinally 'orthodox': the mystics, women and heretics (not least, Evagrius's fellow heretic and theological teacher, Origen). On this, see Sarah Coakley, 'Prayer, Politics and the Trinity: Vying Models of Authority in Third–Fourth-Century Debates on Prayer and "Orthodoxy"', *Scottish Journal of Theology*, 66.4 (2013), 379–99. In Chapter 3, we say more about the 'prayer-based' trinitarianism of Romans 8 uncovered by Coakley.

tradition that reached back at least to Clement of Alexandria in the early third century.[46] It quickly became the go-to metaphor in early Christianity for speaking of the mystery of prayer. For many centuries to come countless theologians after Evagrius would draw on 'conversation' as a fitting metaphor for describing what theologically goes on in prayer.[47]

But what sort of conversation is prayer? Given the political character of prayer (to explored in Chapter 6), on first blush 'conversation' can appear too prosaic a metaphor for describing what is at stake in prayer. Does conversation really capture the part played by prayer in what someone like Barth would call the great 'revolt' against the disorder of the world? There are also significant agential complexities at stake in prayer that push the metaphor of conversation to its limits, and other issues that complicate matters further still. For example, from a sociological perspective conversations are said to be organized around certain 'rules'. In his ground-breaking *Lectures on Conversation*, the distinguished American sociologist Harvey Sacks suggested that one such rule is that of 'turn-taking'. In order for a conversation to count, the dialogue should follow a strict 'A-B-A' format. The format is designed to avoid interruption, protect the respective 'spaces' of the speaker and hearer and minimize 'overlapping' (talking over each other).[48] Mapped onto prayer, conversation with God would look like this: I speak (and God listens), God responds (and I listen), I speak (and God listens). But for Evagrius and many others, prayer does not neatly fit these conventions. Prayer is not so much a polite back-and-forth between the human pray-er and God as a messy 'polyphony' of voices intersecting each other in ways that break the mould of what would ordinarily count as conversation.[49]

In a further breaking of the conventions of conversation, the very words the pray-er speaks in the conversation of prayer are not the pray-er's own words. 'If you want to pray', Evagrius says, 'you need God who gives prayer to the one who prays' (*On Prayer* 59). The gift of prayer takes dominical form in the

---

[46]Clement of Alexandria, 'Stromata – Book 7', in *ANF*, vol. 2, 524–57 (533).

[47]Calvin deploys the metaphor more than once in his lengthy dealings with prayer in Chapter 20 of Book III of the *Institutes*, 850–920. Similarly, Balthasar says that at its root prayer is divine 'dialogue' and structures his classic book on contemplative prayer around the motif of conversation, see Balthasar, *Prayer*.

[48]Harvey Sacks, *Lectures on Conversation – Volumes 1 and 2* (Oxford: Blackwell, 1992), 523–34.

[49]Carol Harrison, *The Art of Listening in the Early Church* (Oxford: Oxford University Press, 2013), 183–228.

giving of the Lord's Prayer. Moreover, God not only gives prayer to the pray-er as 'gift' but even prays 'in' the pray-er. To say that prayer is 'conversation with God', therefore, is to make a Christological statement in which to pray 'truly' is to be caught up in the Son's eternal conversation with the Father. This is why Evagrius is concerned throughout the treatise with encouraging his readers to clear their minds of all wandering distraction – whether image, thought or passion. Prayer is about clearing the idle clutter of the mind in order to be attentive to the divine conversation that is already occurring 'in' us. For Evagrius, it would seem that the human pray-er is more like an active 'eavesdropper', to use Carol Harrison's term, who 'listens in' on the divine conversation already in play.[50] All this makes for a very odd sort of conversation indeed. It is for reasons such as these that D. Z. Phillips judges the use of the metaphor of conversation in the context of prayer to be inappropriate.[51]

Thinking metaphorically of prayer as a sort of exchange of speech between the pray-er and God is only one of the ways the term 'conversation' is used by Evagrius. The more fundamental role conversation plays in Evagrius's schema draws on an earlier definition of the term in circulation in the vocabulary of early monasticism. According to this definition, 'conversation' meant something far richer than the exchange of speech. It meant 'keeping company with'. Here the metaphorical slips into the literal. Saying that prayer is conversation, Evagrius was saying that in prayer we converse with God as if we would talk with a loved one and that, more literally, we 'keep company' with God. We intercourse with the divine, cohabit with the divine – in short, the pray-er cultivates a 'love affair' with God and with all who dialogue with God.[52] In a later qualification of *On Prayer* 2, Evagrius adds that conversing with God in prayer is about 'being engaged in being with him' (*On Prayer* 34). To sum up what Evagrius means by the 'conversation of prayer' in one word, that word would probably be 'union'.

His understanding prayer as union with God might have had something to do with the seriousness with which Evagrius took the command to 'pray always' (Lk. 18.1). The Christian life was about praying 'without ceasing', as Paul urged the Thessalonians (1 Thess. 5.17). There would, of course, have been set times of formal prayer structuring the monastic

---

[50]See Harrison, *The Art of Listening in the Early Church*, 201–4.
[51]D. Z. Phillips, *The Concept of Prayer* (New York: Routledge, 2015), 50.
[52]Gavin D'Costa, *Theology in the Public Square: Church, Academy and Nation* (Oxford: Blackwell, 2005), 112.

day during which prayer would have been more particularly understood as supplication, intercession, thanksgiving and so on. At root, however, Evagrius imagined prayer as something much more expansive than any one practice of prayer. Not limited as it often is today to momentary performances, Evagrius saw prayer as a continuous, unceasing event that would integrate times of formal prayer with the work of copying manuscripts, manual labour, chanting the psalmody, meditating on texts and, especially, reading the Bible. True prayer was reached when the entire Christian life is set to and ordered by the rhythm of the pray-er's uninterrupted dialogue with the divine.

In practice, being united with God through the conversation of prayer likely meant entering into dialogue with the text of scripture in which the purifying Word of God acts and speaks. Dialoguing with God's voice as heard in scripture requires attentiveness, openness and receptivity, all of which depended on the practice of prayer. From the frequent appeals to scripture in his writings on prayer it is clear that Evagrius was a serious reader of the Bible. The exact number of chapters is wittingly derived from the Gospel of John, his metaphor of sapphire light is a result of his meditative reading of Exodus, as is his appeal to prayer as the 'place of God', and a vast number of the chapters in *On Prayer* both directly and through allusions and turns of phrase refer to the Bible. Because a large part of his practice of theology involved the meditative reading of scripture, and in particular meditation on the psalmody,[53] any temptation to separate off the study of the Bible from the study of theology would have been as incomprehensible to Evagrius as the divisions between the practice of prayer and the study of theology some see in modern theology.

We have now reached the nub of Evagrius's argument about the connection between theology and prayer. Although appearing early in the chronology of the text, the notion of prayer as the 'mind's conversation with God' (*On Prayer* 3) corresponds most closely with the final stage of spiritual ascent – *theologia* – in which the impossibility of the theological task is made possible.

One tends to think of 'theology' today as something one studies, something read in a book or examined in a classroom. Theology is

---

[53]See Luke Dysinger, *Psalmody and Prayer in the Writings of Evagrius Ponticus* (Oxford: Oxford University Press, 2005).

an academic enterprise, scholastic in the literal sense of the word. ...
Evagrius ... had a quite different view. According to Evagrius, theology
is a knowledge of God gained from first-hand experience. It comes not
from books, but from prayer. Evagrius did not doubt the value of reading, of study, of reason; nor did he doubt the profound value of dogma,
of liturgy, or of ecclesiastical authority. Far from it. But for him, theology in the strict sense is the encounter of the praying mind with God.[54]

We are able to know God, and speak theologically of God, because we are in
dialogue with God. Prayer is the site where the divine and the human meet;
and that is why prayer matters for theology. As Carol Harrison explains, for
Evagrius, prayer 'makes us theologians – those who, having talked *with* God
in prayer, can talk *about* Him'.[55] Evagrius makes it very explicit that apart from
the sustained practices of conversing with God in prayer true knowledge
of God is simply off limit. Outside of prayer, the idolatries of thought that
dull the mind remain unchecked and the true heights of theological activity
unreachable. But if one is engaged in the kneeling work of prayer the theologian
is unloosed from the idolatrous pull downwards and the true possibilities of
theology are made available in conversational company with God.

This leads to a final loose end that must be faced before going any further.
Earlier we noted that Evagrius sits in the ostensibly awkward position of
being instrumental in the flourishing of desert spirituality while also being
a heretic. To put the paradox more pointedly: how can it be that Evagrius
is praying truly if his doctrine has been determined to be false? Does
Evagrius's doctrinal heresy make him a false ally when it comes to prayer?
Besides the historical and political factors that influenced the reception
and condemnation of his doctrine (which prove too complex to unravel
here but have been covered reliably elsewhere),[56] might it be the case that
what Evagrius offers in his integrated vision of prayer and theology is the
reconfiguring of both 'practice' and 'belief'. The Christian practice of prayer
becomes less the thing I do and more God's practice 'in' me and Christian
belief, under the conditions of Evagrius's pedagogy of prayer, becomes less
an authority that demands my propositional assent and more a life into

---

[54]Harmless and Fitzgerald, 'The Sapphire Light of the Mind', 498.
[55]Harrison, *The Art of Listening*, 191.
[56]Casiday, *Reconstructing the Theology of Evagrius Ponticus*, 46–71 and several of the essays
in Joel Kalvesmaki and Robin Darling Young (eds), *Evagrius and His Legacy* (South Bend:
University of Notre Dame Press, 2016).

which I enter and by which I am transformed.[57] The original meaning of *orthodoxia*, after all, is 'right prayer'.

Summary

Evagrius's pedagogy of prayer, resolved as it is on explicating the theologically disclosive effects of true prayer and the practice-shaping effect of true belief, introduces many of the central themes that are taken up over the course of this book: contemplative training is a programme of intellectual formation; right speech about God and right prayer to God are irreducibly entangled; a deepening in knowledge of God goes hand in hand with a deepening in holiness; prayer is iconoclastic; the kneeling work of the theologian involves the expansion (rather than the suppression) of the mind; and prayer and theology are not two distinct activities that might occasionally collide but should be held together. For Evagrius, the question of how one speaks *to* God is precisely a question of how one speaks *about* God. It is this interaction between speaking to and speaking about that lies at the heart of Evagrius's pedagogy of prayer.

In the next chapter, although we step away from a focused attention on Evagrius, many of the themes explored above feed into the chapter's 'motifs on prayer'. These motifs seek to describe more broadly, and with some contemporary relevancy, the integrity of prayer and theology. But first we need to consider why some believe that the kind of pedagogy of prayer imagined by Evagrius proved ultimately unsustainable under the conditions of modern theology.

---

[57]For an account of prayer as complexifying the definitions of both practice and belief, see Sarah Coakley, 'Deepening "Practices": Perspectives from Ascetical and Mystical Theology', in *Practicing Theology: Beliefs and Practices in Christian Life*, ed. by Miroslav Volf and Dorothy C. Bass (Grand Rapids: William B. Eerdmans, 2001), 78–93.

CHAPTER 2
ON THE 'INTEGRITY' OF
PRAYER AND THEOLOGY

'For the sake of Christian theology,' A. N. Williams implores, 'for the sake of a genuinely Christian spirituality and for the sake of the ministers of the church, both clergy and lay, we must find a way back to the integration of theology as a discipline both systematic and contemplative.'[1] This chapter has two main tasks. First, it investigates what happened to the 'integrity' of prayer and theology that in Evagrius's day was completely unproblematic but if Williams is correct can no longer be assumed. As Williams implies, many have found that developments in theology's self-understanding so successfully carved new lines of demarcation around prayer and theology that their mutual mediation, as imagined by someone like Evagrius, is at risk of being lost altogether. After considering the consequences of this perceived breakdown, it then explores some of the contemporary 'turns to prayer' that have managed to swim against the stream of conventional wisdom in finding a way back to an understanding of theology as a discipline 'both systematic and contemplative'. Drawing from the writings of three contemporary theologians (Sarah Coakley, Rowan Williams and Nicholas Lash), these turns to prayer are consolidated into three 'motifs' on the integrity of prayer and theology.

The disintegration of prayer and theology

No longer should it be assumed that prayer and theology share the same goal. Paul J. Griffiths, for example, has recently argued that prayer and theology

---

[1]A. N. Williams, 'Mystical Theology Redux: The Pattern of Aquinas' *Summa Theologiae*', *Modern Theology*, 13.1 (1997), 53–74 (55).

are two appropriately separate ways of relating to God.[2] They have distinct aims and require different sets of skills. It is entirely possible for theologians to conduct theology with great success, he says, without praying just as it is entirely appropriate for the pray-er to pray truly without engaging in formal theological discourse. Theology desires what Griffiths calls 'cognitive intimacy' with God, while prayer seeks 'affective intimacy'. 'Theological discourse', Griffiths writes, 'aim[s] for a kind of intimacy with the Lord, but it's cognitive intimacy rather than fleshly or affective intimacy.'[3] Distinguishing prayer and theology in this way removes some of the difficulty we came up against in the previous chapter regarding the clearly awkward position to which history has consigned Evagrius – at once heretic and hero. Evagrius was deeply spiritual and clearly prayed truly. His theology, however, was confused and wrong. If Griffiths is correct, this is less problematic because the two seek different ends. However, as others have argued, this stark separation of prayer and theology presents a further set of problems, some of which will be discussed later in this chapter. The more immediate question to be asked is: how did we get from Evagrius's frictionless understanding of prayer and theology to the sharp distinction between the cognitive/affective we encounter in Griffiths and others?

'When and how this division entered theology is a question on which many different views are held,' says the Orthodox theologian Andrew Louth.[4] The emergence of the university, the rise of secularity, the disenchantment with the sacred, the perceived shifts in the function of theology and its tools of enquiry and the consolidation of metaphysics have been variously cited as some of the contributing factors, each knotty in their own right, that have led theology away from its 'contemplative end'.[5] There is a similar level of disagreement about precisely when this false turn occurred. Some argue that from as early as the end of the thirteenth century developments in the method of theology set the discipline on a path towards the disappearance of what Balthasar calls 'the "complete" theologian ... the theologian who is also a saint'.[6] Yet the approaching consensus among commentators is that

[2]Paul J. Griffiths, *The Practice of Catholic Theology: A Modest Proposal* (Washington: The Catholic University of America Press, 2016), 18–23.

[3]Griffiths, *The Practice of Catholic Theology*, 20.

[4]Louth, *Discerning the Mystery*, 4.

[5]John Webster, *God without Measure: Working Papers in Christian Theology – Volume 1: God and the Works of God* (London: T&T Clark, 2015), 220.

[6]Balthasar, 'Theology and Sanctity', 187. Gutiérrez also pinpoints the 'divorce ... between theology and spirituality' to around the same time. See Gutiérrez, *We Drink from our Own Wells*, 36.

these developments in theological method saw their culmination in the period of history known broadly as 'modernity'. As McIntosh explains, we have 'to speak of the *relationship* between theology and spirituality today for a simple reason: for most of modernity they have in fact existed separately'.[7] John Webster agrees, and offers the following explanation:

> It is no exaggeration to claim that a good deal of modern theology has been reluctant to consider contemplation a proper end of theological intelligence. The marks of this reluctance are not difficult to find. It may be seen, for example, in the remarkable prestige enjoyed by literary-historical science in the study of Holy Scripture; or in presentations of Christian doctrine which are devoid of metaphysical ambition and treat dogma as ancillary to the science of Christian practice which is first theology. The assumption (sometimes the explicitly articulated conviction) in both cases is that only the historical is the real, that intellect can extend itself no further than the economy of texts or moral practices. It is an impatient assumption, but one which has proved remarkably adept in shaping the purposes with which theological study is undertaken. Its elimination of the contemplative is an inhibition of theology's theological character.[8]

A full investigation into the disintegration of prayer and theology lies a good deal beyond the scope of the present chapter. It would require asking some probing questions not only of the origins of modernity but of the very nature of theology itself. Nevertheless, it is important still to touch, albeit selectively, on some of the headlining factors that many of the commentators feel sit behind the apparent disappearance of the 'complete' theologian.

Andrew Prevot's *Thinking Prayer: Theology and Spirituality amid the Crisis of Modernity* is one of the most comprehensive investigations to date of exactly the interlocking issues at stake. For Prevot, as for others, the 'ostensible division of theology and spirituality' is an invention of modern theology.[9] The progressive disconnection of 'thinking' and 'prayer',

---

[7]Mark A. McIntosh, 'Theology and Spirituality', in *The Modern Theologians: An Introduction to Christian Theology Since 1918*, ed. by David F. Ford and Rachel Muers (Oxford: Wiley-Blackwell, 2005; 3rd edn), 392–407 (392).

[8]Webster, *God without Measure*, 220.

[9]Prevot, *Thinking Prayer*, 5.

Prevot narrates, comes with significant and indeed violent consequences: it throws modern theology into nothing short of a 'crisis'. We will return to these consequences at the end of this section. In the interim, in terms of the presenting question of how this division entered the theological scene, Prevot names the 'rise of secularity' as one of the key factors contributing to the onset of modernity's 'prayer-denying intellectual culture'.[10] Working from Charles Taylor's thesis that the destabilization of the connection between religious practice and theory is one of the defining marks of secularity,[11] Prevot argues that 'many modern intellectual traditions tend to distort, conceal or marginalize the mystery of prayer through the exclusive promotion of various forms of secularity, that is, forms of worldliness that can be theorized and practiced without any interaction with the living God'.[12] That prayer is treated variously under the categories of superstition, magic and irrationality by some of the architects of modern philosophy – such as, Kant, Hegel and Nietzsche – confirms for Prevot that modern philosophical culture, and the kind of 'secular reason' it promotes, constructs thinking as antithetical to praying. Nietzsche's comment that prayer was 'invented for those who really never have thoughts of their own' becomes a case in point.[13]

The theme of secularization as a contributing factor to the breakdown of 'thinking' and 'prayer' is also visibly at work in much of the literature devoted to the emergence of the stomping ground of this new found 'secular reason': the modern university. For example, Gavin D'Costa argues in *Theology in the Public Square* that the evolution of the modern university is part and parcel of a wider project of secularization.[14] The shift from sacred to secular is described by D'Costa accordingly:

> The foundation of the universities took place in a universe with a sacred canopy, whereby people understood their practices to relate to

---

[10]Ibid., 19–21.

[11]See Charles Taylor, *A Secular Age* (Cambridge, MA: Harvard University Press, 2007), 25–41 and 303–4.

[12]Prevot, *Thinking Prayer*, 5.

[13]Friedrich Nietzsche, *The Gay Science: With a Prelude in Rhymes and an Appending of Songs* (New York: Random House, 1974), 184; and for Kant's denigration of prayer as a 'superstitious delusion' far removed from the frontiers of truth, see *Religion within the Boundaries of Mere Reason and Other Writings* (Cambridge: Cambridge University Press, 1998), 186 – hereafter, *Religion*.

[14]D'Costa, *Theology in the Public Square*, 1–37. For a supporting view, see Philip F. Sheldrake, *Explorations in Spirituality: History, Theology, and Social Practice* (New York: Paulist Press, 2010), 54–74.

an organic and cosmic pattern participating in the nature of reality. This reality was divinely created for the good of men and women, for the flourishing of human society, and for participation in truth and love. The modern university, with some exceptions, in contrast, develops its programs and practices without any reference to a sacred canopy.[15]

For D'Costa, the transition to secularism went hand in hand with the implementation of a new set of intellectual presuppositions that developed in contrast from those pursued under the 'sacred canopy' of earlier ways of learning. Under the canopy of the modern university, and its distinct patterns of reasoning, 'the discipline of theology becomes separated from the practices that are required for its undertaking: prayer, sacraments, and virtue.'[16]

Given the unique pressure the emergence of the modern university is said to have placed on the earlier bond of thinking and praying, a plotting of some of the most significant milestones in the history of the university's evolution may be helpful in getting a handle on the prayer–theology breakdown. This is not to say that the emergence of the university is the only or the most significant factor in the story of the detangling of prayer and theology but it is one that brings into sharper focus many of the main issues at stake. To tell this story we will follow D'Costa's narration and plot the evolution of the university in three historical stages: the monastic, the medieval and the modern, focusing at each stage on the position prayer found itself in.[17] It is important to emphasize from the outset that D'Costa's is just one way of telling the story of the origins of the university. There are others (one of which is discussed below) that identify in the kinds of practices of reason cultivated under the canopy of the modern university

---

[15]D'Costa, *Theology in the Public Square*, 2.
[16]Ibid., 5.
[17]The story of the origins of the university is complex, and the literature that investigates theology's role in the story is vast. For a sample of the most recent contributions to the now burgeoning field of university studies, see David F. Ford, *Christian Wisdom: Desiring God and Learning in Love* (Cambridge: Cambridge University Press, 2007), 304–49; Thomas Albert Howard, *Protestant Theology and the Making of the Modern German University* (Oxford: Oxford University Press, 2006); Mike Higton, *A Theology of Higher Education* (Oxford: Oxford University Press, 2012); and Johannes Zachhuber, *Theology as Science in Nineteenth-Century Germany: From F. C. Baur to Ernst Troeltsch* (Oxford: Oxford University Press, 2013).

far greater continuity with the intellectual practices associated with older forms of theological learning than does D'Costa. But first to D'Costa's classification, as representative of the majority voice.

Monastic

For much of the history of Christianity, theological learning was undertaken within a broadly monastic setting – whether in the monasteries themselves or later in the cathedral schools of the great European cities. In either case, theological learning was often arranged around and integrated with the spiritual practices of psalm-singing, chanting, meditation and the daily liturgy. When it comes to the integrity of prayer and theology, monastic learning represents for many the gold standard. Jean Leclercq, in his acclaimed account of learning in monastic culture, *The Love of Learning and the Desire for God*, paints a picture of the monastery as bound to a sapiential (which means 'wisdom-led') kind of learning that promoted the formation of character and celebrated the Greek concept of *paideia* (the process of 'cultivating the soul').[18] In monastic reasoning, he writes, 'it is God really who does the teaching; consequently, it is to Him that we must pray. In this light, just as there is no theology without moral life and asceticism, so there is no theology without prayer.'[19] The mind and its practices of reason are purified, regenerated and, by the grace of God, turned towards the gospel of Jesus Christ so that in the context of the liturgy, theology and its 'holy reason' is seen to acquire its true vocation, intelligibility and practical bearing.[20] As far as D'Costa sees it, the 'greatest strength' of this form of theological learning 'was the unity of theology with prayer and practice.'[21]

Medieval

As the venue of learning shifted from the monastery and cathedral school into the context of the medieval university, this earlier understanding of

---

[18]See Leclercq, *The Love of Learning and the Desire for God*, 5. See also, G. R. Evans, *Old Arts and New Theology: The Beginnings of Theology as an Academic Discipline* (Oxford: Clarendon Press, 1980).

[19]Leclercq, *The Love of Learning and the Desire for God*, 5.

[20]I am borrowing the term 'holy reason' from John Webster, *Holiness* (London: SCM Press, 2003), 23–4.

[21]D'Costa, *Theology in the Public Square*, 8.

theology as formation in holiness (*paideia*) also began to show signs of movement. According to McIntosh, the 'academic mission of these new venues for learning was quite different from the monastic schools – where growth in Christian knowledge had taken place in the context of practising Christianity as a way of life. In the new universities, Christian discourse migrated from exegetical contemplation of biblical texts into a rational argument about logical propositions.'[22] In the most famous university of the medieval period, the University of Paris, founded in the twelfth century, patterns of reasoning based on disputation, rational argument and the scholastic methods of logic and dialectics came to dominate the intellectual agenda. The result of these new patterns of learning, D'Costa reports, was the widening of the gap between prayer and theology, which to this point had been narrow. 'Theology became disassociated from prayer and contemplation,' he writes.[23] Additionally, the institutional organization of Paris anticipated what many now call the 'fragmentation' of knowledge. The study of theology became dissociated from other academic pursuits (such as the arts, medicine and law) as well as from the liturgy.[24] The fragmentation of theology came to reflect externally the internal fragmentations of the self in which the body and mind (the 'affective' and the 'cognitive', to use Griffiths's terminology) were increasingly being pulled apart.

Modern

The distinction between prayer and theology is customarily thought to have sharpened at the beginning of the nineteenth century and the new age of academic learning it heralded. From monastery to cathedral school through to the medieval era, the final resting place of theological learning was the modern university. The University of Berlin, widely regarded as the first modern university, was founded in 1810 on the mandate to reflect the Enlightenment-inspired ideals of the modern age. The gatekeeper for

---

[22]McIntosh, 'Theology and Spirituality', 394.
[23]D'Costa, *Theology in the Public Square*, 14.
[24]On this, see Edward Farley, *Theologia: The Fragmentation and Unity of Theological Education* (Philadelphia: Fortress Press, 1983). For studies from the same era, see David H. Kelsey, *Between Athens and Jerusalem: The Theological Education Debate* (Grand Rapids: William B. Eerdmans, 1993) and The Mud Flower Collective, *God's Fierce Whimsy: Christian Feminism and Theological Education* (New York: Pilgrim Press, 1985), which highlights feminist concerns with the state of theological education in the North American seminary context.

the inclusion of theology into Berlin's new sociality of learning was the principle of *Wissenschaft*. According to D'Costa's definition, *Wissenschaft* 'intentionally defined itself against the earlier model of *paideia* which had characterized ecclesial forms of education (and dominant forms of pre-Christian Greek education) and instead emphasized a critical, orderly, and disciplined science of research'.[25] As D'Costa suggests, the Berlin model appeared to clash quite considerably with the older, ecclesial ways of education in which theological learning was deepened through prayer and prayer through learning. This threw the discipline of theology into something of an identity crisis: it needed to adapt or face exclusion. Like other disciplines seeking entry into Berlin, Christian theology, Hans Frei explains, found itself 'in the position of having to demonstrate that it was truly *wissenschaftlich* and had a right to citizenship in [the] university'.[26]

The work of demonstrating Christian theology's right to citizenship largely fell into the hands of the father of modern theology, sometime rector of Berlin and designer of its theology faculty: F. D. E. Schleiermacher. To rise to the new standards of the *Wissenschaftsideologie*, under Schleiermacher's leadership the discipline of theology distanced itself from the ecclesially driven forms of education by way of a complex process of internal and external reconstitution. Internally, in careful conversation with Enlightenment thought, Schleiermacher sought to shift the ground of theology from the traditional sense of 'revealed religion', which had been rendered newly suspicious by modern thinking, to the category of religious 'feeling'. Experience rather than revelation was famously at the heart of his vision for the kind of investigation to which the faculty of theology in Berlin would be committed.[27] Christian theology, thus, revolutionizes itself from within by shifting its concern from describing 'God' to describing, as it were, the 'experience' of God. Externally, theology had to abdicate its position as the queen of the sciences, and all the self-confidence that that brought, to take up shop at the less regal fringes of the university as a humble provider of 'professional training'. The case for the inclusion of theology within the university was pitched, therefore, on the basis of the increasingly deal-breaking notion of the 'public good'. Just as the university

---

[25]D'Costa, *Theology in the Public Square*, 16.
[26]Frei, *Types of Christian Theology*, 99.
[27]For Schleiermacher's systematic outworking of this, see *The Christian Faith* (London: T&T Clark, 1999).

had a public responsibility to provide high-grade professional training for lawyers and doctors, Berlin had an equivalent responsibility for the provision of the training of the church's professionals: its ministers. But what happened to prayer within these tectonic shifts that took place in early nineteenth-century renditions of theology?

It was not the case that the Berlin theologians suddenly stopped praying. No doubt prayer continued both privately and corporately. Rather, the question concerns how the practice of prayer, which had not ceased, now relates to the formal task of theology: and what Berlin offered was a way of doing theology that was no longer absolutely reliant on the practice of prayer. Prayer could be newly isolated from the academic study of theology, distinguished into a separate category of 'private devotion' and kept out of the public space of the university. Under the hermeneutics of suspicion within which much of modern theology operated, there was a lost confidence in prayer's premodern capacity to disclose theological truth. Belonging to a long since crumbled world, prayer (and its relation to critical thought) was now seen to intrude where it was no longer welcome, blunting the sharpness of critical inquiry with an uncritical, anti-rational piety. To take an example from the discipline of biblical studies, the long-held tools of the biblical exegete of contemplation and prayer were displaced by rigorous and universally accountable research methodologies drawing from historical–critical rather than theological–doxological categories. If the idea of the modern university was founded on 'universal canons of evidence and inquiry',[28] the doxological commitments bound up in prayer meant that prayer could no longer reliably secure the *wissenschaftlich* conditions to study the Bible objectively – in fact, it was judged to get in the way. The contemplative and the academic came to conflict in other areas of the study of theology too. Take Christology as another example in which a sharp discontinuity emerged in the debate at the time about the Jesus of history (as an academic quest) and the Christ of faith (as a spiritual priority).

The need for individual disciplines, such as biblical studies, to prove their *wissenschaftlich* credentials was part of the realization of the 'fragmentation' of theology, as mentioned above. Although admirably aiming to stimulate disciplined, specialized dialogue, some have argued that the fragmentation programme sowed the seeds, perhaps fatally, for

---

[28]Farley, *Theologia*, 40.

the final separation of prayer and theology. In earlier forms of theological learning 'theology' was taken to be a single enterprise. As Philip Sheldrake comments, theology once 'encompassed a synthesis of exegesis, speculative reasoning and mystical contemplation'.[29] But in the modern university, the single enterprise of theology would be carved up into distinct disciplinary areas, each dedicated to specialist conversation. The disciplinary areas would develop to include biblical studies, doctrinal theology, historical theology, moral theology, philosophical theology and practical theology. And the subject of prayer, as part of the practical business of the church, would find a natural home in practical (or pastoral) theology but crucially not in something like doctrinal theology or theological ethics. Wherever it landed in the curriculum reshuffle, the contemplative and the systematic ended up on either side of a carefully patrolled disciplinary divide.

In an unfortunate sense, it could be said that prayer was caught in the grip of a process of double marginalization. Whereas prayer had once pulsed through all branches of knowledge, it had now been pushed to the margins of the university along with all else theological. From there, prayer was then pushed to the margins of the already marginal, finding home in the practical theology that was at risk of appearing intellectually second rate to its more 'academic' siblings. As Stanley Hauerwas and Samuel Wells explain: what was once the highest function of the mind was 'relegated to the lower divisions of the academy, regarded as the realm of the "merely pious", open to sociological and psychological investigation certainly, but remote from the frontiers of truth'.[30] When, sometime later, the professional training of the ministers of the church migrated from the modern university to separate institutions altogether – with the birth of the theological seminary in the late nineteenth century – these disciplinary distinctions would solidify into institutional barriers that had the potential to compound even further the detachment of theology from its 'contemplative end'.

The subject of prayer, however, would eventually make its way back into the modern university under the auspices of the emerging discipline of 'spirituality studies'. In being unseated from its position as

---

[29]Philip Sheldrake, *Spirituality and History: Questions of Interpretation and Method* (London: SPCK, 1995), 46.
[30]Stanley Hauerwas and Samuel Wells, 'Christian Ethics as Informed Prayer', in *The Blackwell Companion to Christian Ethics*, ed. by Stanley Hauerwas and Samuel Wells (Oxford: Wiley-Blackwell, 2011; 2nd edn), 3–12 (4).

the indispensable practice upon which all knowledge was reliant, prayer re-enters the university as a focus of study in its own right. Within the study of spirituality, practices such as prayer are now treated as religious phenomena that can be analysed 'objectively' under 'universal canons of evidence and inquiry'.[31] Prayer, as a practice of popular devotion, might be investigated from perspectives such as the historical, psychological, anthropological and sociological but not necessarily integrated into the task of systematic theology. In fact, the pioneers of the field insist on a strong methodological distinction between the study of spirituality and the study of theology – one dealing with practice, the other with belief. Despite showcasing prayer as generative of academic debate, some have argued that the outsourcing of 'spirituality' to a discrete sub-discipline, distinct from say systematic theology, risks reproducing the perceived nineteenth-century failure of theology to recognize that its very raison d'être should be found in concerns that are ultimately those of the spiritual life. In 'sub-contracting' prayer out, theology loses sight of its intrinsically spiritual nature. 'What an irony it would be', McIntosh writes, 'if the academicians finally allowed the return of spirituality as a conversation partner in the university, only to consign it … to a non-theological realm labelled, appropriately, "private devotion".'[32] The study of spirituality, as articulated by some of its principal theoreticians, would seem to reinforce (albeit from the other side) exactly the methodological separation between theology and prayer this book is trying to problematize. Even 'with the most well-meaning intentions', the anthropological approach of much of commitment-free spirituality studies, McIntosh concludes, seems likely to perpetuate 'the divorce between spirituality and theology' and prevent the recovery of the genuine reciprocity that sees prayer not

---

[31]Sandra M. Schneiders is a leading voice in this field, see Schneiders, 'Approaches to the Study of Christian Spirituality', in *The Blackwell Companion to Christian Spirituality*, ed. by Arthur Holder (Oxford: Blackwell, 2005), 15–34. The anthropologist Marcel Mauss, well known for his game-changing study on the 'gift', assumes a similar approach to prayer to that represented by Schneider. Like Evagrius and Origen (whose *De oratione* is credited as 'among the very best discussions' of prayer) before him, Mauss too wrote a 'La Prière'. It was his unfinished doctoral thesis. Published posthumously, he says in the first sentence of the study that he seeks to examine prayer 'from the outside' – that is to say, objectively. See Marcel Mauss, *On Prayer: Text and Commentary*, ed. by W. S. F. Pickering (New York: Durkheim Press, 2003), 22.

[32]McIntosh, *Mystical Theology*, 23. See also, Prevot, *Thinking Prayer*, 30–2.

simply as a self-contained subject of study but as supplying the intellectual framework for theological discourse itself.[33]

In learning to be *wissenschaftlich*, D'Costa feels that theology had forgotten something of its original meaning. The pedagogy of prayer imagined by a figure such as Evagrius and the theological habits of thought such a pedagogy implied were displaced by a fully secularized, fully *wissenschaftlich* account of reason. In other words, in the modern university regularized practices of prayer and the very venture of theological thinking are set to pull in fundamentally opposing directions: they simply do not mix. Because 'institutional university theology [to this day] bears many of the marks of this secularized process', D'Costa feels compelled to conclude that 'properly understood, [theology] cannot be taught and practiced within the modern university'.[34] Theologians, therefore, 'must pray for release' from the 'Babylonian captivity' of the modern university.[35]

D'Costa's account of the rise of the university and the construction of theology as distinct from the practice of prayer presumes a particular reading of the history of the origins of the university. Other readings of the same events suggest that 'university reason' might not be as oppositional to the kind of reason rooted in the contemplative culture of monastic theology as D'Costa implies. In *A Theology of Higher Education*, for example, Mike Higton tells a revisionist story of university origins that understands in certain practices of corporate reasoning developed in the medieval University of Paris 'a form of meditative spiritual discipline' that although no longer 'tied to monastic life' remained very much grounded in virtue and 'ordered towards the establishment of well-ordered individual and public life before God'.[36] It should be remembered that Thomas Aquinas, a product of a Parisian medieval education, represents a prime

---

[33]McIntosh, *Mystical Theology*, 21.

[34]D'Costa, *Theology in the Public Square*, 17.

[35]Ibid., 112–44.

[36]Higton, *A Theology of Higher Education*, 36. This accords with Walter Rüegg, the great historian of university origins, who includes within the seven core values of the medieval university the need for continual 'modesty, reverence, and self-criticism' in the course of improving knowledge – themes that Ford relates to the Christian practice of penitential prayer. See Walter Rüegg, 'Themes', in *A History of the University in Europe – Volume 1: Universities in the Middle Ages*, ed. by H. De Ridder-Symoens (Cambridge: Cambridge University Press, 1991), 3–34 and Ford, *Christian Wisdom*, 307.

example of the monastic flowering of the patristic unity of prayer and theology.[37]

These spiritual traits would survive in modified form within the University of Berlin.[38] The practices of intensive dialogue and disagreement and the pursuit of critical clarity prized by Berlin can be understood as forms of *spiritual* practice. For Higton, 'academic study is a form of spiritual formation – in the sense that (at its best) it is a process in which one is stripped of illusions of control and mastery, and overwhelmed by a subject matter that does not fit neatly into one's life. It is a process in which one both repeatedly has to risk interpretations, but in which one is also repeatedly opened up to judgment.'[39] Moreover, 'it is a process in which the learner is – or can be – trained precisely in *contemplation*: in patient, risky, transformative exposure to an as-yet-ungrasped truth which can only be encountered with a humility that is willing to lay down preconceptions and fixed ideas'.[40] In this sense, Higton contests the dominant narrative that constructs reason as antithetical to prayer and concludes that 'university reason emerges not *over against* Christian devotion, but *as a form of Christian devotion*'.[41] Far from being held captive by *wissenschaftlich* ideals, modern university theology can be about the training in the very practices of virtue that order the mind to the contemplation of God. Curiously, if Higton is right, it may well be that the modern university contains exactly the resources needed to overcome the opposition between the contemplative and the systematic that the university is often blamed for introducing into modern theology.

Whether the emergence of the university brought about a complete separation (D'Costa) or more of a modification of an earlier union (Higton), the factors contributing to the breakdown of the integrity of prayer and theology remain multiple and complex. As Webster writes, 'One could arrange an entire history of modern theology around that theme: the intellectual afflictions which had attended the progressive detachment of

---

[37]For an exploration of the spirituality of Thomas's dogmatic theology, see Jean-Pierre Torrell, *Saint Thomas Aquinas – Volume 2: Spiritual Master* (Washington: Catholic University of America Press, 2003).

[38]Higton, *A Theology of Higher Education*, 43–78.

[39]Mike Higton, 'Can the University and the Church Save Each Other?' *CrossCurrents*, 55.2 (2005), 172–83 (179) – emphasis removed.

[40]Higton, 'Can the University and the Church Save Each Other?' 179.

[41]Higton, *A Theology of Higher Education*, 13.

reason from piety.'[42] However the shifting understanding of the nature of theology might have arrived on the theological scene, its consequences are significant.

Making good on our earlier promise to return to Prevot's important study, one of the principal symptoms of the disintegration of prayer and theology outlined in *Thinking Prayer* is the suppression of 'black doxology'.[43] This is part of a broader package of structural 'violence' that Prevot finds underlying much of modern theology. The theological marginalization of black doxological voices, and the concomitant promulgation of Eurocentrism and white supremacy, Prevot argues, 'conspires with long-standing intellectual, cultural, and political processes of denigration, which both conceal and perpetuate the deadly consequences of modernity's antiblack idolatry'.[44] Informed by the black liberation theology of James Cone (whose theology dialogued deeply with the black spiritual traditions of prayer), Prevot argues that the songs of the enslaved and the lived spiritual experience of marginalized communities contain exactly the counter-violent tools that are required to navigate theological thinking's escape from the intersecting crises of modern theology and its ties to Western metaphysics. Black doxology, Prevot concludes, offers 'a genuinely peaceful communion between God and all of God's creatures'.[45] In an Evagrian sense, the 'Spirit-filled songs of the slaves' are truly 'disclosive' of theological truth. 'The prayers ... become an indispensable source of intellectual and practical insight regarding the mysteries of God and the world.'[46] To suppress these voices is to suppress the liberative voice of God. Prevot's is a complex and provocative argument, particularly concerning his 'doxological alternative' to metaphysics,[47] and one that requires more unpacking than can be undertaken here. It should, nevertheless, signify that the ramifications of the disintegration of theology and prayer are considerable and far-reaching, perhaps more so than might initially be expected.

A differently problematic set of consequences of the breakdown of prayer and theology is identified by McIntosh:

---

[42]Webster, *Holiness*, 30.
[43]Prevot, *Thinking Prayer*, 280–325.
[44]Ibid., 281.
[45]Ibid., 323.
[46]Ibid., 280.
[47]See Part I of *Thinking Prayer* for Prevot's account of the counter-violent move 'from metaphysics to doxology'.

Put as bluntly as possible, theology without spirituality becomes ever more methodologically refined but unable to know or speak of the very mysteries at the heart of Christianity, and spirituality without theology becomes rootless, easily hijacked by individualistic consumerism. Part of the difficulty of the ramifications of such a divorce are obscure until one sees the proper integrity of contemplative encounter and dogmatic theology; for apart from their mutual interaction the true functioning of each becomes easily misconceived. In other words, when a culture has grown used to the divorce between theology and spirituality, between doctrine and prayer, then the mutually critical function of the two breaks down. Neither is in sufficiently dialogue with the other to keep it honest. And after a long period of such separation it becomes increasingly difficult to see what is missing in so much of the pale pretenders that pass fairly often for theology and spirituality today. But if one can catch sight of their natural interrelationship, then, the problems inherent in their divorce become painfully apparent.[48]

For McIntosh, the disconnection of prayer and theology seems to immobilize true theology. It prevents it from getting going. Williams paints a similarly bleak picture of what happens to the category of 'spirituality' when it becomes theologically footloose and historically fancy free.

Contemporary works on spirituality are as bare of theological insight as theological ones are uninterested in spirituality: they float free of explicit theological grounding, some even actively discouraging intellectual engagement (though admittedly, few evince interest in ascetical disciplines, either). Indeed, a good deal of contemporary spirituality overtly suggests that thinking damages prayer, that modern people think too much in general, and that they need to unlearn the latter bad habit if they are to become prayerful or holy persons.[49]

---

[48]McIntosh, *Mystical Theology*, 10.
[49]A. N. Williams, *The Divine Sense: The Intellect in Patristic Theology* (Cambridge: Cambridge University Press, 2007), 1–2.

As we have seen with Prevot, under the conditions of modernity prayer was thought to damage thinking. What we are seeing now with Williams is that thinking is thought to damage prayer: the beliefs that are inherently bound up with practices are seen to get in the way of prayer. Indeed, it is a truism to say that we are living in a 'spiritual age'. In the exponential embrace of (duly modified) practices such as prayer in the increasingly crowded market place of 'Christian spirituality', what is invariably taken up is exactly that: the *practice* of prayer. The beliefs associated with prayer are left behind. Take, as an example among many, the contemporary spiritual practice of 'mindfulness' which can be seen to borrow aspects from the Evagrian practice of 'imageless prayer' but leave behind, in a way that would be utterly abhorrent to Evagrius, the doctrinal theory to which the practice refers. The associated belief is made optional at best and untrustworthy at worst. This leaves the practice of prayer suspended rather precariously in mid-air, somewhere between belief and non-belief, and vulnerable to all the distortions described above.[50] Recovering a more integrated account of belief and practice makes extracting practices from the complicated nexus of belief and tradition in which they are historically situated that bit more complicated than is often assumed within the 'supernova' of spirituality in which contemporary culture is said to be engulfed.[51]

Prevot, McIntosh and Williams agree that the cost of a theology that bypasses prayer on the way to belief is also high. The risk is to fulfil exactly the prophecy of contemporary works on spirituality that theology 'thinks too much'. Theology becomes a highly intellectualist, cognitive endeavour that risks undertaking its business in abstraction from the Christian life. As Balthasar comments, 'Theology at prayer was superseded by theology at the desk, and this brought about the cleavage now under discussion. "Scientific" theology became more and more divorced from prayer, and so lost the accent and tone with which it should speak of what is holy, while "affective" theology, as it became increasingly empty, often degenerated into unctuous, platitudinous piety.'[52] It is for reasons such as this that Andrew Louth, citing

---

[50]For a careful exposition, from which McIntosh draws, of what happens to the spiritual category of 'experience', as understood in the mystical traditions, when practice is abstracted from theory, see Denys Turner, *The Darkness of God: Negativity in Christian Mysticism* (Cambridge: Cambridge University Press, 1995).

[51]Taylor, *A Secular Age*, 300.

[52]Balthasar, 'Theology and Sanctity', 208.

Evagrius, insists that while theology is necessary to keep prayer to its true vocation, prayer presents a reciprocal challenge to theology 'to keep *it* to *its* proper vocation'.[53] In reuniting prayer with theology, theology is most comprehensively stimulating. It is a 'way of life' that stirs up the mind, body and soul, and in so doing overcomes the disjunctive divide introduced between the cognitive and the affective.[54]

Having plotted some of the factors and consequences of the disintegration of prayer and theology, the task ahead is to 'catch sight of their natural interrelationship' through three 'motifs' on the integrity of prayer and theology.

Motifs on the integrity of prayer and theology

Despite the perceived breakdown of the integrity of theology and prayer in modern theological studies discussed above, there are moves within contemporary Christian theology that attempt to keep together the contemplative and the systematic. In what follows, we engage these 'turns to prayer' through the writings of three contemporary theologians who not only take prayer to be an unavoidably theological undertaking but see prayer as inextricably entangled with the theological task, seek to integrate prayer with high-grade theological reflection and refuse the caricature of prayer as a movement of intellectual detachment.[55] The following three motifs experiment, then, with the thesis that prayer and theology are best

---

[53] Andrew Louth, *Theology and Spirituality* (Oxford: Fairacres Publications, 1976), 4.

[54] This or that theological statement stands or falls, as Simeon Zahl argues in his investigation of the 'affective salience' of Christian doctrine, 'not just on whether it is right or wrong but also on how it shapes Christian affective experience'. Zahl concludes that 'doctrinal disputes in the history of theology are rarely purely exegetical, logical, or traditional, but often relate to a whole vision of what it is to be a Christian person in the world, and take for granted that one cannot make a wise decision about whether to support a doctrine without taking its full practical impact and affective shape into account'. See Simon Zahl, 'On the Affective Salience of Doctrines', *Modern Theology*, 31.3 (2015), 428–44 (432, 434).

[55] The motifs explored in this chapter do not aim to be comprehensive in scope. Indeed, there are three recent systematic projects that do not feature below despite according prayer, in diverse and interesting ways, significant weight: Paul R. Hinlicky's systematic theology contains a long chapter on prayer, see *Beloved Community: Critical Dogmatics after Christendom* (Grand Rapids: William B. Eerdmans, 2015), 613–90; the first volume of Graham Ward's systematic project is shot through with prayer, see *How the Light Gets In: Ethical Life I* (Oxford: Oxford University Press, 2016), 173–80; and Katherine Sonderegger describes her

understood not as distinct activities but as 'integrally' related. As Prevot explains:

> The desired integration might be conceived of entailing not only a reciprocal influence upon the other but also a significant degree of inseparability: ... we may be dealing not so much with the reciprocity of the two ... realities but with one complex reality glimpsed from different angles.[56]

It is in this mutual mediation that theology is at its most 'theological'.[57] The first motif, in dialogue with Sarah Coakley, discusses prayer's role in the resistance to 'systematic foreclosure'. The second develops this theme through the prayer-soaked writings of Rowan Williams, utilizing his categories of 'dispossession' and 'honesty'. The third and final motif explores through the writings of Nicholas Lash the relation between prayer, theology and idolatry. It is important to note that the thinkers engaged with below are under no illusion that theology must uncritically return to the golden age of the (Evagrian) unity of prayer and theology – where prayer was the principal expression and generator of theology. Their shared concern instead is about renegotiating theology according to a pedagogy of prayer for the contemporary context in which systematic theology operates.

Prayer and the resistance to systematic foreclosure

One of the most prolific forces behind the recent recovery of the theological significance of prayer is Sarah Coakley. Coakley has written extensively on the extraordinary theological power of prayer and its relation to a diverse set of thorny issues, including: gender, ethnicity, sexuality, desire, pain and the

---

Systematic Theology – Volume 1: The Doctrine of God (Minneapolis: Fortress Press, 2015) as an exercise in 'intellectual prayer'.

[56]Prevot, *Thinking Prayer*, 18.

[57]This kind of mutual meditation between prayer and theology bears similarities with Webster's vision for a 'theological theology', which is a call for theology to attend to its own distinctive habits of thought in a way that is unashamed of its unavoidably spiritual character. For Webster's articulation of 'theological theology', see *God without Measure*, 213–24.

doctrine of the Trinity.[58] Across her writings is to be found perhaps the fullest contemporary articulation of a way of doing systematic theology that is urgently reintegrated with prayer.

There are three broad features of Coakley's theological commitment to prayer discussed below. First is the personal commitment to the practice of prayer. By 'prayer' Coakley means a particular kind of disciplined 'contemplative waiting on God', a deep attention to God. As the theologian waits before God, the mind is emptied of all that is not God in order to be filled with the knowledge of who God 'is'. The repetitive practice of contemplative prayer, undertaken over the long haul, is the training through which one inhabits the process of what Coakley might call 'epistemic transformation' – that is to say, in transforming the mind, prayer provides '*new* levels of perception and sensation, *new* ways of "perceiving God"'.[59] Prayer, here, is about belief-production. We will encounter an example of the kind of theological opportunities produced by prayer when we explore her 'prayer-based' approach to the doctrine of the Trinity in the next chapter. The point to be emphasized now is that Coakley insists on the integration of the experience of God in prayer with the task of systematic theology: prayer resources the theologian and their work. In fact, systematic theology goes astray when this kind of integration is thwarted or denied. Systematic theology 'without contemplative and ascetic practices comes with the danger of rending itself void'.[60] Therefore, for Coakley, the practice of theology when rerouted in this way is *more* not less sophisticated, more not less critical, more not less intellectually demanding. Second, and relatedly, is the commitment to prayer as a source of theology. According to Coakley, the writings associated with prayer that have tended to be sidelined in modern theology also need to be integrated with the task of systematic theology. As either resource or source, rather than keeping prayer at a safe distance, Coakley unleashes it on the systematic project, allowing prayer to direct, shape and

---

[58]Details of Coakley's most important writings on prayer to date can be found in the Appendix. Coakley's writings on prayer are not uncontroversial. For a recent critique, see Linn Marie Tonstad, *God and Difference: The Trinity, Sexuality, and the Transformation of Finitude* (New York: Routledge, 2016).

[59]Sarah Coakley, 'Dark Contemplation and Epistemic Transformation: The Analytic Theologian Re-meets Teresa of Ávila', in *Analytic Theology: New Essays in the Philosophy of Theology*, ed. by Oliver D. Crisp and Michael C. Rea (Oxford: Oxford University Press, 2009), 280–312 (304).

[60]Sarah Coakley, *God, Sexuality, and the Self: An Essay 'On the Trinity'* (Cambridge: Cambridge University Press, 2012), 45.

enrich the task of systematic theology from beginning to end. The third feature of Coakley's theological commitment to prayer is the recasting of the project of systematic theology as a contemplative exercise. What should drive theology is neither systematic neatness nor conceptual resolution but nothing less than a desire for God. Theology, when cast in prayer, becomes a way of life: it becomes a sort of prayer. Working from these broad features, the focus in what follows is Coakley's methodological insistence that prayer is the wellspring for the sort of critical regeneration not only of individual doctrines but of the project of systematic theology itself, a regeneration that some have argued is long overdue. It is here that we locate the first of our three motifs on prayer: prayer and the resistance to systematic foreclosure.

For some, Coakley reports, the days of systematic theology have long been numbered.[61] She cites two key interlocking criticisms of the systematic task:

> The first resistance to systematic theology resides in the philosophical critique of so-called 'onto-theology': it claims that systematic theology falsely, and idolatrously, turns God into an object of human knowledge. The second resistance arises from the moral or political critique of so-called 'hegemony': it sees systematic theology (amongst other discourses that provide any purportedly complete vision of an intellectual landscape), as inappropriately totalizing, and thereby necessarily suppressive of the voices and perspectives of marginalized people.[62]

Often played out in postmodern discourses, the first critique says that as long as systematic theology remains in the business of seeking to present an integrated and coherent vision of Christian theology, it will inevitably succumb to the idolatrous tendency to 'over-systematize' God. There is a common risk across the various guises of the systematic project to tie up loose ends, iron out messy creases and ultimately domesticate into the constraints of a system the uncontainable God who always lies beyond our comprehension or control. If this critique is that the enterprise of systematic theology is too systematic, the second critique Coakley identifies is that

---

[61]See Coakley, *God, Sexuality, and the Self*, 42–51 for her account of the current state of the discipline.

[62]Coakley, *God, Sexuality, and the Self*, 42. To these two, Coakley adds a connecting third: the history of the project of systematic theology has been concerned with particularly 'male' patterns of 'phallocentric' thought that are obsessed with control and mastery and therefore 'inherently repressive of "feminine" imagination'. See Coakley, *God, Sexuality, and the Self*, 49.

systematic theology is not systematic enough. The history of systematic theology, in its bid for systematization, has been 'inappropriately totalizing' in the way it has closed down possibilities for fruitful theological conversation from voices that classically fall outside of the systematic mainstream.[63]

In the argument that lies at the heart of the first instalment of her projected five-volume systematic odyssey, *God, Sexuality, and the Self: An Essay 'On the Trinity'*, Coakley suggests that these two critiques lose their edge when the systematic task is rerouted through regularized practices of prayer. For Coakley, only in prayer can the systematic project gain its meaning: prayer makes available new theological discoveries in a way that does not contradict but strengthens critical freedom.

Regarding prayer's blunting of the first critique of the systematic task (to be considered in more detail under the next motif's category of 'dispossession'), in prayer the desire to control the 'object' of theology within an all-too-systematic system is 'kenotically' reworked from within by the interruptive work of the Holy Spirit.[64] The theory of prayer we investigated in conversation with Evagrius similarly calls into question the idea that God is an 'object of knowledge'. God is 'imageless', as Evagrius is at wont to remind us. A theology grounded in prayer loosens theology from the hard grip of epistemological security and renders it constantly in flux – 'in via' as Coakley puts it.[65] In prayer, God is experienced not as an object to be grasped, controlled or even understood, but as the eventful subject who, as that which is beyond all concept and image, grasps us. Knowledge of God, forged in the context of the 'dark night' of prayer, is about sharing, therefore, in God's own knowledge. And that sharing in what God 'is' involves the humility that even then, even in the most acute 'experience' of the divine, God remains beyond the theologian's experiential or conceptual reach – so far beyond that the attempt to systematize God into a controllable system is not simply rendered impossible but the longing towards systematization itself is chastened by the reforming work of the Holy Spirit. In a very Evagrian sense, Coakley insists that the task of theological understanding is inseparable from the ongoing project of the purification of desire; a purification that takes place on one's knees, in contemplation.

---

[63]Coakley, *God, Sexuality, and the Self*, 42.
[64]'Kenosis' appears across Coakley's writings. See the essays on the subject collected in Part I of her *Powers and Submission: Spirituality, Philosophy and Gender* (Oxford: Blackwell, 2002).
[65]Coakley, *God, Sexuality, and the Self*, 15–20.

The response to the second critique, which concerns systematic theology's failure to be robustly systematic, has to do with the broader methodological move Coakley makes in the volume. The methodology developed by Coakley – again, informed by prayer and structured around a contemplative waiting on the divine – that does much of the heavy lifting in this new paradigm for systematic theology is dubbed '*théologie totale*'. This is Coakley's explanation of her methodology, and it is worth citing in full:

> The method of *théologie totale* … is … rooted in an exploration of the many mediums and levels at which theological truth may be engaged. It is in this sense that it deserves the appellation *totale*: not as a totalizing assault on worldly power, but as an attempt to do justice to every level, and type, of religious apprehension and its appropriate mode of expression. Thus it is devoted precisely to the excavation and evaluation of what has previously been neglected: to theological fieldwork a variety of illuminating social and political contexts (not merely those of privilege, in fact especially not); to religious cultural productions of the arts and the imaginations; to neglected or sidelined texts in the tradition; and to explanation of the differences made to theology by such factors as gender, class, or race. In short, *théologie totale* makes the bold claim that the more systematic one's intentions, the more necessary the exploration of such dark and neglected corners; and that, precisely as theology *in via*, *théologie totale* continually risks destabilization and redirection. In an important sense, then, this form of systematic theology must always also remain, in principle, *unsystematic* if by that one means open to the possibility of risk and challenge. This playful oxymoron ('unsystematic systematics') applies just to the extent that the undertaking renders itself persistently vulnerable to interruptions from the unexpected – through its radical practices of attention to the Spirit.[66]

Théologie totale promises a great deal. Systematic theology, particularly in its Protestant incarnations, is often informed by a monolithic canon of literature that leaves spiritual sources insufficiently surveyed. A *théologie totale*, however, opens theology up to a theological bombardment from

---

[66]Ibid., 48. A fuller description of the methodology can be found at 44–51, and is developed again at 88–92.

multiple interdisciplinary directions in an effort to integrate systematically robust doctrinal thinking with embodied practices, critical theory, gender and feminist studies, neglected patristic texts, the visual arts, the social sciences, fieldwork and, above all else, prayer. In a *théologie totale*, all is primed for theological grabbing but especially the spiritual writings, devotional texts, tracts on prayer and the lives of the mystics. No longer banished to the 'realm of the merely pious' or simply regarded as the stuff of 'spirituality', prayer is celebrated as a core, indispensable source of theological insight.

By reconceiving the project of systematic theology through the practice of prayer, the spiritual texts that have been pushed to the parameters of theological discourse are now also brought closer to the centre of the task of theology. This formed part of the rationale for re-engaging the work of Evagrius of Ponticus, himself marginalized by conciliar theology, in the previous chapter. But the process of the migration of prayer from the edges to the centre is not simply to include the voices and texts that are otherwise vulnerable to marginalization into a now larger but just as closed systematic fold. Instead, *théologie totale* is about having the systematic project disrupted and transformed by those voices and texts.[67] It is in that disruption that systematic theology's conceptual 'foreclosure' is further resisted. And it is in prayer, as understood by Coakley, that the 'radical practices of attention' required to identify and hear those neglected voices are cultivated, along with the conditions of humility that make those 'interruptions from the unexpected' possible.[68] Whether the unexpected interruptions come through

---

[67]Although Coakley does not herself make this explicit, there is a connection to liberation theologies to be made. Liberation theologians have long said that the voices of the people that might otherwise be silenced must be brought to bear on the theological task because in these voices the (disruptive) voice of God's revelation in history is heard. See Jon Sobrino, *Spirituality of Liberation: Toward Political Holiness* (Maryknoll: Orbis Books, 1985), 46–79. A similar commitment to the theologically marginalized can be found in Prevot's study. Drawing on postcolonial theory and the writings of James Cone in particular, an underlying argument of *Thinking Prayer* is that the sidelining of spirituality is a product of the white supremacy that Prevot argues contaminates much of modern theology. We said earlier that Prevot suggests, with Evagrian undertones, that the 'prayers of the slaves', and the 'black doxological tradition' more generally, should be allowed to become 'an indispensable source of intellectual and practical insight regarding the mysteries of the world'. If Coakley explores prayer at the intersection of gender and sexuality primarily in dialogue with the patristic tradition, Prevot explores the complex relationship between prayer, ethnicity, oppression and liberation in dialogue with the post-metaphysical tradition.

[68]Coakley, *God, Sexuality, and the Self*, 49.

creative engagements with a wider variety of genres of writings, through the arts, or through the cries of the marginalized other, the attention required to listen to these voices is cultivated in prayer as the pray-er waits silently on the voice of God.[69]

In sum, for Coakley, in the crucible of prayer systematic theology is able most fully to live up to its namesake: prayer expands the possibility for a genuinely systematic kind of theology that is at once more protected against systematic foreclosure and more 'vulnerable' to be disrupted by the voices that are not always heard in mainline systematic theology.

Prayer, dispossession and 'honest' theology

The second of our three motifs requires returning to the first critique of the project of systematic theology mentioned above: its lure towards over-systematization. It is suggested in this motif that the desire to over-systematize the systematic project is checked as the theologian most acutely experiences the radically unsystematizable subject matter of theological discourse in prayer. In the long game of prayer, the mind's idolatrous longing for a comprehensive structure of knowledge is disrupted. This is not only hard work, but will become the pray-er's unrealized task of a lifetime, realized only in the ultimate disruption of the coming of the kingdom.

Rowan Williams, this motif's primary interlocutor, interprets this experience under the contemplative category of 'dispossession'. Throughout Williams' theological writings there is a profound commitment to the rerouting of theology through prayer. 'The integrity of a community's language about God', he writes, 'the degree to which it escapes its own pressures to power and closure, is tied to the integrity of the language it directs *to* God.'[70] Indeed, 'the meanings of the word "God" are to be discovered by watching what this community does – not only when it is consciously reflecting in conceptual ways, but when it is acting, educating or "inducting," imagining and worshipping'.[71]

In the prologue to *On Christian Theology*, Williams cites three 'styles' within which theological work operates – the 'celebratory', 'communicative'

---

[69]For Simone Weil's classic treatment of prayer and attention, see *Waiting for God* (New York: Harper Perennial, 2009), 57–65.
[70]Williams, *On Christian Theology*, 7.
[71]Williams, *On Christian Theology*, xii.

and 'critical'. If the 'celebratory' involves delighting in the possibility of human language about God and is most alive in doxology, and if the 'communicative' is about how Christian theology and its distinctive integrity gains a new perspective on itself through dialogue with other perspectives, the 'critical' is about being perennially alert to tensions, paradoxes and the inner instability of human language. The contemplative experience of dispossession is theology at its most 'critical'.[72] So, citing Williams:

> It remains true that a doxological theology which is not critically aware of its own fragile position – like the hazelnut in the hands of Christ in Julian of Norwich's 'showing', fragile and tiny but ultimately secure as an object of love – will be liable to distortion; it may become what Luther castigated as a 'theology of glory', an assertion of the triumph of the theologizing mind as opposed to the theology of the cross which is drawn back to dispossession.[73]

The critic finds a home in contemplation and the 'contemplative is thus a critic of the ideological distortion of language'.[74] Prayer sounds a 'warning note against the idea that we could secure a firm grip upon definitions of the divine' and in so doing cautions against the temptation to glib satisfaction with the images and concepts we have grown comfortable using to speak of God.[75]

For Williams, an over-systematic theology leaves God familiar, known, able to be 'possessed', and brought under the insatiable control of human language. However, you are likely to lose a great deal, Williams writes, 'when you try to tidy up an unsystematized speech'.[76] For Williams, the tidying up of language into something that is comfortable and 'easy' is nothing short of what the early church called 'heresy'. As we shall see in Chapter 3, Arianism, for example, is thought by Williams to be a

---

[72]Ibid., xii–xvi. For an explanation of the threefold theological methodology of the celebratory, communicative and critical styles, see Mike Higton, *A Difficult Gospel: The Theology of Rowan Williams* (London: SCM Press, 2004), 10–3.

[73]Rowan Williams, 'Theology as a Way of Life', in *The Practice of the Presence of God: Theology as a Way of Life*, ed. by Martin Laird and Sheelah Treflé Hidden (London: Routledge, 2017), 11–16 (13).

[74]Williams, *On Christian Theology*, 12.

[75]Ibid., xv.

[76]Ibid., xii.

rendering of the paradoxes of faith into arguments that missed the mark of the strangeness of the Christian gospel. Heresy errs on the side of neatness, whereas ortho*doxy* resides in the messier world of prayer and doxology. It was easier (conceptually neater, less systematically strained), says Williams, for Arius to argue that because God remains mysteriously unknowable, pure and eternally uncontaminated by the messy realities of relationship with creation, Jesus Christ cannot possibly be divine. It was much harder (conceptually messier, more systematically disordered) to say that God, in all that transcendence, enters into history as a creature in the person of Jesus Christ.[77] In the particular experience of prayer, according to Williams, which is always awkward, difficult and messy (think of John of the Cross' long dark night of the soul), the strangeness of human language about God is most darkly felt and the dispossession of language most acutely 'happens'. To 'use a word like "dispossession" is to evoke the most radical level of prayer, that of simple waiting on God, contemplation'.[78] Offered as prayer, language is ventured in humble recognition of its fractured self.

It is here, in the space opened up by the simple waiting on God, that theology gains, in Williams' terms, its 'honesty'. Within an honest theology possibilities for theological completion are closed down, the idolatrous urge to know all things is smashed, the ambition to master is abandoned, the desire to control is surrendered and language itself is purged of its self-indulgence: it is left unfinished. From John of the Cross' *The Dark Night* to Barth's treatment of prayer in *The Christian Life* and even Marcel Mauss' incomplete anthropological study *On Prayer*, it is somewhat characteristic of texts on prayer to remain themselves unfinished. 'Prayer ... is precisely what *resists* the urge of religious language to claim a total perspective: by articulating its own incompleteness before God, it turns away from any claim to human completeness.'[79] When all else is stripped away what remains is an encounter with the radically uncontrollable God that leaves the pray-er in an epistemic state of what Williams, along with a chorus of mystical writers, would recognize as 'unknowing'. This is not to know nothing; but it is to know something of the 'no-thingness' of God. The *krisis* of language,

---

[77]On this, see Rowan Williams, *Arius: Heresy and Tradition* (London: SCM Press, 2009; 2nd edn).
[78]Williams, *On Christian Theology*, 11.
[79]Ibid., 13.

which is ever-intensified in prayer, strips us of control of the subject matter of theology and leaves us spiralling out of control. 'And the greatness of the great Christian saints,' Williams writes, 'lies in their readiness to be questioned, judged, stripped naked and left speechless by that which lies at the centre of their faith.'[80]

This motif has so far dwelt in the negative side of dispossession: the critical stripping, speechlessness and silence. It has spoken of how the path of (un)knowing described by prayer is ineradicably penitential. The theologian is brought to their knees in humble confession of the limitations (indeed, impossibilities) of human speech about God. It could be assumed that theological discourse stays there, in the darkness of Gethsemane, where language is most strained and strange, and where categories of thought are constantly in flux and continually being made and remade. However, contemplative dispossession also takes place under and issues in Williams' 'celebratory' style. What is learnt in prayer is both the impossible character of theological speech (that 'it does not claim to be, in and of itself, final') but also, paradoxically, that human speech about God is possible as our words are given over to God in the context of the liturgy (it is still *God* being spoken of).[81] Offered as prayer, there is a transformation of human language from within (*à la* Evagrius's *On Prayer* 63).

When freed from the desire to confuse God with a controllable datum, Williams describes how language is 'handed over' to God, offered not as words that seek control but as liturgy – as the oblation of praise. The language of prayer 'ascribes supreme value, supreme resource or power, to something other than the worshipper, so that liturgy attempts to be a "giving over" of our words to God (as opposed to speaking in a way that seeks to retain distance or control over what's being spoken of).'[82] On this basis, theology is supremely positive. It is full of delight, confidence, celebration and resounds in songs of praise. Christian language is most alive when it delights in doxology.

For Williams, the path of knowing described by prayer is at once penitential ('critical') and adorational ('celebratory'). Prayer is the eschatological interaction between the impossible and the possible, dwelling as it does on the edge of despair and hope. In this sense, prayer imbues the theolo-

---

[80]Williams, *The Wound of Knowledge*, 1.
[81]Williams, *On Christian Theology*, 5.
[82]Ibid., 7.

gian with exactly the eschatological hope required to resist the crippling failure of human language that, somewhat paradoxically, had been identified in prayer. A good example of theology at is most hopeful is Hans Urs von Balthasar's *Prayer*, in which he insists, with an ample dose of Evagrian confidence in the certainty of theological discourse, that prayer confers on the theologian the 'right to say "everything"'.[83] His study of prayer can be read as a doctrinal outworking of this hope. Here Balthasar conducts theology at the heady heights of prayer, investigating doctrine after doctrine with the renewed clarity disclosed to him in the experience of contemplation. As we encountered in the previous chapter, one of the key moves Evagrius makes in his treatise is to locate prayer at the very summit of intellectual activity (and therefore as far as possible from the kind of anti-intellectualist realm of inner piety to which it is often exiled). Prayer sets the mind free to be 'like a young eagle soaring in the heights', he says (*On Prayer* 82). In the space-making practice of prayer, the very structure of one's thinking is dispossessively broken open by the unfathomable mysteries of God but also remade in order to say something 'honest' about God: for Evagrius and Williams alike, dispossession and the expansion of the mind, both wrought in prayer, go hand in hand.

Amen! Prayer as a 'protocol against idolatry'

Putting the first two motifs on prayer together presents an intriguing thesis. In the crucible of prayer systematic theology can simultaneously avoid the charge of over-systematization and pursue its systematic task more rigorously. It can present a more coherent picture of the full realities of human existence that braces more systematically the spiritual, dogmatic, practical, ethical and political. But without prayer the systematic project risks both closing down the possibilities for disruptive conversation and domesticating the wildly uncontainable subject matter of theology into ready-made systems of thought. Nicholas Lash's interrogative, critical theology names this kind of system-making, and its desire to harness, tame and domesticate God, a form of the greatest biblical sin: idolatry. 'The concept of "system", with its seductive, promethean overtones of panoramic organization, allows the theologian too easily to lose sight of the fact that his

---

[83]Balthasar, *Prayer*, 45.

work, like that of the philosopher, is irreducibly interrogative in character.'[84] Under these conditions, prayer – like the creed – can be seen to function as one of the church's 'protocols against idolatry', which is our final motif on the integrity of prayer and theology.[85]

Both Lash and Evagrius agree on the ever-present danger of idolatry. The church must be permanently iconoclastic, according to Lash, and Evagrius's treatise on prayer at root is one long training session for the vigilant awareness of and battle against the idolatry of the 'image'. The propensity for idolatry takes many different forms. The idol can be made of anything: the material (a golden calf) but also the non-material (a 'system', for example, or an 'image'). Whatever form it takes, and the covert operations of unobvious idols are all the more dangerous of course, idolatry commits the common mistake of 'getting the reference wrong: of taking that to be God which is not God'.[86] Importantly, both Lash and Evagrius agree that the activity of 'getting the reference wrong' takes fundamental form not outside but inside the praying communities of faith. Evagrius, remember, is warning the one seeking instruction in prayer (the very practice that stands at the height of Christian piety) of the pervasive reach of idolatry. Idolatry here cannot be externalized as the domain of the idolatrous other; and yet it is suggestive that both Evagrius's and Lash's response to the inevitable idolatry of prayer is not to stop praying but to pray more.[87]

How prayer, the very site of idolatry, functions as a 'protocol *against* idolatry' can be brought into sharper focus through the logic of the 'Prayer of Preparation', which occurs towards the beginning of many Anglican Eucharistic liturgies.

Almighty God,
to whom all hearts are open,
all desires known,
and from whom no secrets are hidden:

---

[84]Nicholas Lash, *Theology on Dover Beach* (London: Darton, Longman and Todd, 1979), 12.
[85]Lash, *Theology on Dover Beach*, 3–23.
[86]Nicholas Lash, *The Beginning and the End of 'Religion'* (Cambridge: Cambridge University Press, 1996), 134.
[87]A cross reference can be made at this point to Barth's blistering critique of religion (which also forms a critique of idolatry) delivered in *CD* I/2, §17. For Barth, nothing escapes the bounds of religiosity. In fact, the practices that stand at the height of piety (such as prayer) are most religious and therefore most in need of 'judgment'.

cleanse the thoughts of our hearts
by the inspiration of your Holy Spirit,
that we may perfectly love you,
and worthily magnify your holy name;
through Christ our Lord.
Amen.[88]

The 'Prayer of Preparation' contains three moves that are relevant to prayer's performance as a 'protocol against idolatry'. Mapped onto the aforementioned three styles of theological work described by Williams, the first can be seen to fall into Williams' 'critical' mode, the second into 'celebratory' and the third into both.

First, prayer has a (critical) role to play in the identification of idolatry. The prayer is addressed to the God 'to whom all hearts are open, all desires known, and before whom no secrets are hidden'. As said above, the idols fashioned by our hands are perhaps easier to identify than the idols that are constructed conceptually – ones that lurk deeply in our hearts, dwell subtly in our desires and remain hidden in our secrets. But in the contemplative waiting on the divine, the devices and desires of the heart that otherwise remain hidden are 'unmasked' and laid to bear. In prayer, the idolatries of desire that morph and shift in shape to hide their destructive force finally stand still. They are prized open and exposed for what, in a fallen world, they are: disordered, malformed and misdirected.

Second, prayer has a (celebratory) role in the iconoclastic reordering, reforming and redirecting of the desires of our hearts towards that which God intends: the love of God. As the 'Prayer of Preparation' continues, we pray, 'Cleanse the thoughts of our hearts by the inspiration of your Holy Spirit.' Without this cleansing – without being caught up in the sanctifying presence of God – theology is without vocation. It is suggestive that this cleansing work, which brings order to a disordered mind (Rom. 12.2), is accorded to the work of the Holy Spirit. In the previous chapter's investigation of the workings of Evagrius's theory of prayer, we noted that his logic of 'prayerful knowing' is also expressed pneumatologically. The Holy Spirit stirs up desire and progressively purifies human desire into the likeness of divine desire (*On Prayer* 63). The call to unceasing prayer (1

---

[88]*Common Worship: Services and Prayers for the Church of England* (London: Church House Publishing, 2000), 168.

Thess. 5.16) means that this cleansing is not a 'quick fix' but involves the long-term process of identification, purgation and constant alertness. The point of the identification and pneumatological cleansing of human desire is revealed as the 'Prayer of Preparation' reaches its climax: all this so 'that we may perfectly love you, and worthily magnify your holy name; through Christ our Lord'. Desire for God is finally put above all other desires. Or better, all desire is finally directed towards its proper end and 'through Christ' is brought into alignment with the desire of God. For Lash, human language is used well when it is used doxologically; this is the kind of language that 'magnifies' the holy name of God.

Third, prayer has a (critical and celebratory) role in saying 'Amen'. Lash begins his book on the Apostles' Creed not, as might be expected, with the first article of the creed, the 'I believe in God the Father', but with the word 'Amen'.[89] This is an odd place to begin a work of theology. 'Amen' is usually the word that brings a prayer to an end. It signals finality, completion; a finality and completion that prayer, it has been suggested, rules out. However, styled the 'critical' mode of theological work, the reverse is true. The critical, interrogative move the 'Amen' makes accepts that the conversation has not finished but has only just begun. In saying 'Amen' the theologian is drawn beyond the boundaries of the self into a much wider community of continuing conversation, of 'endless learning', of corporate self-correction, undoing and redoing, making and breaking.[90] As D'Costa writes, 'Prayer facilitates a complex cohabitation and participation with a "living tradition" of saints, sinners, fasts and feast days, dogmas and doctrines, the repressed and the explicit emblems of what communing with God might mean. ... In joining this prayer, the theologian participates in and contributes to this on-going, unfinished tradition.'[91] To say 'Amen' is to admit that theological speech is not 'new speech' but is undertaken in the 'acknowledgement of God's "Amen", which always goes before'.[92] It is to confess that 'none of us begins at the beginning' but take off from where others have ended.[93] Theology begins, as it were, in medias res – in the midst of things, in the midst of prayer.

---

[89] Nicholas Lash, *Believing Three Ways in One God* (London: SCM Press, 1992), 1–3.
[90] Lash, *Believing Three Ways in One God*, 4–16.
[91] D'Costa, *Theology in the Public Square*, 119.
[92] Lash, *Believing Three Ways in One God*, 3.
[93] Ibid., 2.

Following the logic of the 'Prayer of Preparation', in prayer the idols of the heart are made known, cleansed and incorporated into the praise of God. 'Amen' is offered in the celebratory hope that despite the fragility of language, the inevitable risk of idolatry, the propensity for human language to control and 'master', the recurring temptation to resolution and neatness, despite all this, human speech about God is made possible by its very speech *to* God. And in the doxological praise of God, our speech about God is 'given back' to God to be sanctified: to be reshaped with new meaning and significance.[94] Amen!

Summary

The motifs on prayer offered above have tried to capture something of the dialectical opportunities an integrated understanding of prayer and theology might provide. In prayer, the theologian kneels in contemplation. In the openness of prayer, space is made for the attentive listening to the voice of God – the interruptive, disruptive, wildly uncontainable voice of God. The theologian kneels in confession. Human language about God is offered to God in prayer under the confession that the words we use of God are not wholly adequate; they need to be broken open and remade. But a kneeling theology also speaks of praise and thanksgiving. Transposed into this celebratory key, the posture of prayer also changes. The pray-er is no longer penitentially incurved: kneeling with hands clasped and heads bowed – the humbling posture that counters the sin of pride. The pray-er's posture is now eccentrically expanded: upstanding, hands lifted, outstretched and heads raised in adoration of the divine. The theologian adopts the positions of the 'orans' – on this, more in Chapter 6. The head, no longer focused downwards (at the devises and desires of the heart), is turned upwards, heavenwards, facing God in adoration and drawn into the always-attractive 'poiesis' of God.

Each of the motifs discussed above agree that prayer is unavoidably tied up with the task of theology. To detangle theology from prayer is to lose a great deal. But it must be emphasized before going any further that a theology conceived in the logic of prayer must avoid going too far in the

---

[94] Ibid., 81.

opposite direction in its repair of modernity's progressive subordination of prayer to theology. It is not the case that the hierarchy can be stood on its head so that theology is now subordinated to prayer. The hierarchy must be genuinely toppled to make way for the better integration of theology as a discipline truly contemplative, genuinely systematic, 'honest' and always alert to idolatry.[95] The chapters that follow shift gear to examine something of this 'integrity' as it plays out in the doctrines of the Trinity, Christology, providence and the Christian life.

---

[95]Graham Ward is particularly attentive to the kind of reciprocity I am envisaging in *How the Light Gets In*, 174–80.

CHAPTER 3
'ENLARGE OUR MINDS':
PRAYER AND THE TRINITY

Holy God,
faithful and unchanging:
enlarge our minds with the knowledge of your truth,
and draw us more deeply into the mystery of your love,
that we may truly worship you,
Father, Son and Holy Spirit,
one God, now and for ever.

Collect of Trinity Sunday[1]

The mention of idolatry in the previous chapter raises probably one of the most fundamental questions Christian theology can ask: who is the God to whom Christians pray? For Nicholas Lash, the creed functions as a 'protocol against idolatry'.[2] The creed guides thinking about the word 'God'. More specifically, saying the creed guides thinking about God according to the paradoxical unity of Father, Son and Holy Spirit. To paraphrase Lash, believing in God is to believe three ways about one thing that is not a thing (as we know things to be) but that which stands before all things. Our minds are 'enlarged', to cite the Collect of Trinity Sunday, to see God in three ways – not one way will do.[3]

God's trinitarian 'no-thingness' will become important later in this book when we consider the vexing issue of God's providential action in the world

---

[1] *Common Worship: Additional Collects* (London: Church House Publishing, 2004), 19.
[2] Lash, *The Beginning and the End of 'Religion'*, 90.
[3] Gregory of Nyssa's account of prayer as *epektasis* (a 'stretching out') connects well to the Collect's theme of the enlargement of the mind through prayer, see Gregory of Nyssa, *The Life of Moses*, trans. by Abraham J. Malherbe and Everett Ferguson, CWS (New York: Paulist Press, 1978), 12–14.

and its relation to the freedom of human prayer. In the meantime, the point to be emphasized is that an adequate response to the question about the God to whom Christians pray cannot bypass the doctrine of the Trinity. As we have already seen in our initial dialogue with Evagrius, the 'image' implanted on the mind after the purgative breaking and remaking of prayer is the image of the trinitarian God – an image so radiant it shines as blindingly bright as sapphire, the holy colour of the Trinity. Apart from the mind's conversation with God in prayer, Evagrius would say, the theological insight that God is Trinity is not fully reachable. There can be no naked knowledge of God, for Evagrius; only knowledge clothed in prayer, through which the theologian comes into contact with God's own knowledge.[4]

Similarly, an adequate account of prayer cannot bypass the doctrine of the Trinity. No theological enquiry, including enquiries into the nature of Christian prayer, can proceed very far before needing to navigate the doctrine of the Trinity. Again, this has been introduced in the earlier discussion of Evagrius. For Evagrius, prayer is a trinitarian event, involving the experience of Father, Son and Holy Spirit.

This chapter thinks through the relation between the doctrine of the Trinity and the practice of prayer in more detail. To be more specific, it is chiefly interested in two interrelated questions, which will occupy the two major sections in this chapter. The first considers the difference prayer made (and indeed continues to make) in doctrinal thinking about the Trinity, and particularly as the doctrine developed in those formative first few centuries of Christianity. Here we cannot avoid dipping our toes into the fourth-century Christological debate between Arius and Athanasius, keeping a close eye on the role prayer played in those discussions. Then we will consider the role prayer continues to play in the remaking of doctrine in the work of Christian theology today.

Prayer, we will soon discover, is rarely far from doctrinal formulations about Jesus Christ and the Holy Spirit. More than just contributing to the making of the doctrine of the Trinity, this chapter sees that it does so in a *daring* way. Prayer sets about radicalizing the doctrine of God by making it stranger, more perplexing. In terms of dialogue partners, we cast the net widely. The section draws variously on Maurice Wiles's work on the development

---

[4]For a discussion of the interconnection of contemplation and theology as it plays out in Augustine's theology of the Trinity, see Williams, 'Contemplation: Knowledge of God in Augustine's *De Trinitate*', 121–46.

of early Christian doctrine, as well as Josef A. Jungmann's magisterial study on the place of Christ in liturgical prayer, Rowan Williams' work on Arius, Athanasius's doxological combatting of Arianism and the richly pneumatological interpretation of the Lord's Prayer by Gregory of Nyssa and other patristic exegetes. When we come to explore the on-going influence of prayer on the development of the doctrine of the Trinity in contemporary Christian theology, we offer the flourishing field of feminist spirituality and the worldwide movements of Pentecostalism and charismatic Christianity as examples of lively pockets of pneumatological activity. Following these examples is some focused work on two trinitarian 'case studies', both of which major on prayer: Sarah Coakley's 'prayer-based' model of the Trinity and the 'doxological trinitarianism' of Alan J. Torrance and others.

The second question considers the flip side of the first by asking: what does the practice of prayer come to look like when worked out through the doctrine of the Trinity? Just as the word 'God' is 'enlarged' according to a trinitarian logic so too is prayer. Structured according to the logic of the Trinity, prayer becomes ecstatically more complex than the thing I might do on my knees with my hands clasped: it becomes about what God does 'in' me. Or better, understood trinitarianly, the human activity of prayer becomes more expansively about being caught up by the Holy Spirit into the prayer of the praying Son before the Father. In this section, we draw from James Torrance's characterization of prayer as 'gift', Ludwig Feuerbach's reduction of prayer to self-conversation and the 'incorporative' understanding of prayer as divine conversation suggested by Hans Urs von Balthasar and Adrienne von Speyr to point in the direction of a trinitarian account of prayer. But before all this, an incursion into the oft-cited patristic adage – the *lex orandi, lex credendi* – helps to structure the subsequent exploration of the relation of prayer (*orandi*) and the doctrine of the Trinity (*credendi*).

Lex orandi, lex credendi

The results of the previous chapters could lead to the false impression that doctrine might not really matter. So long as the theologian is praying, anything goes. An integrated understanding of theology and prayer must beg to differ. Doctrine provides the indispensable tools to make better sense of what is going on theologically in prayer, to 'regulate' Christian practices of prayer, to anchor them in the broader Christian imagination and to hold them to critique.[5] Without doctrine prayer makes little sense. A fully integrated understanding of theology and spirituality goes further, however. It sees the activity of Christian doctrine itself as 'spiritual practice': shaping and forming us in particular ways. Believing this or that about God makes a difference to the way we understand ourselves and our place in the world. Christian doctrine, then, is not so much a body of theories and ideas that seeks our propositional assent as a 'recommendation for life'.[6] The kind of reciprocity of prayer and doctrine I am imagining is captured in the patristic notion of the *lex orandi, lex credendi*, which is often translated as: 'the law of prayer is the law of believing'.

Reference to the *lex orandi, lex credendi* is likely to be found in scholarship on the development of Christian doctrine.[7] It is often invoked to describe how the liturgy in general (including practices of prayer) shaped the way particular doctrines develop and continue to develop. You are also likely to find reference to the *lex orandi, lex credendi* in the context of discussion about the liturgical movement of the twentieth century. The second half of the twentieth century saw significant revisions to the formal liturgies of many of the world churches. The *Missal of Paul VI* for the Roman Catholic Church, revisions to the *Book of Common Order* for the Church of Scotland, *The Methodist Worship Book* for the Methodist Church of Great Britain and the Prayer Book revisions in the Church of England – to mention just a few landmark liturgical developments of the period. It quickly became apparent in the movement's updating of the liturgy in the light of modern concerns that the theological understanding of how the liturgy relates to doctrine is fundamental. What kind of doctrine is being transmitted in the liturgy? How does the liturgy reflect a particular church's doctrinal perspective? And what has priority?

Around the same time as the liturgical movement was gathering pace, the twentieth century saw a broader recovery of the sources of Christianity, particularly in French-speaking and German-speaking Roman Catholic theology. This '*ressourcement*', as it was known, turned back to the formative texts and writings of the Christian tradition, especially the writings of

---

[5]On doctrine as 'regulating' Christian belief and practice, see George Lindbeck, *The Nature of Christian Doctrine: Religion and Theology in a Postliberal Age* (Louisville: Westminster John Knox Press, 1984).

[6]Coakley, *God, Sexuality, and the Self*, 18.

[7]For example, Maurice F. Wiles, *The Making of Christian Doctrine: A Study in the Early Development of Christian Doctrine* (Cambridge: Cambridge University Press, 1967), 62–93.

the early church, to repair perceived false turns in modern theology. In uncovering theological patterns of thought that preceded modern theology's rupturing of the prayer-theology relation, the *lex orandi, lex credendi* was also rediscovered.

Although the general question of the relation between prayer and belief has always been central to the Christian religion, the particular origins of the term *lex orandi, lex credendi* is customarily accredited to the eighth chapter of the Augustinian dossier 'Official Pronouncements of the Apostolic See on Divine Grace and Free Will', written by the follower of Augustine and sometime secretary to Leo the Great, Prosper of Aquitaine (c. 390–455).[8] Originally appearing as 'let the rule of prayer establish the rule of faith', over the centuries the term has been shortened and adapted to its more familiar form.[9] Generally, the *lex orandi, lex credendi* says that if you observe how a community prays you should be able to get an idea of their beliefs. Prayer focuses doctrinal issues very clearly. For example, if I pray to Jesus Christ then there is a good chance that I believe in the full divinity of Christ. If I pray to Mary then that likewise reveals something of what I believe doctrinally about Mariology. My prayer and my belief are interconnected.

The date of Prosper's dossier ranges between 435 and 442. The context was the semi-Pelagian controversy that was sweeping through the monasteries of now southern France. The presenting issue was the doctrine of grace. According to semi-Pelagian teaching, one can refrain from sin and have faith in God apart from the gift of grace. For Augustine, and therefore for Prosper, however, human action cannot be said to be independent of grace in any way, shape or form: from beginning to end and everything in between, faith is dependent on God and God's grace. It is into this context of doctrinal dispute that Prosper invokes (in a surprisingly casual way,

---

[8]Prosper of Aquitaine, 'Official Pronouncements of the Apostolic See on Divine Grace and Free Will', in *Prosper of Aquitaine: Defense of St Augustine*, ACW, vol. 32 (New York: Newman Press, 1963), 178–85. For a detailed historical analysis of the term, see Paul De Clerck, '"Lex orandi, lex credendi": The Original Sense and Historical Avatars of an Equivocal Adage', *Studia Liturgica*, 24 (1994), 178–200. For other treatments, see Jason Byassee, 'Theology and Worship', in *The Routledge Companion to the Practice of Christian Theology*, ed. by Mike Higton and Jim Fodor (New York: Routledge, 2015), 203–21 and Paul L. Gavrilyuk, 'Canonical Liturgies: The Dialectic of *Lex Orandi and Lex Credendi*', in *Canonical Theism: A Proposal for Theology and the Church*, ed. by William J. Abraham, Jason E. Vickers and Natalie B. Van Kirk (Grand Rapids: William B. Eerdmans, 2008), 61–72.

[9]Prosper, 'Official Pronouncements', 183.

given the attention it would later receive) the 'law of prayer'. He seeks to settle the theological debate on grace by referring to existing practices of prayer and prove by the *lex orandi* the Augustinian doctrine of the priority of grace.

The law of prayer, in this instance, goes something like this. In 1 Tim. 2.1-4 the church is commanded to make intercessions 'for everyone' who 'desires to be saved'. This leads Prosper to argue that 'when the pastors of the Christian people discharge their mandate and mission, they plead the cause of the human race with the divine mercy and, in union with the supplications of the entire Church, beg and pray that faith may be given to unbelievers'.[10] The prayer that 'faith may be given' implies that faith, from the beginning, is a work of divine grace, and that everyone, even 'kings and all who are in high positions' (1 Tim. 2.2), stands in need of that grace. The prayer traditions of the early church suggest that grace logically precedes conversion; and on that basis the prayer for supplication proves Augustine's theory of grace and by implication disproves the semi-Pelagian doctrine.

In the case of Prosper versus the semi-Pelagians the *lex orandi*, in part, is corrective. It seeks to correct and clarify doctrinal thinking that has gone astray. Augustine appealed to prayer in a similar, 'corrective' way in one of his own battles against the Pelagians. Invoking the fifth petition of the Lord's Prayer in his anti-Pelagian treatise, *On Nature and Grace*, he argued that the daily petition for forgiveness implies that we cannot be forgiven apart from the grace of God – else why would we need to pray for daily forgiveness.[11]

However, when the *lex orandi* is taken up in the context of the twentieth-century liturgical movement, the discussion often focuses on questions of power and control.[12] Does prayer control doctrine? Does doctrine control

---

[10]Ibid.

[11]Augustine, 'On Nature and Grace', in *St Augustine: Writings against the Pelagians*, NPNF, series 1, vol. 5 (Edinburgh: T&T Clark, 1997), 121–51 (135).

[12]Take, for example, the work of the twentieth-century liturgical scholar Aidan Kavanagh. In his book, *On Liturgical Theology* (Collegeville: The Liturgical Press, 1992), Kavanagh argues that theological discourse should be distinguished into *theologia prima* (prayer) and *theologia secunda* (doctrine). For Kavanagh, the church finds its true theological voice in its prayer and liturgy – this is 'true' theology in the Evagrian sense of the word. 'Power', then, lies very much in the hands of the *lex orandi*. However, Kavanagh's interpretation of the *lex orandi* appears at points restrictively undialectical. The flow of prayer and doctrine is unidirectional, flowing in the direction from prayer to belief and not in the reverse. An alternative take on the *lex orandi* can be found in the writings of Geoffrey Wainwright and in particular in his systematic

prayer? Where is power located? Is it in the doctrinal teachings of the church or in its prayer life? The very framing of these questions, however, assumes exactly the kind of undialectical relation of prayer and doctrine that we are rejecting. Prosper is certainly doing something more complex in his original deployment of the *lex orandi* than an undialectical assertion of the priority of prayer over doctrine to resolve doctrinal dispute. Consider, for example, the two qualifications he attaches to the use of prayer in the settling of the debate over grace. Prayer can be invoked only so long as it is both founded on scripture (in this case, on 1 Tim. 2.1-2) and expresses tradition (in this case, Augustine and the wider teachings of the church). That the appeal to prayer is a heavily qualified appeal should alert us to the complex ways the *lex orandi* is already and unavoidably muddled with matters of the *lex credendi*. Prayer is knitted into an intricate tapestry of doctrine, theological reflection on scripture and the whole Christian life of discipleship and action. If this is the case, then the kind of chicken-and-egg discourse that is often associated with discussions of the *lex orandi, lex credendi* is somewhat off the mark.

An alternative, perhaps more fruitful interpretation of the *lex orandi*, does not see prayer as the arbiter of dogmatic dispute. After all, the liturgy can accommodate more than one, and sometimes contradictory, doctrinal perspectives. Instead it can be better understood as a way of making legible and then helping to maintain the 'integrity' of belief and practice, of doctrine and prayer. It enquires into both the doctrinal beliefs that underpin practices of prayer and the practices that in turn shape belief. In other words, the *lex orandi* can be interpreted as a methodological resource to help doctrine and prayer 'hang together' the best they can. It helps them interpret one another, to interact with each other and to hold each other to theological

theology written from a liturgical perspective first published in 1980: *Doxology: The Praise of God in Worship, Doctrine and Life: A Systematic Theology* (New York: Oxford University Press, 2008). At the heart of Wainwright's theo-liturgical project is a lengthy investigation of the *lex orandi* (Chapter 7) and its relation to the *lex credendi* (Chapter 8). According to Wainwright, the *lex orandi, lex credendi* is usually construed in one of two ways, which fall along conventional Protestant-Catholic fault lines. In the Protestant tradition, the control generally lies in the *lex credendi* – doctrine controls prayer; and in the Roman Catholic tradition (and presumably also for Kavanagh) the reverse is true. In the ecumenical fashion of the period, Wainwright charts a middle course between the two interpretations. 'The linguistic ambiguity of the Latin tag corresponds to a material interplay which in fact takes place between worship and doctrine in Christian practice: worship influences doctrine, and doctrine worship'. See Wainwright, *Doxology*, 218. My interpretation aligns more with Wainwright's than Kavanagh's.

account. And the protection of this integrity, as we shall see, leads to the radicalization of both belief and practice. When held together, belief in God and the practice of prayer become more radical, more complicated, more daring and more perplexing. With this interpretation of the *lex orandi* and its radicalizing logic in mind, let us see how it plays out in the development of the doctrine of the Trinity.

Prayer and the making of Christian doctrine

The making of the doctrine of the Trinity through councils, creeds and controversies is a long and convoluted story. To risk oversimplifying a complex history, there were two central Christian innovations in the doctrine of God in relation to the Jewish tradition out of which Christianity emerged: the affirmation of the divinity of the Son and the affirmation of the divinity of the Holy Spirit. The divinity of Jesus Christ and the Holy Spirit were agreed creedally at the Council of Nicaea in 325 and affirmed by subsequent ecumenical councils. At those councils, it was determined that the persons of the Trinity relate in a unity-in-distinction. Expressed in more explicitly creedal terms, the three distinguishable 'persons' of the Trinity – Father, Son and Holy Spirit – are united as one divine '*ousia*', one substance.

Intense disagreement, fierce dialogue and bitter dispute accompanied the doctrine of the Trinity throughout its development. This much we know. But what is often undervalued in the story of the development of the doctrine of the Trinity is the various roles prayer played in those debates. For example, prayer played a central role in the *transmission* of doctrinal development from one generation to the next. A fine example of prayer passing on highly developed trinitarian doctrine is this prayer from the Byzantine tradition, which is said to this day on the Feast of Pentecost in the Orthodox Church:

> Come, all ye people, let us worship the deity in Three Persons: the Son in the Father with the Holy Spirit. The Father timelessly begot the Son, of one essence and one reign, and the Holy Spirit is in the Father, glorified with the Son: one power, one essence, one deity. Him we all worship saying: Holy God who hast created all through the Son with the cooperation of the Holy Spirit; Holy Mighty through whom we have known the Father and the Holy Spirit came into the world; Holy

Immortal, comforting Spirit, proceeding from the Father and resting in the Son. Most Holy Trinity, glory to Thee.[13]

Technical trinitarian doctrine is being expressed here: 'one deity in Three Persons', the Son 'of one essence and one reign' with the Father, the Spirit 'proceeding from the Father'. The Orthodox theologian Nicholas Lossky considers this 'at once a prayer and a lesson in a very respectful trinitarian theology. Thus theology and prayer are truly one, inseparable.'[14] But before doctrine could be transmitted, it had to be formulated; and prayer also contributed to the *making* of the doctrine of the Trinity. The following two sections consider the two major doctrinal innovations in the doctrine of God: first Christology, then pneumatology.

Christology

The Council of Nicaea was called by Constantine in the hope that a united Christianity would settle the doctrinal disagreements over the person of Jesus Christ that were dividing his empire. More was at stake in these debates than political cohesion. Also on the line was the very way prayer was to be understood and practised. The fact that the doctrine of the Trinity had enormous ramifications for the prayer life of early Christians gives some explanation as to why its development was carried out with such impassioned intensity. As Maurice Wiles comments in his classic study, *The Making of Christian Doctrine*, theologians 'do not normally feel so deeply over matters of formal doctrinal statement unless those matters are felt to bear upon the practice of their piety'.[15]

To an important extent, the debates that led to the creedal affirmation of the shared substance of the Son and the Father were about coming to terms with the diversity of prayer as already practised in earliest Christianity. Although the historical data around the actual prayer practices of the earliest Christians is admittedly thin, there is enough evidence to suggest

---

[13]From the *Pentekostarion*, Great Vespers of Pentecost, cited in Nicholas Lossky, 'Theology and Prayer: An Orthodox Perspective', in *Ecumenical Theology in Worship, Doctrine, and Life: Essays Presented to Geoffrey Wainwright on His Sixtieth Birthday*, ed. by Lucas Lamadrid, David S. Cunningham and Ralph Del Colle (New York: Oxford University Press, 1999), 24–32 (31).
[14]Lossky, 'Theology and Prayer', 31.
[15]Wiles, *The Making of Christian Doctrine*, 62.

that there was a rich 'constellation' of Christ-shaped practices of prayer in circulation during the earliest periods of Christianity's history.[16]

The Christ-shaped practices of prayer included praying through Christ, praying to Christ, singing to Christ, calling upon the name of Christ in prayer, baptizing in the name of Christ and others still.[17] These practices are clearly not empty of doctrinal significance: indeed, they make daring theological claims relating to the divine status of the Son. In particular, the Maranatha ('Oh Lord, come!') in the final few verses of Paul's first letter to the Corinthians (1 Cor. 16.22), which was probably first used in a liturgical context, is customarily cited as an early example of a tradition of prayer that raised huge questions of the relation of Jesus to God. To invoke Jesus with the same name ('Lord') that was until then reserved for Yahweh and for Yahweh alone had considerable, and indeed radical, implications for the doctrine of God. 'Somehow', Stephen Holmes comments, 'right at the beginning of the church, the exclusive loyalty and worship demanded by God alone in the Old Testament was assumed to be upheld and not violated by worship offered to Jesus.'[18] When the early church eventually sought more precise theological formulation of these implications, whatever doctrinal settlement that would be reached needed to correlate with what was already Christologically going on in the 'constellation' of Christ-shaped practices of prayer. According to the logic of the *lex orandi*, doctrine and prayer had to 'hang together'. Read this way round, the creedal affirmation of the divinity of the Son, as agreed at Nicaea, provides the doctrinal rationale for the already established doxological practices of rendering praise and prayer to Jesus Christ.

---

[16]On this, see Larry W. Hurtado, *Lord Jesus Christ: Devotion to Jesus in Earliest Christianity* (Grand Rapids: William B. Eerdmans, 2005), 137–38. Commenting on early Pauline Christianity, Hurtado concludes that 'we get the impression of a remarkably well established pattern of prayer in which Jesus features very prominently, either as a recipient or as unique agent through whom prayer is offered. Moreover, there is simply no analogy in Roman-era Jewish groups for the characteristic linking of Jesus with God in the prayer practice reflected in Paul's letters'. See Hurtado, *Lord Jesus Christ*, 140. For a rich collection of prayers to Jesus Christ, see Benedict J. Groeschel, *Praying to Our Lord Jesus Christ: Prayers and Meditations Through the Centuries* (San Francisco: Ignatius Press, 2004).

[17]For more on Christ as the 'object' of worship, see Larry W. Hurtado, *One God, One Lord: Early Christian Devotion and Ancient Jewish Monotheism* (London: Bloomsbury, 2015), 99–100 and *At the Origins of Christian Worship: The Context and Character of Earliest Christian Devotion* (Grand Rapids: William B. Eerdmans, 2000), 74–6.

[18]Stephen R. Holmes, 'Classical Trinity: Evangelical Perspective', in *Two Views on the Doctrine of the Trinity*, ed. by Jason S. Sexton (Grand Rapids: Zondervan, 2014), 25–48 (33).

In addition to prayer, the role of heresy cannot be underestimated in the formation of the doctrine of the Trinity. For Wiles, along with scripture, the experience of salvation and prayer, heresies form the building blocks of early Christian doctrinal development.[19] Heresies – the doctrinal 'near-misses' – challenged early Christianity into thinking more clearly, more energetically and more wisely about its core beliefs. The clash between Arianism and Athanasius, in which the Christian world was embroiled in the early fourth century, was one of the early church's great Christological debates that helped to consolidate the orthodox formulations of the person of Jesus Christ. Now is not the time to detail the complex historical and theological factors at play during the Arian controversy; there are existing studies that have done this work more carefully than is possible here.[20] But what should not escape our attention is prayer's role in the battle against the Arian heresy.

For the Arians, following the Alexandrian priest Arius, the Son cannot be considered divine without Christianity abandoning the hallowed tradition of monotheism and from there falling into idolatry. At best, the Son is like God but not intrinsically God, not fully divine and therefore not a worthy recipient of prayer. Arianism citied liturgical evidence in support of its cause. Jesus' practice of directing prayers to the Father indicated to the Arians that Jesus cannot himself be divine. Instead, the Son was thought to be a created intermediary who stands between the uncreated God and the created world. Doctrinally, then, compared to what was eventually agreed at Nicaea, the Arian position presented an eminently straightforward option. It was more convenient to think of the Son as a kind of mediatory figure who is neither fully divine nor fully human than it was to think through the vexing logistics of multiple divinities. Arianism has the virtue of making some conceptual sense but the vices of being theologically undaring and indeed doxologically rather muddled.

Because of the rejection of the full divinity of Christ, one might expect Arius and his followers to have insisted that prayers of an Arian flavour were to be directed to God alone and perhaps through the Son. This would have

---

[19]Wiles explores these elements of doctrinal development in *The Making of Christian Doctrine* and *The Remaking of Christian Doctrine* (London: SCM Press, 2011).

[20]Scholarly treatments of the history involved include Lewis Ayres, *Nicaea and its Legacy: An Approach to Fourth-Century Trinitarian Theology* (Oxford: Oxford University Press, 2004), 430–5; Stephen R. Holmes, *The Holy Trinity: Understanding God's Life* (Milton Keynes: Paternoster, 2012), 82–96; and Williams, *Arius*.

been consistent with the doctrinal teaching on the subordination of the Son to a mediatory figure somewhere between full divinity and full humanity. In meditating the prayers of the world to God, Jesus is not worshipped with God as a second object of devotion but points to the worship of the one true God. As Josef A. Jungmann argues in his seminal study *The Place of Christ in Liturgical Prayer*, the practice of praying through Christ would have 'provided the Arian with a welcome argument for his heresy'.[21] Furthermore, praying through the Son would have been consistent with what Jungmann considered to be the customary prayer practice of the time. For Jungmann, of the Christological constellation of Christ-shaped practices of prayer, the dominant doxologies of the ante-Nicene period were those that addressed 'the Lord God "through Jesus Christ"'.[22] The early liturgical manual, the *Didache*, and its reference to praying through Christ, helps to build Jungmann's case, as does Origen and his insistence that we pray 'in' rather than to the Son (*De oratione* 15–6). 'It was not until the end of the fourth century', Jungmann believes, 'that we meet ... prayers *to* Christ the Lord,' which reflects a higher Christology of the Son as the divine recipient of devotion.[23] For Jungmann, the massive liturgical swing occurring in the fourth century (from praying *through* to praying *to* the Son) was part of an extensive, Christianity-wide suppression of all things Arian.

Given all this, it is somewhat curious that in addition to praying through the Son as the paradigm intercessor, Arius also appeared to permit the presumably un-Arian practice of praying *to* the Son. As Rowan Williams discovers: 'While Origen notoriously discouraged prayer to the Son (Christian prayer should be made *in* the Son *to* the Father), Arius and his followers apparently allowed it.'[24] Perhaps the Arians prayed to Christ

---

[21]Josef A. Jungmann, *The Place of Christ in Liturgical Prayer* (Collegeville: Liturgical Press, 1989), 162.

[22]Jungmann, *The Place of Christ in Liturgical Prayer*, 144.

[23]Ibid., 164.

[24]Williams, *Arius*, 144. For further textual evidence of the retention of Christ as the object of worship in some of Arius's followers, see Jon M. Robertson, *Christ as Mediator: A Study of the Theologies of Eusebius of Caesarea, Marcellus of Ancyra, and Athanasius of Alexandria* (Oxford: Oxford University Press, 2007), 137–216. It should be further noted that although Jungmann's thesis for the late fourth-century liturgical swing was initially received positively, it has not continued to claim widespread approval. It is now considered that the practice of praying to (rather than through) the Son was not as uncommon in the years that preceded the Arian watershed than suggested by Jungmann's study. Many of the hesitations around Jungmann's

because, as that which is more than human but less than divine, the Son still towered imposingly above his fellow creatures. But in any case, if Williams is right and Arius prayed to the Son, then somewhere near the heart of the Arian controversy is not simply a matter of doctrinal disagreement but a mismatch in the way doctrine and practice relate: prayer and doctrine no longer 'hang together' in Arian Christology; and this discrepancy needed ironing out.

The cost of the doctrinal convenience of avoiding the vexing question of multiple divinities was liturgical confusion. It would have been more coherent for Arius to reject outright the practice of praying to Christ and insist on directing prayers exclusively through Jesus. But he did not. And even if he did, Athanasius, his arch-opponent, pinned much of his anti-Arian argument on questioning the capacity of the Arian Christ to provide any real mediation in prayer. If Christ is less than divine then Christ cannot mediate the divine any more than you or I can. For Athanasius, it is 'because we invoke no originate thing, no ordinary man, but the natural and true Son from God, who has become man, yet is not the less Lord and God and Saviour' that the logic of mediation works and we can pray to the divine.[25] But more gravely, so Athanasius argued, if the Son is identifiably separate in being from the Father, and if the Arians nevertheless permitted prayers to be directed *to* the Son, the Arians were guilty of praying to two separate recipients of worship. So Athanasius: 'Why, then, ... do they [the Arians] not rank themselves with the Gentiles? For they also, as these, worship the creature rather than the Creator of all.'[26] This would, rather ironically, Athanasius notes, lead Arius and his followers into exactly the idolatry they

---

thesis concern the swiftness of his omission of alternative early liturgical sources that do not fit neatly in his narrative of the early church's unilateral movement from praying 'through' to praying 'to' the Son. For an explication of the critiques, see Bryan D. Spinks, 'The Place of Christ in Liturgical Prayer: What Jungmann Omitted to Say', in *The Place of Christ in Liturgical Prayer: Trinity, Christology, and Liturgical Theology*, ed. by Bryan D. Spinks (Liturgical Press, Collegeville 2008), 1–19 and Hurtado, *At the Origins of Christian Worship*, 63–97. These revisionist readings add further weight to the case for the Arian Christ as an object of prayer and devotion.

[25]Athanasius, 'Four Discourses against the Arians', in *St Athanasius: Select Works and Letters*, NPNF, series 2, vol. 4 (Edinburgh: T&T Clark, 1980), 306–447 (411). On the doxological factors that contributed to the formation of Athanasius's doctrinal understanding of the Trinity, see Thomas G. Weinandy, *Athanasius: A Theological Introduction* (Farnham: Ashgate, 2007), 103–20.

[26]Athanasius, 'Four Discourses against the Arians', 402.

so obsessively sought to avoid in their denial of Christ's full divinity.[27] The key iconoclastic move made by Athanasius in his response to Arian Christology was not to deny the fully divine status to Jesus Christ did but to deny the distinction between Jesus and God. The Son must be fully divine and 'of one substance with the Father' for him to be legitimately prayed to as God.

For the present purposes, it is important that one of the critical issues on the table during the Arian controversy was the relation of prayer to doctrine to the extent that it was bound up with the doctrinal issue of the relation of the Son to the Father. It could even be said that what secured Athanasius's Christology over Arius's was neither the conceptual clarity of his doctrinal argument nor his biblical fidelity. He won the debate because his doctrinal account of the person of Christ more successfully measured up to the Christ-shaped patterns of prayer already in practice in the early church. Here we catch sight of the *lex orandi* in action. As said above, the *lex orandi* is misunderstood as an undialectical appeal to prayer to trump doctrinal argument. Instead, the *lex orandi* functions as a way of maintaining the 'integrity' of that which rightly belongs together and thereby making legible the inherent relationship of prayer and doctrine. And in so doing, prayer radicalizes previously held assumptions about the divine: in the long dark nights of prayer the doctrine of God is made more complex.

The Arian versus Athanasius saga helps to illustrate, then, that prayer not only contributed to the making of early Christological doctrine but did so *daringly*. This puts a different spin on the notion of 'orthodoxy'. It is easy to think that orthodoxy is the intrinsically conservative agenda that stifles innovation: it sets the boundaries to that which is doctrinally possible. But as Williams has argued, it was Arius who represented the conservative position and favoured a 'theology of repetition' over the risker labour of doctrinal innovation.[28] Athanasius was the progressive. He was more willing to improvise on the doctrinal implications of the Christ-shaped praying practices of the church even if those improvisations would lead to the inconvenient doctrinal truth of Christ's divinity. The problem with Arius was not that his Christology did not make sense but that it made too much sense of the mystery of God, whereas orthodoxy defers to the odd, to the strange. Rather than simply repeating the past, orthodoxy defaults to the more

---

[27]Athanasius, 'To Adelphius', in *St Athanasius: Select Works and Letters*, NPNF, series 2, vol. 4 (Edinburgh: T&T Clark, 1980), 575–78 (575).
[28]Williams, *Arius*, 235.

perplexing option presented by prayer. The radical theological innovations to the doctrine of God, pioneered by early Christian theologians from Paul and the Gospel writers onwards, were propelled and pushed forward by the experience and practice of prayer.

Pneumatology

We have so far considered prayer's role in the making of early Christological doctrine. But what role, if any, did prayer have in the making of the second major innovation in the doctrine of God: the divinity of the Holy Spirit? Conveniently, an immediate answer can be drawn from the creed itself. Whereas the divinity of the Son is expressed creedally through the technical terminology of *homoousios* (which translates as 'of the same substance' or 'one being'), the Nicene-Constantinopolitan Creed of 381 establishes the divinity of the Spirit through a direct appeal to prayer. The Holy Spirit, the creed states, 'is worshipped and glorified together with the Father and the Son'. The divinity of the Spirit is secured doxologically. It is because the Spirit is venerated alongside the Father and the Son in the doxology of the church that the Spirit is considered divine. The fourth-century Greek theologian Gregory of Nazianzus displays the moves of the early argument for the divinity of the Spirit well when he says that 'if He [the Spirit] is to be worshipped, surely He is an Object of adoration, and if an Object of adoration He must be God'.[29]

As with Christology, there is liturgical evidence to suggest that the divinity of the Holy Spirit was part of the practice of Christian prayer long before it received full doctrinal affirmation. One of the key pieces of liturgical evidence associated with the development of early pneumatology is the inclusion of the Holy Spirit in the triadic baptismal formula (Mt. 28.19). The invocation of 'the name of the Father, and of the Son and of the Holy Spirit' in the commission to baptize implied the divinity of the Spirit: only the divine can save; and if the Spirit is soteriologically active then the Spirit must be divine, so ran the patristic argument. Another piece of liturgical evidence is the *epiclēsis* of the Holy Spirit. The practice of invoking the Spirit over the people of God (and later over the elements) in

---

[29]Gregory Nazianzen, 'The Fifth Theological Oration: On the Holy Spirit', in *St Cyril of Jerusalem: Catechetical Lectures; St Gregory Nazianzen: Orations, Sermons, Letters, Prolegomena*, NPNF, series 2, vol. 7 (Edinburgh: T&T Clark, 1980), 318–28 (327).

the Eucharistic liturgy to make them holy implied the divinity of the Spirit: only the divine can sanctify, the patristic argument continued.

In addition to assuming the divinity of the Spirit, there is further evidence from the early traditions of Christian prayer that brings clarity to the distinctiveness of the Holy Spirit's work. The biblical association of the Spirit with the Spirit-infused practices of prayer and charismatic gifts (such as prophecy, speaking in tongues and ecstatic vision) suggests a vibrancy to the work of the Spirit. The Holy Spirit here is associated with the work of sanctification and perfection. It is fiery, feisty, dazzling – transformative.

However, in his account of the development of Christian doctrine, Wiles is concerned that prayer practices such as these contributed too much to the early church's doctrinal thinking on pneumatology. 'In the case of the Holy Spirit', he argues, 'there is even less in the text of the New Testament to compel belief in a third, co-equal person of the godhead. ... Indeed the paucity of scriptural evidence was something of an embarrassment to the Church's theologians when they sought to demonstrate the Spirit's full divinity in the closing years of the fourth century.'[30] On this occasion, for Wiles, the *lex orandi* led the early Christian theologians astray. The biblical evidence to warrant the hypostatization of the Holy Spirit assumed by the church's practices of prayer simply does not stack up. So Wiles concludes: 'Undoubtedly the practice of prayer has had its effect on doctrine; undoubtedly the practice of prayer should have its effect on doctrine. But that is not to say that the effect which prayer has actually had is at every point precisely the effect which it should have had.'[31]

While for Wiles prayer led the church astray, there are others who are concerned that early Christian theology did not make enough of the pneumatologically rich practices of prayer of earliest Christianity. Take the Lord's Prayer as an example. It is well known that in the New Testament there are two versions of the Lord's Prayer – one in the Gospel of Matthew and another, slightly shorter version in the Gospel of Luke. Although these versions differ in length, they generally agree in terms of content. However, there is evidence to suggest that there was at least a third version of the Lord's Prayer in circulation in the early church. This third version is mentioned by Tertullian, Gregory of Nyssa and Maximus the Confessor

---

[30]Wiles, *The Making of Christian Doctrine*, 78.
[31]Ibid., 93.

in their commentaries on the Lord's Prayer.[32] Tracing the petition to some manuscript variants in Luke's version of the Lord's Prayer, some modern scholars have claimed that this version might even be the most original version of the Lord's Prayer.[33]

The difference between the versions of the Lord's Prayer we recognize today and this third, lost version is the suggestive inclusion of an *epiclēsis*-style reference to the Holy Spirit in place of the second petition. As Gregory of Nyssa explains:

> When [Luke] desires the Kingdom to come, [he] implores the help of the Holy Spirit. For so he says in his Gospel; instead of *Thy Kingdom Come* it reads 'May Thy Holy Spirit come upon us and purify us'.[34]

The pneumatological reference gives Maximus the Confessor ample licence to interpret the Lord's Prayer in a decidedly trinitarian manner. Along with Gregory, he sees more than a fleeting nod to the Holy Spirit here. While the creeds end with the Spirit, this tradition of the Lord's Prayer begins there and the subsequent petitions should be read in this pneumatological light, as the patristic exegetes instruct. This Lord's Prayer accords primacy and priority to the Holy Spirit: it gives the Spirit pride of place as the first petition and of similar significance, by implication, as the coming of the kingdom of God. Thus Gregory cites this variant of the second petition of the Lord's Prayer to combat those, such as the late fourth-century Macedonian heretics, who seek to 'drag Him [the Holy Spirit] down into a subject creature, placing Him with the ruled, instead of with the ruling Nature'.[35] So, countering the Macedonian denial of the divinity of the Spirit, what follows in his commentary on the *Pater Noster* is a technical defence

---

[32]On this, see Roy Hammerling, *The Lord's Prayer in the Early Church: The Pearl of Great Price* (New York: Palgrave, 2010), 28–30. For primary text evidence, see Gregory of Nyssa, *The Lord's Prayer*, 52–6 and Maximus Confessor, 'Commentary on the Our Father', in *Maximus Confessor: Selected Writings*, trans. by George C. Berthold, CWS (New York: Paulist Press, 1985), 99–125 (106).

[33]There is evidence that Evagrius referred to the petition in his lost commentary on the Lord's Prayer. Citing the renowned patristic scholar, Irénée Hausherr, George C. Berthold notes that 'certain Coptic documents say that Evagrius composed a treatise on the Our Father where the Holy Spirit is spoken of the kingdom that is prayed for'. See the notes to Berthold's CWS translation of Maximus's 'Commentary on the Our Father', 122 n.44.

[34]Gregory of Nyssa, *The Lord's Prayer*, 52.

[35]Ibid., 53.

of the Spirit's divinization built on exactly the doxological evidence he finds in the Spirit petition of the Lord's Prayer. On Gregory's reasoning, because the pray-er calls on the Holy Spirit to 'cleanse sin' and 'the very same thing' is said of the cleansing work of the Son, it is logically the case that the Holy Spirit and the Son are the same in 'power and operation'.[36] Thus,

> if the Son is by nature united to the Father, and if the Holy Spirit has been shown not to be alien from the nature of the Son on account of the identity of operations, it necessarily follows, I say, that the nature of the Holy Trinity has been shown to be one, though not fused as regards the properties which belong to each Person as His special characteristic, since their special features are not changed into each other.[37]

Despite the liturgical suggesting a vibrant theology of the Spirit, some have argued that pneumatology failed to materialize doctrinally. The Holy Spirit has long been considered the 'forgotten God'.[38] Contrary to Wiles, it would seem that prayer did not do enough to generate the lively pneumatological thinking it was due. Some feel that the same kind of intense, heated debate did not accompany the development of early pneumatology as it did the patristic negotiation of the person of Christ. The Council of Nicaea of 325, for example, while devoting substantial doctrinal attention to the status of the person of Christ, said comparably little about the Holy Spirit and was even coyer about exploring the distinctiveness of the Spirit's work. It affirmed, almost as an afterthought, belief 'in the Holy Spirit'. It was not until 381 that the pneumatological imbalance in the creeds would be redressed by finally working out how the Spirit fits into the *homoousian* unity of the Father and the Son relation. But even at Constantinople the Spirit would be subordinated (as least in the ordering of the creed) to the other persons of the Trinity and its controlling interest remained that of the Father-Son relationship. Some have also argued that even when pneumatology was worked out in the new trinitarian orthodoxy, the doctrinal version of the Spirit was tamer than the fiery, transformative pneumatology found in

---

[36]Ibid.

[37]Ibid., 54.

[38]The term is borrowed from Elizabeth A. Johnson, *Women, Earth, and Creator Spirit* (New York: Paulist Press, 1993), 19.

the practices of prayer mentioned above.[39] The fire in the pneumatological belly had been (doctrinally) snuffed out. The Holy Spirit was scrambling around for something left to do, destined variously to become the 'bond' of union between the other more important persons of the Trinity or a sort of 'bridge crosser' tasked with the communication of information about the doctrinally more interesting relation the Son shares with the Father.

One of the implications of a subordinated doctrine of the Spirit is the 'linearism' it introduces into the Godhead. Rowan Williams worries that sometimes the Trinity is thought of as 'a *sequence* of divine persons, successively revealed in a kind of hierarchically ordered illumination'.[40] This linearism is even implied in the shaping of the liturgical year (also discussed at Nicaea), in which Pentecost is tucked onto the tail end of a rather busy year of Christ veneration. As we shall soon see, a linear account of trinitarian relations has knock-on effects concerning the question of divine human participation, which of course lies at the heart of the theology of prayer.

Although prayer clearly had a role to play in the doctrinal affirmation of the divinity of the Holy Spirit, there remains a sense that the creedal proclamations did not go far enough in tapping the deep pneumatological wisdom offered by prayer in which the Spirit was most transformatively alive. Once again, we can detect an unsatisfying disconnect in the way doctrine and prayer 'hang together': the doctrinal thinking around the nature of the Holy Spirit could not keep up with the Holy Spirit as it was experienced and practised in prayer. The stakes here, of course, are significantly lower than they were with the Arian disconnect between doctrine and prayer. The full divinity of the Holy Spirit is not under question in the way that Arianism questioned the divinity of the Son. Nevertheless, the problem of subordination remains the same: the Spirit's subordination to the Son and the Father rather than the Son's to the Father.

Prayer and the remaking of Christian doctrine

The key issue now to be probed is whether a focus on prayer can reveal new understandings, emphases and dimensions in the doctrine of the Trinity. It

---

[39]On this, see Geoffrey Wainwright, 'Holy Spirit', in *The Cambridge Companion to Christian Doctrine*, ed. by Colin Gunton (Cambridge: Cambridge University Press, 2000), 273–96.
[40]Williams, *On Christian Theology*, 115.

has been suggested that the conciliar negotiations of the doctrine, despite the overarching vision of *homoousian* equality, led to the unorthodox temptation to subordinate the doctrine of the Holy Spirit to a third. The ramifications of this subordination extended well into modern theology.[41] This section identifies some resources from within the traditions of Christian prayer in which the Holy Spirit is alive and kicking. Then it presents two trinitarian 'case studies' that capture the kind of theological opportunities that are possible when the doctrine of the Trinity is redirected through the practice of prayer.

A good example of a resource for the remaking of the doctrine of the Trinity according to the logic of prayer is the flourishing field of feminist spirituality. As mentioned in the introduction, feminist theology, and its rejection of the separation of theory and practice, is a subterranean influence on this book's methodological committment to the integrity of prayer and theology. In feminist theology the embodied spiritual experiences of women are not only given voice but are celebrated as core theological resources – not least for the kind of pneumatology yielded by those spiritual experiences. Nicola Slee, for example, makes a convincing case that 'much creative thinking about the person and work of the Spirit is to be found within … the rapidly expanding field of feminist spirituality'.[42] The spiritual experiences of women have, however, 'gone largely unrecorded down the ages'.[43] This is because they were recorded in 'journals, letters, hymns, poems, or crafts which have not accorded public recognition' and because of 'more overt male suppression'.[44] A recovery of these experiences of prayer, then, points in the direction of a lively and robust doctrine of the

---

[41]Sarah Coakley has developed a rough typology of modern trinitarianism, four of which include a subordination of the Holy Spirit. The subordination can take many forms: questioning the need to hypostize the Spirit in the first place; taking the hypostization of the Spirit for granted but subordinating the Holy Spirit to a completer and communicator of the revelation of God in the Son; reducing the Spirit to a 'bond' of union between the two more important persons of the Trinity; or requiring the Spirit but only as the third that enables better relationships between God and between us and God. See Sarah Coakley, 'Why Three? Some Further Reflections on the Doctrine of the Trinity', in *The Making and Remaking of Christian Doctrine: Essays in Honour of Maurice Wiles*, ed. by Sarah Coakley and David A. Pailin (Oxford: Clarendon Press, 1993), 29–56 (31–9).
[42]Nicola Slee, 'The Holy Spirit and Spirituality', in *The Cambridge Companion to Feminist Theology*, ed. by Susan Frank Parsons (Cambridge: Cambridge University, 2003), 171–89 (172).
[43]Slee, 'The Holy Spirit and Spirituality', 172.
[44]Ibid., 173.

Holy Spirit that can revitalize theological understandings of the doctrine of the Trinity.[45]

Another pneumatological resource made available by a more integrated understanding of theology and prayer, which similarly grants theological priority to spiritual experience, is the contemporary phenomenon of the worldwide Pentecostal and charismatic movements.[46] These movements, in their various stripes, have seen an explosive growth over the past half-century or so. It is not coincidental that over the same period there has been a parallel explosion of high-quality theological reflection on the doctrine of the Holy Spirit.[47] It might be too early to determine the causal link between the pneumatologically driven practices of these traditions of spirituality and the broader renewal of doctrinal interest in the theology of the Holy Spirit but what is certain is that the Spirit-centric practices of prayer inherent to these doxological traditions makes it difficult to sideline theologically the third article of the creed.[48]

A common feature in both of these examples is the shared implication that lively pockets of pneumatological activity have a habit of dwelling at the edges of Christianity, on its boundaries. An integrated account of theology and prayer, we have said before, should be committed to the exploration of precisely these neglected areas of Christianity and the sidelined genres of theological writing that can be found in feminist spirituality and the Pentecostal and charismatic traditions of Christianity.

---

[45]On this, see Anne Claar Thomasson-Rosingh, *Searching for the Holy Spirit: Feminist Theology and Traditional Doctrine* (London: Routledge, 2015).

[46]For resources on the relation between the Holy Spirit and Pentecostalism, see example, Wolfgang Vondey, *Pentecostal Theology: Living the Full Gospel* (London: Bloomsbury, 2017); and Allan Heaton Anderson, *An Introduction to Pentecostalism: Global Charismatic Christianity* (Cambridge: Cambridge University Press, 2014; 2nd edn). For a sociological account of the relation between and the Holy Spirit and practice of 'soaking prayer' in the charismatic revivals of the 1990s, see Michael Wilkenson and Peter Althouse, 'The Embodiment of Prayer in Charismatic Christianity', in *The Sociology of Prayer*, ed. by Giuseppe Giordan and Linda Woodhead (Farnham: Ashgate, 2015), 153–76. 'Soaking prayer' is where 'people would appear to spontaneously fall to the floor and "rest" in the Spirit for great lengths of time' (153), which is sometimes articulated with reference to Romans 8.

[47]For a collection of contemporary essays on the Holy Spirit that evidences some of this pneumatological rethinking, see Eugene F. Rogers (ed.), *The Holy Spirit: Classic and Contemporary Readings* (Chichester: Wiley-Blackwell, 2009).

[48]This point is made in Michael Welker, *God the Spirit* (Minneapolis: Augsburg Press, 1994) and *The Work of the Spirit: Pneumatology and Pentecostalism* (Grand Rapids: William B. Eerdmans, 2006).

The first of our trinitarian 'case studies', now to be discussed, is also located in somewhat forgotten and underexplored strands in the history of Christian spirituality.

The 'prayer-based' model of Trinity

As we mentioned in the previous chapter, Sarah Coakley has worked hard to bring the practice of prayer more intimately into the discussion of doctrinal and philosophical theology than is often conventional. The fruit of this theological commitment to deep prayer as central to the practice of theology is the 'prayer-based' model of the Trinity.[49]

This underexplored trinitarian strand in the history of Christian spirituality finds its textual root in Paul's tantalizing reflections on prayer in Romans 8 and 'its description of the cooperative action of the praying Christian with the energizing promptings of the Holy Spirit'.[50] In Romans 8, Paul says:

> For all who are led by the Spirit of God are children of God. For you did not receive a spirit of slavery to fall back into fear, but you have received a spirit of adoption. When we cry, 'Abba! Father!' it is that very Spirit bearing witness with our spirit that we are children of God, and if children, then heirs, heirs of God and joint heirs with Christ – if, in fact, we suffer with him so that we may also be glorified with him. ...

> Likewise the Spirit helps us in our weakness; for we do not know how to pray as we ought, but that very Spirit intercedes with sighs too deep

---

[49]For Coakley's most developed rendition of the 'prayer-based' model of the Trinity, see *God, Sexuality, and the Self*, 100–51. Other examples of similar, Romans 8 inspired approaches to the doctrine of the Trinity include: Robert W. Jenson, *The Triune Identity: God According to the Gospel* (Philadelphia: Fortress Press, 1982), 44; Eugene Rogers, *After the Spirit: A Constructive Pneumatology from Resources outside the Modern West* (Grand Rapids: William B. Eerdmans, 2005), 75–97; and Thomas G. Weinandy, *The Father's Spirit of Sonship: Reconceiving the Trinity* (London: T&T Clark, 1995), 33–8. The 'prayer-based' model can also be seen in the mystical writings of the Swiss Catholic Adrienne von Speyr. In *The World of Prayer* (San Francisco: Ignatius Press, 1985), Speyr develops a fascinating 'trinitarian mysticism' which is rich with pneumatological insight. On this, see Matthew Lewis Sutton, *Heaven Opens: The Trinitarian Mysticism of Adrienne von Speyr* (Minneapolis: Fortress Press, 2014).

[50]Coakley, *God, Sexuality, and the Self*, 112.

for words. And God, who searches the heart, knows what is the mind of the Spirit, because the Spirit intercedes for the saints according to the will of God. We know that all things work together for good for those who love God, who are called according to his purpose. For those whom he foreknew he also predestined to be conformed to the image of his Son, in order that he might be the firstborn within a large family. And those whom he predestined he also called; and those whom he called he also justified; and those whom he justified he also glorified. (Rom. 8.14-17; 8.26-30)

The model goes somewhat beyond Paul, Coakley recognizes, 'into explicitly trinitarian language'.[51] In addition to Paul, Coakley draws from the wealth of Spirit-centric practices that were in circulation in early Christianity during which formal trinitarian expression was still unfixed, including the charismatic and prophetic practices associated with the second-century Montanism movement, early Christian documents such as the *Shepherd of Hermas* and the writings of many mystics down the ages who speak vividly of the transformative potential of the indwelling Spirit.[52] Supremely, though, the model owes its allegiance to one of Romans 8's principal patristic exegetes: Origen.

Unlike some of the other patristic figures Coakley surveys (such as Irenaeus and Tertullian) it is Origen who offers the most striking manifestation of the Romans 8 model in the early church. This is for at least two reasons:

First, the treatise starts (*De oratione* 1) with an insistence on the priority and primacy of the Holy Spirit in understanding the nature and purpose of prayer; and it stresses the capacity of the grace of God to take us beyond the 'worthless' 'reasoning of mortals' to a sphere of unutterable mysteries (see 2 Cor. 12), where 'spiritual prayer' occurs in the 'heart' (*De oratione* 2.5). Already, then, there is the explicit willingness to allow that the Spirit – though from the start a 'fellow worker' with the Father and Son – escorts the pray-er to a realm beyond the normal constraints of human rationality. Second, the exegesis of Romans 8 is central to the argument from the start,

---

[51]Ibid.
[52]Ibid., 120.

and citations are reiterated more than once; it is through prayer, and being 'mingled with the Spirit', that we become 'partakers of the Word of God' (*De oratione* 10.2).[53]

Although most explicitly associated with Origen, we have also seen a rendition of sorts of the Romans 8 approach to the doctrine of the Trinity in the writings of one of his most distinguished pupils. At a significant stage in his argument on prayer (soon after the famous *On Prayer* 61), we recall that Evagrius of Ponticus inserts a telling nod to the Pauline tradition he likely inherited from Origen:

> 63. The Holy Spirit, sympathising with our weakness [cf. Rom. 8.26], regularly visits us even when we are impure. And if he should find the mind praying to him alone from love of truth, he lights upon it and obliterates the whole battle-array of thoughts or representations that encircle it, advancing it in the love of spiritual prayer.

These often forgotten (or actively suppressed) streams of Christianity's spiritual traditions reached into the Western theological imagination through neglected strands of Athanasius's theology and then reflowered in the mysticism of John of the Cross and Julian of Norwich both of whom, Coakley argues, present rich accounts of the relation between prayer and Spirit-led incorporation in the trinitarian life of the divine.[54] However, beyond these figures, the 'prayer-based' model of the Trinity did not prove historically forthcoming. Because of the danger it posed to 'ecclesiastical stability', Coakley concludes, it was pressed to the fringes of Christianity and buried in history.[55]

What are the distinctive features of this approach to the Trinity? According to Coakley, although the experience of God in prayer is too subtle an experience to allow the unpicking of agency in any neat way (prayer remains an experience of the one God), the 'prayer-based'

---

[53]Ibid., 127.

[54]See John of the Cross, 'Spiritual Canticle', in *Selected Writings*, ed. by Kieran Kavanaugh, CWS (New York: Paulist Press, 1987), 219–83.

[55]Coakley, *God, Sexuality, and the Self*, 117. More specifically, the perceived political danger is that 'the transformative view of the Spirit might expand the reference of the redeemed life of "Sonship" even beyond what the church could predict or control'. See Coakley, *God, Sexuality, and the Self*, 121.

model suggests a way of making sense of this experience according to a distinctively threefold pattern. The pray-er's 'total "perception" of God is here found to be ineluctably and equally trifaceted: the "Father" is both source and ultimate object of divine desire; the "Spirit" is that (irreducibly distinct) enabler and incorporator of that desire in creation – that which makes the creation divine; the "Son" is that divine and perfected creation'.[56] Additionally, argues Coakley, the model of the Trinity that developed out of the context of the spiritual experience of prayer much more effectively speaks of the full equality of the three 'persons' of the Trinity in one 'substance' than the creedal confessions, which despite their propositional protection of *homoousian* equality almost inevitably rendered the Holy Spirit a third in a line of three. In what is in effect a diametric reversal of the ordering of the creed, then, the prayer-inspired model of the Trinity begins with the Holy Spirit rather than ends there.

For Coakley, therefore, Paul's tantalizing writings on prayer in Romans 8 and the fiery renditions of the Spirit found in the writings of his mystical exegetes are rich with pneumatological implications. Far from struggling to find any work for the Holy Spirit to do, the Spirit takes primacy as the recipient of prayer ('praying to him', as Evagrius has it), the one who 'does' the praying ('interceding with sighs too deep for words', as Paul has it), the one who helps 'us to think and speak rightly of so great a subject' as prayer (as Origen explains in *De oratione* 3.6) and the one who transforms us ('incorporating' the pray-er into the life of the divine, as Coakley has it).

The 'prayer-based' model, and its primary stress on the incorporative work of the Spirit, Coakley writes, is to be contrasted with the straightforward 'linear' model of the Trinity we mentioned earlier. 'The Holy Spirit is construed not simply as extending the revelation of Christ, nor merely as enabling Christ's recognition, but as actually catching up the created realm into the life of God (making it "conformed to the likeness of his Son", to use Paul's memorable phrase in Romans 8.29)'.[57] If what we are talking about in pneumatology is the agency that constitutes us as children of God, draws out of us the cry of 'Abba' and catches us up into the life of the

---

[56]Coakley, *God, Sexuality, and the Self*, 114. Robert W. Jenson argues similarly by saying that 'the whole doctrine of the Trinity can be explained by simply remarking that Christians pray to the Father, with the Son, in the Spirit, and are convinced that by so doing they are properly caught up in the story that God lives with his people'. See Robert W. Jenson, *A Theology in Outline: Can These Bones Live* (Oxford: Oxford University Press, 2016), 51.
[57]Coakley, *God, Sexuality, and the Self*, 111–12.

divine, then it makes little sense, under the conditions of prayer, to speak of the Holy Spirit as a third. As such, there is an interesting irony, not lost on Coakley, in the argument that among those most resourced to rescue the doctrine of the Trinity from a deflated third article are the very ones condemned by the church for, among a litany of abuses, an indefensible subordinationism.[58]

On Coakley's rendition, the minority 'prayer-based' tradition of the doctrine of the Trinity addresses in one fell swoop the pneumatological poverty that is detectable in much of modern trinitarianism, while asking challenging questions regarding the nature of ecclesiastical authority. It also raises questions regarding the very nature of Christian prayer and Christian belief. Within this kind of trinitarianism, as 'something precisely not done by oneself', the practice of prayer becomes itself more perplexing – on this, more later – and so too for that matter does belief.[59] In prayer, the doxologically reconstructed doctrine of 'the Trinity is no longer seen as an obscure though authoritative ecclesial doctrine of God's nature, but rather a life into which we enter and, in unbreakable union with Christ, breathe the very Spirit of God'.[60]

Doxological trinitarianism

The second of our trinitarian case studies operates under the name 'doxological trinitarianism'. As we shall see, it shares a family resemblance with Coakley's 'prayer-based' model of the Trinity in terms of both its commitment to rerouting the doctrine of the Trinity through prayer and its textual loyalty to Romans 8. 'Doxological trinitarianism' features in the writings of theologians such as Jürgen Moltmann, Catherine Mowry LaCugna and Alan J. Torrance – for the sake of space and for its critical edginess, Torrance's *Persons in Communion* will be our primary focus.[61]

---

[58]Ibid., 140.

[59]Ibid., 113.

[60]Coakley, 'Deepening "Practices"', 93.

[61]See Jürgen Moltmann, *The Trinity and the Kingdom of God: The Doctrine of God* (London: SCM Press, 1981), 151–61; Catherine Mowry LaCugna, *God for Us: The Trinity and Christian Life* (New York: Harper Collins, 1991), 319–75; and Alan J. Torrance, *Persons in Communion: An Essay on Trinitarian Description and Human Participation* (London: T&T Clark, 1996), 307–71.

'Doxological trinitarianism' is developed by Torrance as a doxological alternative to Karl Barth's doctrine of the Trinity as presented in the early volumes of his *Church Dogmatics*. Torrance characterizes Barth's doctrine of the Trinity as a 'revelation model' to the extent that the early Barth locates one of his principal investigations of the Trinity within a discussion about the nature of revelation, epistemology and theological language. Torrance writes that 'the Trinity itself is witnessed in the structure of revelation, as is reflected, Barth argues, in the statement, "*God* reveals Himself. He reveals *Himself through Himself*. He reveals *Himself*." This is to say that God is the Revealer, the Revelation and the Revealedness.'[62] By wedding the Trinity to the doctrine of revelation, Torrance sees in Barth's early account of the Trinity an unsatisfying subordination of the Holy Spirit. More specifically, he means that despite protestations to the contrary Barth cannot help rendering the Spirit the third in a threefold event of revelation (Revealer, Revelation and only then Revealedness). In making known the revelation of God in Jesus Christ, the identity of the Holy Spirit is established in terms of its service to the other more significant persons of the Trinity. 'Attributing to the Holy Spirit the role or function of Revealedness is insufficient,' Torrance concludes: it does damage to the full *homoousian* unity of the Godhead and weakens the sense of divine-human participation.[63]

By relocating, as Torrance does, the doctrine from a context of revelation to doxology the Trinity starts to look very different. For Torrance, the only means of speaking of the relations of God is by being in relation with God. But Barth's revelation model of the Trinity appears to Torrance to obscure the reality of our communion with God. It is about knowledge rather than fellowship; and knowledge alone does not constitute relationship.[64] The relationship with God, Torrance says, is doxologically rather than epistemologically driven: it is principally by way of prayer and praise. To speak truly of God means participating in the life of God, and that means praying – which is both 'in Christ' and 'through the Spirit'. This experience of God in prayer is the source from which a more participative, pneumatologically driven doctrine of the Trinity springs.

---

[62]Torrance, *Persons in Communion*, 89 (citing Barth, *CD* I/1, 340).

[63]Torrance, *Persons in Communion*, 222.

[64]It is important to note that 'knowledge' and 'fellowship', as theological categories, are more connected in Barth's theology than Torrance lets on.

Torrance's alternative 'doxological' model, he concludes, 'leads to a rather different conception of the divine Triunity by offering a) a closer integration of the *trinitas ad intra* and the divine economy – and thus greater emphasis on the grounds of human participation in the intra-divine life – and b) a more dynamic conception of personhood with respect to both the divine and also the human realms'.[65] As with Coakley so here too: prayer daringly pushes Christian doctrine into articulating a more generously participative account of the God-world relation. How prayer achieves this takes us to the next section of this chapter, for its answer lies in the way the doctrine of the Trinity, so Torrance argues, is not only shaped and structured by prayer but itself shapes and structures the practice of prayer.

Prayer shaped by the doctrine of the Trinity

We have so far traced the entanglement of prayer in the making and remaking of the doctrine of the Trinity. Stephen Holmes sums things up well by saying that the doctrine of the Trinity developed to provide logical expression of 'primitive practices of worship. At the risk of oversimplifying, the church always knew how to speak *to* God. Yet it took four centuries or so to work out how to speak *about* God in ways that were compatible with this.'[66] Our task now is to consider the other side of the relation between the Trinity and prayer: that is, what a theology of prayer shaped by the doctrine of the Trinity might look like. As we shall see, just as prayer makes the doctrine of God more complex, a confession of God as Trinity also complexifies prayer, expanding it into something intensely perplexing.

'Everything looks – and, indeed, is – different in the light of the Trinity,' Colin Gunton argues.[67] If Gunton is right then thinking trinitarianly about God fundamentally alters our thinking about prayer. The difference trinitarian thinking makes to prayer can be illustrated by a contrast James Torrance sets up in his 1994 Disbury Lectures published as *Worship,*

---

[65]Torrance, *Persons in Communion*, 308.

[66]Holmes, 'Classical Trinity', 33.

[67]Colin Gunton, *The Promise of Trinitarian Theology* (London: T&T Clark, 1997; 2nd edn), 4–5.

Community and the Triune God of Grace.[68] There he contrasts two different views of worship: the 'unitarian' and the 'trinitarian'. Torrance's argument is as follows:

> Probably the most common and widespread view is that worship is something which we, religious people, do – mainly in church on Sunday. We go to church, we sing our psalms and hymns to God, we intercede for the world, we listen to the sermon (too simply an exhortation), we offer our money, time and talents to God. No doubt we need God's grace to help us to do it. We do it because Jesus taught us to do it and left us an example of how to do it. But worship is what *we* do before God. In theological language, this means that the only priesthood is our priesthood, the only offering is our offering, the only intercessions our intercessions. Indeed this view of worship is in practice unitarian, has no doctrine of the Mediator or sole priesthood of Christ, is human-centred, has no proper doctrine of the Holy Spirit, is too often non-sacramental, and can engender weariness. ... It is not trintiarian.[69]

A fully trinitarian view of worship, however, 'means participating, in union with Christ, in what he has done for us, once and for all, in his self-offering to the Father. ... Is this not the meaning of life in the Spirit, of that important New Testament word *koinonia*, which can be translated "communion", "fellowship", "sharing", "participation"? "God has sent the Spirit of his Son into our hearts whereby we cry: *Abba* Father" (Gal. 4.6).'[70] If we substitute 'worship' for 'prayer' then the gist of Torrance's argument is that once the Trinity recedes from view, prayer loses a sense of the 'priestly mediation' of Jesus Christ (on this, more to follow in Chapter 4), emerges as an exclusively human action (it 'is what *we* do before God') and results in the introduction of an unhelpful dualism into the divine–human relation (prayer is the thing that we do 'down here' to attract the attention of God 'up there'). Without an adequate trinitarian structuring of prayer, Torrance would say, we get prayer 'wrong'.

---

[68]James B. Torrance, *Worship, Community and the Triune God of Grace* (Carlisle: Paternoster, 1996).
[69]Torrance, *Worship, Community and the Triune God of Grace*, 7.
[70]Ibid., 8–9.

The German philosopher of religion Ludwig Feuerbach presents an example of something of what it means to get prayer 'wrong'. In *The Essence of Christianity* of 1841, Feuerbach famously proclaimed that the concept of God is based on a 'projection' of the human imagination. The God who creates humanity becomes the God created by humanity. The classical doctrine of the Trinity, under these conditions, becomes a projection of an 'essential need of duality, of love, of community' onto a figment of the imagination we name as God.[71] God is an 'alter ego' and 'theology is anthropology', he announced.[72] Curiously, despite his reduction of God to the essence of the self, Feuerbach retained a space for prayer within his projectionism-thesis. Prayer is understood by Feuerbach to be the practice through which the pray-er 'turns to the Omnipotence of Goodness'. But the source of the 'Omnipotence of Goodness' here is not the divine, as is the case in classical understandings of prayer, but that which is found in the pray-er's 'own heart'.[73] Prayer becomes some sort of therapy to alter the inner state of the self. While in the Evagrian sense prayer might be 'the mind's conversation with God' (*On Prayer* 3), under Feuerbach prayer remains conversational but the subject of the conversation has changed from God to the self. Prayer becomes 'a dialogue of man with himself', he concludes.[74] In this sense Feuerbach brings Torrance's 'unitarian' model of worship to its logical completion: prayer is monological.

If Feuerbach evinces an arguably straightforward example of getting prayer 'wrong', Alan Torrance finds in the approach to prayer assumed by some accounts of the ever-popular 'social' models of the Trinity a subtler example of the same problem. Some renditions of social trinitarianism make the internal relations of the Trinity the exemplum, the celestial blueprint, as it were, for all other relationships – personal, social and indeed the relationship of prayer. Our prayer is 'modelled', as it were, on the prayer of the imitable life of the Trinity. Because the Son prays to the Father so must we. To cite Moltmann, 'Praying simply means doing ... what God himself does in the world through his Spirit.'[75] Moltmann offers a way of casting prayer

---

[71]Ludwig Feuerbach, *The Essence of Christianity* (Cambridge: Cambridge University Press, 2011), 66.

[72]Feuerbach, *The Essence of Christianity*, 267.

[73]Ibid., 124.

[74]Ibid., 122.

[75]Jürgen Moltmann, *The Source of Life: The Holy Spirit and the Theology of Life* (London: SCM Press, 1997), 133.

in a deliberately trinitarian mould. But the way of the social trinitarianism he represents, at least according to Torrance, remains underpinned by an assumption that comes uncomfortably close to the 'unitarian' model of worship identified and rejected by James Torrance. He concludes that social trinitarianism 'assumes that worship is essentially something which *we* do and initiate – albeit by the Spirit and in the fellowship of Jesus'.[76] In short, prayer is self-propelled, on a slippery slope to Feuerbach via Pelagius. Social trinitarianism, on Torrance's reading, does not go far enough in restructuring prayer as divine 'gift' rather than human 'task'.[77]

If Torrance is right and a non-trinitarian account of prayer 'minimizes' prayer as a self-initiated human action, then a trinitarianly reconfigured theory of prayer, along the lines offered by both Torrances and others, 'maxes' prayer out. A 'maximalist', or 'enlarged' to use the language of the Collect of Trinity Sunday with which we began this chapter, understands that there is more to the human practice of prayer than meets the eye. Citing Adrienne von Speyr's work on prayer, Balthasar writes, 'There is a *deeper* and comprehensive sense in which the trinitarian conversation is the prototype of all prayer. When God stands before God we can say … "Worship as we know it is a grace that comes from the triune worship. Nothing is more rooted in God than worship."'[78] Speyr also stands in the tradition of Romans 8, to which we referred earlier, having written a punchy meditation on the subject.[79] On this Pauline logic, the more I pray, Speyr would say, the more I realize that it is not me praying but the divine who prays in me. The Holy Spirit, with groans too deep for words, catches me up into the prayer of

---

[76]Torrance, *Persons in Communion*, 311.

[77]Wading any further into the now burgeoning industry of defending or rejecting the social Trinity is not our concern. Yet it is worth saying that, if nothing else, the strange experience of prayer sounds a warning note of the deep complications of probing too precisely the internal constitution of 'God', let alone mapping those conclusions onto human prayer. For important contributions to these debates, see Karen Kilby, 'Perichoresis and Projection: Problems with Social Doctrines of the Trinity', *New Blackfriars*, 81.957 (2000), 432–45; Sarah Coakley, '"Persons" in the "Social" Doctrine of the Trinity: A Critique of Current Analytic Discussion', in *The Trinity: An Interdisciplinary Symposium on the Doctrine of the Trinity*, ed. by Stephen T. Davis, Daniel Kendall and Gerald O'Collins (Oxford: Oxford University Press, 1999), 123–44; and Janet Martin Soskice, 'Trinity and "the Feminine Other"', *New Blackfriars*, 75.878 (1994), 2–17.

[78]Hans Urs von Balthasar, *Theo-Drama: Theological Dramatic Theory – Volume 5: The Last Act* (San Francisco: Ignatius Press, 1998), 96 (citing Speyr's *The World of Prayer*).

[79]See Adrienne von Speyr, *The Victory of Love: A Meditation on Romans 8* (San Francisco: Ignatius Press, 1990).

the praying Son, incorporates me into the life of the trinitarian divine and releases me from the anxiety of not being able to pray as I ought. Following Romans 8, a trinitarian approach to prayer sees the vocation to prayer as less about replicating the prayer of the Trinity on earth as it is in heaven as actually being 'incorporated' into that prayer. All of a sudden, prayer starts to look a whole lot more complicated, as we mentioned earlier in our discussion of Coakley's 'prayer-based' model of the Trinity. We can now make this more explicit by citing Coakley once again:

> It is the perception of many Christians who pray either contemplatively or charismatically (in both cases there is a willed suspension of one's own agenda, a deliberate waiting on the divine) that the dialogue of prayer is strictly speaking not a simple communication between an individual and a divine monad, but rather a movement of divine reflexivity, a sort of answering of God to God in and through the one who prays (see again Rom. 8.26-7). ... Yet even to call it this – to call it a human (let alone a 'religious') 'experience' – is to risk a serious misunderstanding; for the whole point is that it is a delicate ceding to something precisely not done by oneself. It is the sense (admittedly obscure) of an irreducibly dy-polar divine activity – a call and response of divine desire – into which the pray-er is drawn and incorporated.[80]

Prayer here is not simply something we 'do'; prayer does something to us. By the work of the Holy Spirit, it forms us and shapes us into the life of Christ. Alan Torrance calls this kind of approach to prayer 'theopoiesis'.

> Doxological participation is an event of grace – a concept which barely features in Moltmann's theology – and not, therefore, of any natural human response or innate capacity. As such, worship may be described as an event of 'theopoietic' *koinonia*, which is both 'in Christ' and 'through the Spirit', and one, therefore, in which the Kingdom of God is 'in a manner' actually and freely *present* – and not merely future.[81]

Understanding prayer in these 'theopoetic' terms offers a double-repair of both the doxological shortcomings Torrance sees in Moltmann and

---

[80]Coakley, *God, Sexuality, and the Self*, 112–13.
[81]Torrance, *Persons in Communion*, 313.

the trinitarian disappointments he identifies in Barth's early doctrinal thinking discussed above. In respect of the former, he would agree with Coakley that prayer is undervalued if assumed to be minimally about my action rather than maximally a work of divine–human participation. In respect of the latter, he concludes that the doxology of prayer gives a 'fuller characterization of the *agency* of the Spirit' and its work of incorporation and as a consequence presents a more 'inclusive communion of the Trinity' than is otherwise possible.[82] So Torrance: prayer is not 'task' but 'the gift of participating, through the Spirit, in what Christ has done and is doing for us in his intercessions and communion with the Father.'[83]

Summary

Andrew Louth writes that 'it is in prayer that the question, "Who is this God?" is answered'.[84] This chapter has seen that the answer prayer yields is trinitarian in shape and structure. We have seen that prayer complexifies the doctrine of God: prayer led early Christian theologians to confront complex questions around monotheism, and in their answers made the language of God stranger – trinitarianly strange. The doctrine of the Trinity helps us to be clearer about the confusions and complications in our speech about God; tensions that are not resolved in prayer but intensified. Just as prayer complexifies belief in God as Trinity, the practice of prayer itself is re-modulated by trinitarian belief: no longer understood as a self-propelled human practice, the centre of gravity shifts to make space for prayer to be seen as the divinely inspired practice 'in' us, which involves the divine and the human in a messy, entangled web of incorporation. Located in the Christian imagination of Father, Son and Holy Spirit, prayer is made more – in a word – perplexing. Further questions are presented by this now perplexed theory of prayer: can prayer really be a genuinely human action if it is also the work of the divine? How does divine agency and human agency relate in prayer? These questions take us into new territory, and especially the doctrine of Christology, the subject of the next chapter.

---

[82]Ibid., 314–15.
[83]Torrance, *Persons in Communion*, 311 – original emphasis removed.
[84]Louth, *Theology and Spirituality*, 3.

CHAPTER 4
CHRIST THE PRAY-ER,
CHRIST THE PRAYER

As we discovered in the previous chapter, when set to the grammar of the Trinity the practice of prayer becomes a good deal more perplexing. It becomes about nothing less than participation, by the grace of God, in the prayer of the Trinity. More specifically, prayer is about the pray-er's incorporation by the Holy Spirit into the praying life of the Son, the second person of the Trinity, the one who shares our humanity and the focus of the present chapter. We have already seen how the practices of praying to Jesus Christ acted as catalysts for doctrinal thinking on the divinity of Christ. As we are now to find, prayer also helped to shape doctrinal reflection on Christ's human nature. Because prayer was often directed 'through' Christ, in the name of Jesus, it was critical for the early church to speak of Jesus Christ as fully human, fully one of us. Complementing the themes explored in the previous chapter, the kind of Christology of prayer this chapter is pursuing, then, requires an investigation of Jesus Christ as the one who offers as well as receives prayer.

Two Christological 'moves' frame our exploration. The first plays with the theme of Jesus Christ as 'pray-er'. What does the New Testament say about Jesus' practice of praying to God? What does Jesus Christ, through his practice of prayer, teach us about our practices of offering prayer to God? What does Jesus Christ continue to do for us in prayer in his office as mediator? These questions lead us into some of the key New Testament texts on prayer, which include Luke's version of the Lord's Prayer (Lk. 11.2-4), his account of Christ's prayer in the Garden of Gethsemane (Lk. 22.39-46) and Paul's description of the ongoing intercession of Jesus Christ in Romans 8. Once again, we cannot avoid dipping our toes into the fourth-century debates around the person of Jesus Christ, and this time those concerning his human nature provoked by the Apollinarian heresy. In this section, we begin to scratch the surface of the endlessly rich body of interpretation surrounding what is perhaps Christian theology's most prayed prayer: the

Lord's Prayer. Additionally, we touch on Karl Barth's compelling exegesis of Christ's prayer in the Garden of Gethsemane, T. F. Torrance's magisterial essay on Apollinarianism and worship and John Calvin's famed account of Christ's priestly mediation. The second Christological 'move' requires thinking through the more perplexing notion that Jesus Christ is not only the one who offers prayer but, as complexly fully divine and fully human, he is the very embodiment of what it means to pray. As the paradigm prayer, the source as well as the teacher of prayer, Jesus Christ *is* prayer. Again, this claim takes us deep into the logic of prayer in the New Testament, and this time the key text is John 17 read through the interpretive lens of Cyril of Alexandria's commentary on John. The final section utilizes classical Christological categories to begin to think through the relation between divine and human agency in prayer.

Christ the pray-er

Prayer is an important theme in each of the Gospels, and especially in the Gospel of Luke.[1] The verb 'to pray' (*proseuchomai*) appears more times in Luke than it does anywhere else in the New Testament. The Gospel of Luke begins with two scenes that relate to the theme of prayer: the corporate prayer of the assembly of God gathered outside the temple in Jerusalem (Lk. 1.10) and the personal prayer of Zachariah inside the temple. The first spoken word of the gospel relates to prayer (Lk. 1.13). The opening two chapters include several references to the prayer life of significant gospel characters: the prayers of Zechariah and Elizabeth for a child (Lk. 1.13), Mary's hymn of praise (Lk. 1.46-55), Zechariah's Spirit-inspired prophesy of his child's role in relation to the Messiah (Lk. 1.68-79), the old priest Simeon's great prayer of thanksgiving (Lk. 2.29-32) and the prophet Anna's steadfast prayer (Lk. 2.36-38). The canticles contained in the first two chapters of Luke (Mary's *Magnificat*, Zechariah's *Benedictus* and Simeon's *Nunc Dimittis*) continue to structure the prayer life of many Christians around the world today.

---

[1] See I. Howard Marshall, 'Jesus – Example and Teacher of Prayer in the Synoptic Gospels', in *Into God's Presence: Prayer in the New Testament*, ed. by Richard N. Longenecker (Grand Rapids: William B. Eerdmans, 2002), 113–31.

Just as prayer begins Luke's gospel, it also ends it. As Jesus is breaking and 'blessing' bread in prayer, the post-resurrection identity of Jesus is revealed to the two disciples (Lk. 24.29-31). In the final scene of the gospel, as Jesus ascends into heaven, he prays for his disciples (Lk. 24.50-51) and provides them with a final example of the practice of prayer that characterized much of his prayer life on earth: the practice of intercessory prayer. In the same scene, the disciples are described as 'worshipping' Jesus (Lk. 24.52). This is the Gospel of Luke's single example of Jesus receiving prayer. Then there is the final verse of the gospel, which circles back to the setting of the temple in Jerusalem to have Jesus' followers 'continually' blessing God (Lk. 24.53) just as the now ascended Christ is 'at the right hand of God' continually interceding for them (Rom. 8.34). The gospel ends as it begins in prayer.[2] In between the beginning and ending of the Gospel of Luke is an intriguing Christology of prayer, which is discussed below around three themes: Jesus' teaching on prayer, his activity as pray-er and his role as mediator in prayer.

Jesus Christ: Teacher of prayer

Paul's injunction that 'we do not know how to pray as we ought' (Rom. 8.26) suggests that in order to pray we need first to be taught how to pray. The New Testament provides a wealth of teaching on prayer, not least by Jesus himself. According to James Dunn, of all the things Jesus taught in the New Testament prayer is 'one of the most consistent themes'.[3] This is particularly the case in the Gospel of Luke. As I. Howard Marshall says, the sheer 'quantity and content of the material on prayer in Luke's gospel suggests that the third evangelist was consciously aware of the significance of prayer in Jesus' ministry and teaching'.[4] In the Gospel of Luke, Jesus teaches his followers to petition God for labourers for the harvest (Lk. 10.2). He teaches about God's promise to answer prayer (Lk. 11.9) and about the need to be persistent in prayer (Lk. 11.5-8), a theme repeated in the parable

---

[2]The theme of prayer is picked up again by Luke in the Acts of the Apostles, which begins with a description of the disciples at prayer during the choosing of Matthias, Judas's replacement (Acts 1.14). For the material on Luke and Acts, I am grateful to conversations with Hannah Cocksworth.

[3]James D. G. Dunn, 'Prayer', in *Dictionary of Jesus and the Gospels*, ed. by Joel B. Green, Scot McKnight and I. Howard Marshall (Downers Grove: InterVarsity Press, 1992), 617–25.

[4]Marshall, 'Jesus – Example and Teacher of Prayer in the Synoptic Gospels', 115.

of the unjust judge (Lk. 18.1-8). There is also teaching about the relation between prayer and 'being alert' and on the relation between prayer and 'strength' (Lk. 21.36).

Undoubtedly, though, the capstone of Jesus' teaching on prayer in the Gospel of Luke is the Lord's Prayer (Lk. 11.2-4). As the disciples approached Jesus after he had finished praying they asked: 'Lord, teach us to pray', and Jesus said to them, 'when you pray, say ...', and he prayed the Lord's Prayer (Lk. 11.1-2). 'Here', Leonardo Boff writes, 'we find a crystallization of the very essence of Jesus' experience and the basic landmark of his teachings.'[5] For Origen, one of the interesting things about the Lord's Prayer is that Jesus' central teaching on prayer is by way of example. In praying, Jesus provides a pattern of 'how we ought to pray' (*De oratione* 18.3).

As Christianity spread, the Lord's Prayer spread through the Christian world like wildfire.[6] So too did the task of interpreting the Lord's Prayer. Initially, its individual petitions were the primary subjects of interpretation (for example, those by Clement of Rome, Irenaeus, *The Epistle of Polycarp to the Philippians* and Clement of Alexandria) but by the third century commentaries on the entire prayer began to appear and since then the Lord's Prayer has continued to seize the imagination of countless Christian theologians. A small sample of engagements with the Lord's Prayer include those by Tertullian, Cyprian, Origen, Cyril of Jerusalem, Gregory of Nyssa, Ambrose of Milan, Theodore of Mopsuestia, John Cassian, Augustine, Maximus the Confessor, Francis of Assisi, Aquinas, Teresa of Ávila, Luther, Calvin, Barth, Simone Weil and many others.[7] There are now feminist, liberationist and postcolonial readings of the Lord's Prayer.[8] The Lord's

---

[5]Leonardo Boff, *The Lord's Prayer: The Prayer of Integral Liberation* (Maryknoll: Orbis Books, 1983), 17.

[6]For some helpful surveys of the Lord's Prayer down the ages see, Kenneth W. Stevenson, *The Lord's Prayer: A Text in Tradition* (London: SCM Press, 2004); Karlfried Froehlich, 'The Lord's Prayer in Patristic Literature', in *A History of Prayer: The First to the Fifteenth Century,* ed. by Roy Hammerling, (Leiden: Brill, 2008), 59–77; Hammerling, *The Lord's Prayer in the Early Church*; and Nicholas Ayo, *The Lord's Prayer: A Survey Theological and Literary* (Notre Dame: University of Notre Dame Press, 1992).

[7]See the Appendix for bibliographical details.

[8]For example: Roland Mushat Frye, 'On Praying "Our Father": The Challenge of Radical Feminist Language for God', in *The Politics of Prayer: Feminist Language and the Worship of God,* ed. by Helen Hull Hitchcock (San Francisco: Ignatius Press, 1992), 209–28; Boff, *The Lord's Prayer*; Musa W. Dube Shomanah, 'Praying the Lord's Prayer in a Global Economic Era', *The Ecumenical Review,* 49.4 (1997), 439–50; and Bénézet Bujo, *The Impact of the Our Father on Everyday Life: Meditations of an African Theologian* (Nairobi: Paulines, 2002).

Prayer has inspired sermons, treatises and literary works – for example, the epic stories of the fourth-century poet Caius Vettius Aquilinus Juvencus who produced an extraordinary poetic paraphrase of the Lord's Prayer, the fifth-century poet Coelius Sedulius who followed in his tracks as did Francis of Assisi and Dante in Canto XI of his *Purgatorio*.[9] There are hymns on the Lord's Prayer. The Lord's Prayer has even been translated into the visual arts (such as the series of woodcuts of the 1920s on the petitions of the Lord's Prayer by the German interwar year expressionist painter and printer Max Pechstein) and can be found inscribed into some of the earliest Christian symbolism (such as in the 'Sator-Rotas Square' uncovered in the ruins of Pompeii).[10] It also plays a role in the Christian catechetical tradition. For centuries, the Lord's Prayer has been used as part of the preparation of candidates for baptism and for a while was the reserve of the baptized alone: it communicates the core teachings of the Christian faith and comes to mark the foundation of the Christian life.

According to John Cassian, whom we have already encountered in connection with Evagrius, the Lord's Prayer is 'an example and rule' for all prayer.[11] Similarly, Teresa of Ávila, in her heady exploration of the Lord's Prayer, is marvelled 'to see that in so few words everything about contemplation and perfection is included'.[12] Many of the church's practices of prayer are incorporated into this one prayer, Teresa points out. There is praise, petition, thanksgiving and confession. 'In fact, in the Prayer is comprised an epitome of the whole Gospel', as Tertullian said in probably the first comprehensive commentary on the Lord's Prayer written around the turn of the third century.[13] In the hands of Augustine, who wrote more about the Lord's Prayer than anyone in the early church, the simple prayer Jesus taught his disciples becomes nothing short of sacramental. It both points beyond itself to a higher, holier truth and becomes a channel of

---

[9]For a discussion of the Lord's Prayer as 'poetry', see Hammerling, *The Lord's Prayer in the Early Church*, 47–59.

[10]On the 'Sator Rotas Square', see again Hammerling, *The Lord's Prayer in the Early Church*, 22–4.

[11]John Cassian, 'Conference Nine: On Prayer', in *Conferences*, trans. by Colm Luibheid, CWS (New York: Paulist Press, 1985), 101–24 (116).

[12]Teresa of Ávila, 'The Way of Perfection', in *The Collected Works of St Teresa of Ávila – Volume 2* (Washington: Institute of Carmelite Studies, 1980), 137–204 (183).

[13]Tertullian, 'On Prayer', in *Tertullian*, ANF, vol. 3 (Edinburgh: T&T Clark, 1997), 681–91 (681).

grace 'by which the sacred signified truth becomes a part of the lives of the believer'.[14] Perhaps because of the transforming effect the prayer has on the lives of the faithful, Chapter 8 of the *Didache* instructs Christians to pray the Lord's Prayer three times a day. Cyprian sees this threefold structure of daily prayer as symbolic of the Trinity.[15] Centuries later the Church of England's *Book of Common Prayer* of 1662 would include two recitations of the Lord's Prayer in its liturgy for both Morning Prayer and Evening Prayer and once again in the daily Litany. Five times daily the Lord's Prayer would be said. Furthermore, the order for the Lord's Supper in the Prayer Book begins and ends with the Lord's Prayer. In the baptism liturgy the godparents are exhorted to ensure that the child will 'learn ... the Lord's Prayer ... in the vulgar tongue', at which point the child should be presented for confirmation. And in the catechism prior to confirmation, the catechist asks, 'Let me hear therefore if thou canst say the Lord's Prayer.' It would not be an exaggeration to say that the Lord's Prayer is the most said and interpreted prayer in the history of Christianity.

Although the previous chapter argued that a fully trinitarian theory of prayer means reconceiving prayer as God's action 'through' us – being 'prayed in' – what we encounter in Jesus Christ's teaching is something of the full human reality of prayer. We pray the Lord's Prayer in communion with all who say the Lord's Prayer and indeed in union with Christ the mediator (soon to be discussed) through the Holy Spirit. But the Lord's Prayer is a prayer that you and I really and properly pray: we are given an example of what it means to pray in Christ's modelling of prayer, and, as disciples of Christ, we follow that example. Whatever else prayer is, it is a fully human action. It is perhaps the most human thing that we can do, the very thing that defines us and makes us human.

Karl Barth emphasized strongly the full human reality of prayer across his treatments of the topic. Prayer is 'the true and proper work of the Christian' (*CD* III/3, 265), he insists. The vocation of the Christian is to follow Christ's teaching on prayer and pray; hence the inclusion of a long meditation on prayer in the ethical sections of his doctrine of creation. Barth ended each major volume of the *Church Dogmatics* with an ethics, and the doctrine of

---

[14]Roy Hammerling, 'St Augustine of Hippo: Prayer as Sacrament', in *A History of Prayer: The First to the Fifteenth Century*, ed. by Roy Hammerling (Leiden: Brill, 2008), 183–97 (190).

[15]Cyprian, 'On the Lord's Prayer (Treatise IV)', in *Hippolytus, Cyprian, Caius, Novatian*, ANF, vol. 5 (Edinburgh: T&T Clark, 1995), 447–57 (456).

reconciliation was no exception. But what sets the ethics of reconciliation apart is that the entire part-volume, published posthumously as *The Christian Life*, is unusually structured around the petitions of the Lord's Prayer. He selects prayer as the organizing theme around which to arrange his most mature deliberations on the shape of the Christian life for a simple reason: prayer best expresses 'the fact that some human *action* is at issue in the obedience which the gracious God commands of man' (*ChrL*, 42).

Jesus Christ: At prayer

Jesus gave instructions to his followers about how to pray. As Aquinas says, he also 'elected to pray to his Father' (*ST* 3a, q.21, art.3). Prayer was an everyday practice in first-century Judaism.[16] The temple was a 'house of prayer' (Isa. 56.7; Mk 12.29). There would be personal prayer three times daily – at the third, sixth and ninth hour (Dan. 6.10). There were set corporate prayers in the synagogue. There were prayers before each meal (Deut. 8.10). As a practising Jew, prayer would have been an everyday practice for Jesus.[17] 'We may conclude with all probability that no day in the life of Jesus passed without the three times of prayer.'[18] Although the praying Jesus is found throughout the synoptic tradition, the Gospel of Luke gives a particularly vivid insight into Jesus' prayer life.

According to Luke, Jesus 'was praying' at the beginning of his ministry during his baptism (Lk. 3.21). More than once he retreated 'to deserted places' to pray. He was sometimes alone (Lk. 5.16), sometimes in the company of his disciples (Lk. 9.18) and on occassion he prayed for significant periods of time (Lk. 6.12). Luke records Jesus prayerfully thanking God for the revelation of 'hidden things' after the sending of the seventy-two (Lk. 10.21). There was prayer at the transfiguration when 'he went up on the mountain to pray' (Lk. 9.28-29). There are also examples of Jesus praying for others – including praying for Peter (Lk. 22.32) and for his disciples on the Mount of Olives (Lk. 22.39-46). Jesus prayed before important decisions,

---

[16]On this, see Christopher R. Seitz, 'Prayer in the Old Testament or Hebrew Bible', in *Into God's Presence: Prayer in the New Testament*, ed. by Richard N. Longenecker (Grand Rapids: William B. Eerdmans, 2002), 3–22.

[17]For an exploration of Jesus' practice of prayer from the perspective of liberation theology, see Jon Sobrino, *Christology at the Crossroads: A Latin American Approach* (London: SCM Press, 1978), 146–78.

[18]Joachim Jeremias, *The Prayers of Jesus* (London: SCM Press, 1967), 75.

such as the choosing of the twelve (Lk. 6.12) and during important events, such as at his death when he prayed to God to forgive 'them, for they do not know what they do' (Lk. 23.34) and commended himself to God in prayer using the prayer book of the Hebrew Bible, the Psalter (Lk. 23.46). As mentioned earlier, the final scene of the gospel has Jesus 'blessing' his disciples at his ascension (Lk. 24.50-51). These examples of the regularity of Jesus at prayer are used by Luke to emphasize the piety of Jesus' prayer life: Jesus went far beyond what was expected in prayer.

The focus on the fervency of Jesus' prayer life also, according to Yves Congar, serves to emphasize the full humanity of Christ. 'It is as man, and with a fully human prayer, that Christ prays.'[19] Although, as Congar continues, 'it is difficult to single out the moments of Jesus' prayer, for prayer filled His whole life', one of the most significant occasions of a very human Jesus at prayer in the Gospel of Luke is the prayer in the Garden of Gethsemane.[20]

> He came out and went, as was his custom, to the Mount of Olives; and the disciples followed him. When he reached the place, he said to them, 'Pray that you may not come into the time of trial.' Then he withdrew from them about a stone's throw, knelt down, and prayed, 'Father, if you are willing, remove this cup from me; yet, not my will but yours be done.' … When he got up from prayer, he came to the disciples and found them sleeping because of grief, and he said to them, 'Why are you sleeping? Get up and pray that you may not come into the time of trial.' (Lk. 22.39-46)

Here, at night, Jesus was praying – alone, in agonizing isolation. He 'alone watched and prayed in their place' (*CD* IV/1, 268), as Barth comments in his compelling exegesis of the scene. Having spent so much of his ministry in the company of others, the scene captures a 'pause', a 'moment' in which Jesus Christ is caught frighteningly alone. In the dark hour in the garden, he alone acts as our representative before God. As one of us, fully one of us, Jesus Christ stands, as a brother in arms, in our place, as pray-er.

---

[19]Yves Congar, *Jesus Christ* (London: Geoffrey Chapman, 1968), 87. Andrew Louth makes a similar point in his *Introducing Eastern Orthodox Theology* (London: SPCK, 2013), 55–7.
[20]Congar, *Jesus Christ*, 90.

Luke tries hard to arrange his scene so that Christ's vicarious solitude is accentuated. The prayer takes place in a place of remoteness: a garden or a mount, located outside the city walls. Even then, when Jesus and his disciples arrive in the garden, Luke explains how 'he withdrew from them about a stone's throw' away. The church, represented by the disciples, 'is present', Barth writes, but 'has no part at all in that prayer to God. Jesus makes it alone. There is no one there to bear the burden with Him. There is none to help' (*CD* IV/1, 267). This 'notorious non-participation' (*CD* IV/1, 268) is reinforced by the juxtaposition Luke sets up between the praying Christ and the sleeping disciples. In Luke, Jesus instructs his disciples to pray for themselves (Lk. 22.40). But although the disciples follow Jesus to the Mount none follows him in prayer. Instead, they all are found sleeping (Lk. 22.45). Gethsemane is about the 'frightful loneliness in which they left Him, and in which quite alone – not with them but without them and therefore for them – He had to do and did what had to be done' (*CD* IV/1, 268). Matthew and Mark emphasize the disciples' flight from prayer in even stronger terms for Jesus would find them sleeping not once but thrice. Again and again he found them sleeping, each time lacking the obedience to pray as they ought (Mt. 26.40-45 and Mk 14.37-40). If prayer has to do with the category of human 'obedience', as it does for Luther in his interpretation of the Lord's Prayer,[21] again what is being emphasized in the Garden of Gethsemane is the exemplary character of Jesus' prayer life. Jesus is not only the teacher of prayer, or simply one who prays, but is the paradigm pray-er – who is obedient when others are not.

In his study of the theme of prayer in the Lukan tradition, David Crump argues that one of the distinctive features of Luke's portrayal of Jesus' exemplary prayer life is his activity as 'intercessor'.[22] Jesus Christ is the one who prays for others. Gethsemane provides Crump with a case in point. As the disciples sleep, Christ stands in their place and prays on their behalf. In the hour of need, he does that very human thing and prays, emphasizing again the full humanity of Jesus Christ. In addition to the Gethsemane prayer, Crump also singles out Lk. 22.31-32 as particularly

---

[21]For a helpful compilation of Luther's dealings with the Lord's Prayer and the theme of prayer as obedience, see *Luther's Spirituality*, ed. and trans. by Philip D. W. Krey and Peter D. S. Krey, CWS (New York: Paulist Press, 2007), 183–251.
[22]David Crump, *Jesus the Intercessor: Prayer and Christology in Luke-Acts* (Tubingen: J. C. B. Mohr, 1992), 176.

revealing of Jesus' ministry of intercession since it provides a further example of Jesus disclosing to others the intercessory content of his prayers. Luke tells us what Jesus is praying. 'I have prayed for you,' he says to Peter (Lk. 22.32). These two scenes depicting the prayer life of Jesus illustrate the importance of intercession to Christ's ministry and, consequently, the centrality of intercession to the Christian life more generally. Just as Jesus interceded for us, we are called to stand in the place of others and intercede for them.

Let me try to make sense of this with an example. In the chapel at the theological college from where I am writing this book, the community meets daily for prayer. When those gathered for prayer reach the point of the liturgy at which the Lord's Prayer is said, an invitation is offered to say the Lord's Prayer in the 'language and form that is most familiar to you'. What this invariably means is that my neighbour ends up saying a different version of the Lord's Prayer to me. On some occasions, when my concentration lapses, I find that the version of the Lord's Prayer I am reciting drifts into the version of my neighbour: I might begin praying 'Our Father, which art in heaven' but end 'for the kingdom, the power, and the glory'. On other occasions, I find that I am unable to pray in the first place. This is about being honest about the ups and downs of the human reality of prayer. Yet I am in the presence of those who can pray. And others, on these occasions, intercede for me, on my behalf. My neighbour's prayer becomes *my* prayer, prayed on my behalf in my time of need – just as Jesus is said to intercede for others.

The intercessory character of Jesus' prayer life is evidenced again at the end of the Gospel of Luke, where Jesus' ascension takes place in the context of intercession. 'While he was blessing them, he withdrew from them and was carried up into heaven' (Lk. 24.51). But this final mention of the intercessory activity of Jesus takes on a crucial twist: the ministry of intercession, of praying 'for' others, that began on earth is said to continue in heaven.

In heaven as on earth: Prayer and the mediation of Christ

In addition to the ending of Luke, the theme of the ongoing mediation of Christ is explored in Romans 8. 'It is Christ Jesus, who died, yes, who was raised, who is at the right hand of God, who indeed intercedes for us' (Rom. 8.34). Following the logic of Paul's argument, the 'impossibility of prayer' (of being unable to pray as we ought) is made possible not simply through right teaching but as prayer is meditated through the ongoing intercession of

Jesus Christ. Alongside the Pauline material, the theme of the mediation of Christ in prayer appears in I Jn 2.1, Eph. 2.18 and of course in the Letter to the Hebrews. It can also be detected (among other sources) in the *Didache's* doxology, which renders praise and glory 'through' Jesus Christ 'for ever', and in Origen's early treatise on prayer, which as we have said recommends that prayer should be 'in' rather than 'to' Christ. Jesus 'stands in the midst even of those who do not know Him (cf. Jn 1.26), who is never absent from prayer, and who prays to the Father with the person whose Mediator He is. For the Son of God is a High Priest who makes offerings for us' (*De oratione* 10.2).

Origen is following the Epistle to the Hebrews by allocating the ministry of mediation to Christ's priestly office. It is part of his ministry as 'priest', which began on earth and continues in heaven, to intercede for us. 'In the days of his flesh, Jesus offered up prayers and supplications, with loud cries and tears' (Heb. 5.7). The ferocity of Jesus' prayer life on earth is emphasized by the writer of Hebrews to accentuate the steadfastness of the prayer of Jesus in heaven. 'He always lives to make intercession for them' (Heb. 7.25). Because of his priestly mediation in atonement and in prayer the pray-er can thus 'approach the throne of grace with boldness' (Heb. 4.16). As in the cultic system of Israelite worship, mediation in prayer is dependent on a twofold logic: first, that the high priest represents the people before God and second, that the high priest represents God before the people. It mattered a great deal, then, that the high priest is fully human.[23] 'Therefore he had to become like his brothers and sisters in every respect, so that he might be a merciful and faithful high priest in the service of God' (Heb. 2.17). How could one represent another if they did not share 'the same things' (Heb. 2.14)? In other words, what is being emphasized again in the doctrine of Christ's priestly mediation is the full humanity of Jesus Christ.

Despite the biblical, liturgical and theological evidence associated with the ongoing mediation of Christ, dependent as it is on Christ's humanity, part of Jungmann's (not uncontroversial) argument mentioned in the previous chapter is that an obsessive concern to avoid all things Arian in the fourth century led to one of the early church's great liturgical cover-ups: the mediatorial practice of praying 'through' the Son was replaced with

---

[23]On this, see Bruce L. McCormack, '"With Loud Cries and Tears": The Humanity of the Son in the Epistle to the Hebrews', in *The Epistle to the Hebrews and Christian Theology*, ed. by Richard Bauckham, Daniel R. Driver, Trevor A. Hart and Nathan MacDonald (Grand Rapids: William B. Eerdmans, 2009), 37–68.

practices of prayer that were more explicitly directed 'to' Christ. Fending off Arianism, prayers were now rerouted to Christ, the Son of God, fully *homoousios* with the Father, the worthy recipient of our prayer. A liturgical culture was introduced to emphasize the full divinity of Jesus Christ. The Son would be venerated with the Father, heads would be bowed during the saying of the second article of the creed and the practice of praying 'through' Jesus Christ (as a brother in prayer) was not simply downplayed, says Jungmann, but actively suppressed. In a magisterial essay entitled 'The Mind of Christ in Worship: The Problem of Apollinarianism in the Liturgy', T. F. Torrance argues that as the church was busy redirecting prayer 'to' the fully divine Christ, a Christological problem was beginning to materialize behind the pray-er's back.[24] The problem concerned the full humanity of Christ and took form in another of the early church's Christological heresies: Apollinarianism.

The claim that Jesus Christ is fully human was clearly less controversial than the claims made of his divinity. But the doctrinal pinch point in early Christian theology concerned the extent of Christ's humanity: just how human was Christ? The presenting issue Apollinarianism attempted to tackle was the extent of Christ's humanity as it related to the mind of Christ. Because the mind controls the body, the mind is prey to sin and worldly desires. If Christ is genuinely free from the taint of sin, so Apollinarianism believed, his mind cannot possibly be human. In an overreaction to the Arian rejection of the deity of Christ, Apollinarianism therefore erred on the side of an exaggerated doctrine of Christ's divinity and argued that Christ was human in all but mind, which was divine – thus protecting the purity of the mind of Christ from being contaminated by the murky world of human desire and sin.

Although Apollinarianism seemed to present a convenient response to a thorny doctrinal issue, its cost – as with Arianism – was an apparent mismatch between prayer and doctrine. In order for the practice of praying 'through' the Son to make doctrinal sense, the Son must share human experience in truth and not just in appearance. If Christ is anything less than fully consubstantial with humanity, the ministry of priestly mediation is compromised. As Torrance explains, a less than fully human Christ 'disqualifies Christ from being a priest ... and so cuts away the ground from

---

[24]T. F. Torrance, *Theology in Reconciliation: Essays Towards Evangelical and Catholic Unity in East and West* (London: Geoffrey Chapman, 1975), 139–214.

his mediatorial activity on behalf of and from man towards the Father: it destroys his representative capacity as Man before God'.[25] The mismatch was identified in the first instance, according to Torrance, by Athanasius, then developed by the Cappadocians and brought to culmination in the writings of Cyril of Alexandria who argues at length in his *Commentary on John* (written between 425-28) that in his office of priest Christ '"asks" on our behalf as a human being'.[26] We will draw more from Cyril's commentary on John below but the point to be noted at this stage is that the rejection of Apollinarianism comes down, at least in part, to a matter of the *lex orandi*: the logic of mediation, upon which the practice of prayer depends, assumes the full humanity of Jesus Christ.

Torrance comments that a related consequence of a Christology that de-emphasizes the human nature of Christ by over-emphasizing prayer 'to' rather than 'through' the Son was the 'thrusting' of Jesus 'up into the majesty and grandeur of the Godhead'.[27] It is curious that around the same time as the church was combating Arianism, the posture of prayer was also shifting. As we will see in Chapter 6, some of the earliest depictions (both visual and written) of Christians at prayer have the pray-er assuming the position of the 'orans': upright, upstanding, hands raised, head poised towards the heavens – in 'full stretch', as it were.[28] Slowly, though, as the Arian controversy set in and the divinity of Christ became more important than ever, the body posture shifted and the pray-er was brought gradually to their knees, the head was bowed and hands were clasped in contorted submission to the overwhelming majesty of God. No longer did pray-ers stand alongside their brother in prayer, as fellow humans before God. They found themselves kneeling before their exalted King of Kings.

According to a common interpretation of the history of Christian prayer, with the pray-er on their knees, the search for a replacement mediatorial ministry began. The brief was simple: to bridge the gulf between God and the world that had been left by the now de-emphasized human priesthood of Christ. As the human Jesus was becoming increasingly more regal

---

[25]Torrance, *Theology in Reconciliation*, 148.

[26]Throughout this chapter I am using David R. Maxwell's very readable translation published as Cyril of Alexandria, *Commentary on John – Volume 2*, Ancient Christian Texts (Downers Grove: IVP Academic, 2015), 282.

[27]Torrance, *Theology in Reconciliation*, 142.

[28]The term is borrowed from Don E. Saliers, *Worship as Theology: Foretaste of Glory Divine* (Nashville: Abingdon Press, 1994), 28.

and consequently more 'other' an alternative intermediary was required. Initially, Mary would step in to fill the gap between ordinary human beings and an otherwise unapproachable deity. As the sociologist Martin Stringer explains: 'Devotion to Mary takes over as the means by which ordinary Christians can engage in intimate relations with the divine, as Mary, the mother of us all, intercedes with her, now distant, son. As Mary also becomes more distant, virginal or queenly, so local saints come in to take on that human, immanent, mediating role.'[29] In the devotional traditions in which Mary and the saints are (for whatever doctrinal reason) unavailable to act as mediators, the Holy Spirit can be drafted in to 'bond' the distinction between the created and the uncreated. And the Reformation, and the evangelical revivals that emerged in its wake, Stringer concludes, 'could be seen to be, in part, about bringing Jesus back down to the human level and re-establishing that close, personal, relationship with Jesus that negates the need for other local intermediaries. As the popular hymn proclaims, "What a friend we have in Jesus."'[30] Both T. F. Torrance and his brother James, who as Scottish Reformed theologians stand firmly in the tradition of the Reformation, seek to rescue Jesus from the 'grandeur of the Godhead' and bring him back down to the human level to resume his work as the one, true mediator between God and the world. But moreover, for James Torrance, as we saw in the previous chapter, the issue at stake is not simply the doctrinal question of who can and cannot appropriately act as intermediary but also a matter of the very nature of prayer. Once prayer bypasses the human mediation of Christ, Torrance says, it risks falling into something of a liturgical semi-Pelagianism. If there is no mediation outside of the person of Jesus prayer cannot, so to speak, get off the ground. No longer 'maximally' understood as participation in the life of the divine, prayer becomes more narrowly conceived as the thing that '*we* do before God'.[31] What is required, according to both Torrances, is a recovery of a sufficiently full-bodied Christology of prayer that emphasizes the human priesthood of Jesus in order for our prayer not simply to be presented to God through the work of an intermediary but more complexly to be knitted into the prayer of the praying human Son of God.

---

[29]Martin Stringer, 'Transcendence and Immanence in Public and Private Prayer', in *A Sociology of Prayer*, ed. by Giuseppe Giordan and Linda Woodhead (Farnham: Ashgate, 2015), 67–80 (71).

[30]Stringer, 'Transcendence and Immanence in Public and Private Prayer', 71.

[31]Torrance, *Worship, Community, and the Triune God of Grace*, 7.

Such a recovery of the human mediation of Christ, the kind that (if this aspect of Jungmann's thesis is correct) defined the earliest practices of the church, can be found in several modern figures. The Russian Orthodox theologian Sergius Bulgakov includes a profound meditation on the continuing intercession of Christ in the third instalment of his dogmatic trilogy.[32] The central chapter in the Roman Catholic Yves Congar's *Jesus Christ* concerns 'the prayer of Jesus', which falls within a wider section on the 'mediation of Christ'.[33] A similarly strong sense of Jesus Christ's ongoing intercession is central to the patterns of prayer the Lutheran martyr Dietrich Bonhoeffer instigated at Finkenwalde.[34] But the theme of the mediation of Christ is perhaps most persistent in the Reformed tradition: more than one Torrance, Karl Barth and in particular John Calvin all treat the theme of the mediation of Christ with paramount importance.[35]

Chapter 20 of the third book of the *Institutes of the Christian Religion*, which contains Calvin's long discussion of prayer, begins with a theological puzzle regarding the status of the faith of humanity before God. 'We clearly see how destitute and devoid of all good things man is,'

---

[32]Sergius Bulgakov, *The Comforter* (Grand Rapids: William B. Eerdmans, 2004), 371–2 and 374–6.

[33]Congar, *Jesus Christ*, 86–106; see also *ST* 3a, q.21 for Aquinas's treatment of Christ's prayer, which immediately precedes his treatment of 'the priesthood of Christ', both of which fall within the wider treatment of Christ as 'the one mediator'.

[34]In his remarkable handbook on prayer, *Life Together*, written for the Finkenwalde community, Bonhoeffer describes how the practice of praying the Psalter involves the slow realization that 'here someone else is praying'. This is the 'secret of the Psalter', he writes. And for Bonhoeffer that 'someone else' is the human Jesus. 'The *human* Jesus Christ … is praying in the Psalter through the mouth of his congregation.' Jesus Christ, he continues, 'has become their intercessor'. The Psalter 'is the vicarious prayer of Christ for his congregation'. In this sense, 'we pray on the basis of the prayer of the truly human Jesus Christ. This is what the Scripture means when it says that the Holy Spirit prays in us and for us, that Christ prays for us, that we can pray to God in the right way only in the name of Jesus Christ.' See Dietrich Bonhoeffer, *Life Together and Prayerbook of the Bible*, Dietrich Bonhoeffer Works 5 (Minneapolis: Fortress Press, 1996), 54–5. Bonhoeffer is here tapping into a long tradition of hearing the voice of Christ in the praying of the Psalter. See Richard Price, 'The Voice of Christ in the Psalms', in *Meditations of the Heart: The Psalms in Early Christian Thought and Practice - Essays in Honour of Andrew Louth*, ed. by Andreas Andreopoulos, Augustine Casiday, and Carol Harrison (Turnhout: Brepols, 2011), 1–16.

[35]See Graham Redding, *Prayer and the Priesthood of Christ in the Reformed Tradition* (Edinburgh: T&T Clark, 2003) for a detailed investigation of the theme in the Reformed tradition; for an exploration of the priesthood of Christ outside of the Reformed tradition, see Gerald O'Collins and Michael Keenan Jones, *Jesus our Priest: A Christian Approach to the Priesthood of Christ* (Oxford: Oxford University Press, 2010).

he begins (*Inst.* 3.20.1). Faith, he goes on to say, is impossible because of humanity's 'destitution'. But all is not lost. In good Reformation fashion, Calvin finds the solution to the theological puzzle that lays before him 'outside of himself'. 'If he seeks resources to succor him in his need, he must go outside of himself and get them elsewhere' (*Inst.* 3.20.1). In respect of faith, the 'elsewhere' is located in Christ. It is in Christ's faith that our faithfulness is found. Interestingly, Calvin sees the same theological problem playing out in the puzzle of prayer. As with faith, so too with prayer: taking Paul at his word, Calvin believes that we cannot pray as we ought. Because prayer 'springs from faith' and, according to the title of Chapter 20, is the 'chief exercise of faith' (*Inst.* 3.20.27), Calvin applies the same Christological argument that he developed in response to the problem of faith to think through the problem of prayer. Again, then, all is not lost. The solution to the puzzle of being unable to pray is found 'outside of himself' – that is, in Christ.

At the heart of Calvin's theology of prayer, therefore, is the idea that we can only pray as we ought with a mediated relationship with God (see *Inst.* 3.20.17-20). The work of mediation falls not on the saints (as Calvin fiercely argues over some seven subsections) or even on the church but exclusively on the person of the one true mediator: Jesus Christ. 'Christ is constituted the only Mediator, by whose intercession the Father is for us rendered gracious and easily entreated' (*Inst.* 3.20.19). To bypass the mediation of Christ is 'to dishonor Christ and strip him of the title of sole Mediator, which, as it has been given to him by the Father as a unique privilege, ought not to be transferred to another' (*Inst.* 3.20.21). Therefore, just as one cannot have faith by one's own action alone, one cannot pray without the action of the mediator. 'No prayer is pleasing to God unless this Mediator sanctifies it' (*Inst.* 3.20.27). In the Geneva Catechism, citing again Romans 8, Calvin sums up his richly Christological understanding of prayer in one sentence. 'For he who prays thus conceives his prayers as from the mouth of Christ himself, since he knows his own prayer to be assisted and recommended by the intercession of Christ (Rom. 8.34).[36] All prayer, for Calvin, even wordless prayer, is in a sense *worded* as it is inscribed into the Word of God,

---

[36] John Calvin, 'Catechism of the Church of Geneva (1545)', in *Calvin: Theological Treatises,* The Library of Christian Classics (London: Westminster John Knox Press, 1960), 88–139 (122).

into the very 'mouth of Christ'.[37] For Calvin, Christ's priestly mediation gives us special confidence to offer our prayer with boldness and assurance of being heard. Hence the Lord's Prayer is often introduced with the words: 'Let us pray with *confidence* as our Saviour has taught us'.[38]

Christ the prayer

This chapter has so far explored the teachings of Jesus Christ on prayer, his practice of prayer and his ongoing priestly activity of intercession. We now move from considering Jesus' activity as pray-er to the second Christological move around which this chapter is framed: the rather curious idea that Jesus Christ is both pray-er and 'prayer' – the very embodiment of what it means to pray. Herbert McCabe goes some way in explaining the idea in his claim that Jesus Christ is 'not just one who prays, not even one who prays best' but is 'sheer prayer'.[39] But what does this mean? This section's shift in Christological concentration also marks a shift in textual focus as we move from the synoptic and Pauline traditions of prayer to the Gospel of John and more specifically to John 17. We will read the high-priestly prayer of John 17 in dialogue with Cyril of Alexandria's *Commentary on John*, written towards the beginning of his episcopacy and shortly before the outbreak of the Nestorian controversy.

As with other themes, John's gospel is distinctive when it comes to the theme of prayer. Although John includes references to prayer in the narrative of Jesus' public ministry (at the tomb of Lazarus in Jn 11, for example, and a reference here and there to Jesus praying over food), generally the figure of the praying Jesus receives less frequent attention than it does in the synoptic tradition. John's Jesus not once withdraws to any of his favourite synoptic hangouts – usually a mountain or a desert place – to pray. There is no prayer of dereliction on the cross. There is no formal teaching on prayer. There

---

[37]On the 'wordedness' of prayer as it plays out in postmodern discourse on prayer, see Laurence P. Hemming, 'The Subject of Prayer: Unwilling Words in the Postmodern Access to God', in *The Blackwell Companion to Postmodern Theology*, ed. by Graham Ward (Oxford: Blackwell, 2005), 444–57.

[38]On the theme of confidence and prayer, see Paul Murray, OP, *Praying with Confidence: Aquinas on the Lord's Prayer* (London: Burns and Oaks, 2010).

[39]Herbert McCabe, *God Matters* (London: Continuum, 2005), 220.

are no parables on prayer. Even the Greek word *proseuchomai* ('to pray'), which appears many times in Matthew, Mark and especially Luke, does not appear in the Gospel of John.[40] Perhaps most significantly, the two key scenes on prayer in the life of Jesus, which we said above include the Lord's Prayer and the prayer in the Garden of Gethsemane, are conspicuous by their absence. John's Gethsemane scene (Jn 18.1-11) describes the betrayal and arrest of Jesus but makes no mention of prayer and the intercession of Jesus. This does not mean that John neglects the theme of prayer; prayer is too important a subject to be sidelined. But it does mean that John seems to be up to something theologically distinctive in the Fourth Gospel that does not so much repeat the synoptic material as – to borrow David F. Ford's term – 'improvise' on it.[41]

Improvisations, by nature, do not repeat material in either content or form. Instead, they expand, reappropriate and reimagine themes in a new way. They are variations on the same theme while revealing something new. They are recognizably similar and recognizably different. Ford has described John's prologue as 'non-identical repetition, repetition with variation, a theme with improvisation'.[42] In writing the prologue, John is drawing on the synoptic birth narratives, the Septuagint, the wisdom tradition and other texts from the Torah but in a way that is not straightforward repetition. What is offered is the reading of old texts intensively and the writing of new texts in Spirit-led improvisation. John goes beyond, then, the opening of Genesis by daringly identifying Jesus as the eternal Word, the one who was with God 'in the beginning'. Ford explains that it is about 'taking the plain sense seriously but going beyond it, linking it with other texts, asking new questions of it, extending the meaning, discovering depths, resonances and applications of it that have not been suggested before'.[43]

---

[40]On this, see Andrew T. Lincoln, 'God's Name, Jesus' Name, and Prayer in the Fourth Gospel', in *Into God's Presence: Prayer in the New Testament*, ed. by Richard N. Longenecker (Grand Rapids: William B. Eerdmans, 2002), 155–80.

[41]I am grateful to David Ford for conversations on the ideas explored in this section. In what follows I draw from his category of 'improvisation' as developed in the following works: David F. Ford, *The Drama of Living: Becoming Wise in the Spirit* (London: Canterbury Press, 2014) and *Christian Wisdom*.

[42]Ford, *The Drama of Living*, 90.

[43]Ford, *Christian Wisdom*, 55.

A similar process of intensive reading and wise improvisation can be detected in the extraordinary prayer of John 17 spoken by Jesus on the eve of his crucifixion.[44] To be more specific: in the seventeenth chapter of his gospel, John can be found not simply repeating the synoptic tradition of prayer but improvising on it, repeating it in a 'non-identical' way, and in so doing discovering new depths to the theology of prayer that have not been suggested before. In particular, we find him improvising on the Lord's Prayer and the Gethsemane tradition of prayer. Let us take each in turn.

In terms of the Lord's Prayer, there are several 'non-identical repetitions' to be found in John 17. There are improvisations regarding purpose, structure and language. Regarding purpose, in his exegesis of John 17 Cyril is quite clear that, like the Lord's Prayer, the purpose of the prayer is decidedly didactical. It belongs to Jesus' teaching ministry. As in the Lord's Prayer, 'here too he suggests by his conduct the pattern of an excellent way of life'.[45] Just as Jesus gave an example of how to pray by praying the Lord's Prayer, in John 17 Jesus offers teaching on prayer by praying himself. 'He fashions for us, then, a pattern for prayer.'[46] It is perhaps for this reason that Cyril cites the Lord's Prayer in its entirety in his commentary on the first verse of John 17.

Regarding structure, as commentators down the ages have noticed, the Lord's Prayer follows a three-part structure. There is the opening vocative, followed by a series of petitions concerning God (the hallowing of the divine name, coming of the kingdom, doing of the will of God), concluding with a final set of petitions concerning worldly matters (the giving of our daily bread, forgiving us of debts, leading us not into temptation). John 17 can be seen to follow these same contours. There is the opening vocative to the Father (Jn 17.1), followed by a set of theo-centric prayers for the glorification of God (Jn 17.1-8), concluding with the prayers for his disciples (Jn 17.9-19) and for the world (Jn 17.20-26).

Regarding language, perhaps most curiously, John seems to weave into the prayer of John 17 actual references to the petitions of the Lord's Prayer. Although there is much debate about the extent to which John drew on the text of the Lord's Prayer in the writing of John 17, there are nevertheless

---

[44]Ford made this point himself in one of his as yet unpublished Bampton Lectures delivered in Oxford in January 2015 entitled: 'Reading John as John Reads – Improvising Then and Now'.
[45]Cyril, *Commentary on John*, 269.
[46]Ibid.

intriguing parallels to be found. The most compelling connections between the petitions of the Lord's Prayer and John 17 in their 'improvised' form include:

- The 'Our Father in heaven' of the Lord's Prayer (Mt. 6.9) on which the opening verse of John 17 improvises and where John reports that Jesus – who interestingly seems to adopt the posture of the 'orans' – 'looked up to *heaven* and said, "*Father*, the hour has come; glorify your Son so that the Son may glorify you"' (Jn 17.1).

- The first petition of the Lord's Prayer, the hallowing of the divine name (Lk. 11.2), which finds its improvised parallel in John's repeated reference to glorification (Jn 17.1, 4, 5) and the importance he attaches to the 'name' throughout the gospel.

- The petition concerning the doing of the will of God 'on earth as it is on heaven' (Mt. 6.10), which corresponds with Jesus' words in Jn 17.4 about glorifying 'you on *earth* by finishing the work that you gave me to do'.

- Then there is Matthew's petition to 'rescue us from the *evil one*' (Mt. 6.13), which is repeated almost verbatim in Jesus' petition 'to protect them from the *evil one*' in Jn 17.15.

These are not identical repetitions but rather 'improvisations' on the petitions of the Lord's Prayer. The similarities in purpose, structure and language have even led some commenters to the conclusion that John 17 is 'a type of "midrash" on the … Lord's Prayer'.[47]

In this sense, John can be seen to set an example of what he expects his readers to do for themselves. Following John's example as 'reader' of the Lord's Prayer, our own ways of reading the Lord's Prayer must mean not only repetition but wise 'improvisation'. If the practices of the Lord's Prayer in my college chapel are anything to go by, the Lord's Prayer is a

---

[47]William O. Walker, 'The Lord's Prayer in Matthew and in John', *New Testament Studies*, 28 (1982), 237–56. Similarly Westcott, in his classic commentary, says that John 17 contains 'what may be most properly called the "Lord's Prayer"'. See, B. F. Westcott, *The Gospel according to St John* (London: James Clark, 1958), 238. Raymond E. Brown, *The Gospel according to John XIII-XXI: A New Translation with Introduction and Commentary* (London: Yale University Press, 2008), 747 also notes the parallels. For an opposing view, see Andreas J. Köstenberger, *A Theology of John's Gospel and Letters: The Word, the Christ, the Son of God* (Grand Rapids: Zondervan, 2009), 482.

remarkably adaptable prayer – there are endless local and denominational variations in form, language and indeed theology. There is not, and never has been, a standardized way of praying the Lord's Prayer. Like John, we are to go deeper, go beyond the text, make new connections, reread, improvise and challenge what comes before. The Lord's Prayer has indeed inspired extraordinary rereadings. For example, in addition to the rereading of the Lord's Prayer by the fourth-century Spanish priest-poet Caius Vettius Aquilinus Juvencus, Coelius Sedulius's poetic improvisation in the fifth century and Dante's extraordinary improvisation on the Lord's Prayer in Canto XI of his *Purgatorio* that we have already mentioned, think of Augustine's imaginative rereading of each of the seven petitions of the Lord's Prayer in conversation with the seven beatitudes and the seven gifts of the Holy Spirit in his commentary on the Sermon on the Mount.[48] Think of John Cassian's improvisation on the petitions of the Lord's Prayer to communicate the monastic ideals in Chapters 9–10 of his *Conferences*.[49] Think also of the many feminist and liberationist rereadings that continue to improvise on the Lord's Prayer afresh revealing new depths and resonances.[50] Indeed Boff, in his commentary on the Lord's Prayer, says that it is impossible to read the Lord's Prayer without reading our own histories into the prayer.[51] Boff thinks this is why the Lord's Prayer was transmitted from the beginning in more than one version – by Matthew, Luke and the Holy Spirit version we encountered in Chapter 3. If that is the Lord's Prayer, what about John's handling of the other central strand of the synoptic tradition of prayer: Christ's prayer in the Garden of Gethsemane?

---

[48]Augustine, 'Our Lord's Sermon on the Mount', in *St Augustine: Sermon on the Mount, Harmony of the Gospels, Homilies on the Gospels*, NPNF, series 1, vol. 6 (Edinburgh: T&T Clark, 1996), 3–63 (46).

[49]Cassian, *Conferences*, 101–40.

[50]See the liberationist rereading of the 'kingdom' petition according to the logic of 'kin-dom' by Ada María Isasi-Díaz, 'Defining Our Proyecto Histórico: Mujerista Strategies for Liberation', *Journal of Feminist Studies in Religion*, 9.1 (1993), 17–28. Some other liberationist engagements with the Lord's Prayer offer similar rewritings of individual petitions, such as in the version of the Lord's Prayer cited by Boff in *The Lord's Prayer*, 121, which asks, 'Why do you not give all of us our daily bread?' Others switch traditional names for God, such as 'Father', with more liberative terms. For an example, see the poet-priest Jim Cotter's reimagining of the first petition as 'Eternal Spirit, Earth-maker, Pain-bearer, Life-giver' which has been adopted by, among others, *A New Zealand Prayer Book* (Auckland: Collins, 1989).

[51]Boff, *The Lord's Prayer*, 7.

In terms of the Gethsemane tradition and John 17, further 'non-identical repetitions' can be found.[52] There is a narratival connection between John 17 and Gethsemane: the prayer of John 17 takes place at the end of the final meal he has with the disciples and immediately before they set off across the Kidron valley to the garden of Jesus' betrayal and arrest – the garden on the Mount of Olives (Jn 18.1-9). But the most suggestive connection between John 17 and Gethsemane is the shared theme of the 'vicariousness' of Christ's prayer. In Gethsemane, Christ is alone in the garden doing something 'for others' as they sleep (as explained above with reference to Barth). Likewise, John 17 is known as the 'high-priestly prayer'. In v. 9, Jesus says: 'I am asking on their behalf', and in v. 20 Christ's intercession is extended beyond his disciples to all people, praying, 'I ask not only on behalf of these, but also on behalf of those who will believe in me through their word.' In John 17, Christ is clearly doing something on behalf of others. This leads Cyril to write that Christ is acting as our 'mediator and high priest',[53] which, as we have said above and as Cyril explains in his commentary, depends on an affirmation of the full humanity of Christ. By praying 'for us', Jesus 'once more mediates as a *human being*, the reconciler and mediator between God and human beings'.[54]

John 17 seems to stitch together the two key episodes of prayer in the synoptic gospels. In so doing, he redirects the synoptic themes (Jesus' teaching on prayer in the Lord's Prayer and Jesus' intercessory activity in Gethsemane) into one, rich theology of prayer. But John 17 is more complex still. It is also possible to read John 17, and this comes very naturally to Cyril, as a 'double improvisation' both on the synoptic traditions of prayer and on the logic of 'incorporation' that is central to the Pauline treatment of prayer in Romans 8. These two streams of the Christian tradition of prayer – the synoptic and the Pauline – flow into John's theology of prayer to discover a new depth about what prayer, at its most fundamental level, really means. John is less concerned about Jesus at prayer, which is the synoptic question, and more about Jesus *as* prayer, as the very embodiment of what it means to pray.

---

[52]For further textual evidence, see Barnabas Lindars, *The Gospel of John* (Grand Rapids: William B. Eerdmans, 1981), 517, who argues that John 17 is modelled on the Gethsemane tradition, as does C. K. Barrett, *The Gospel According to St John: An Introduction with Commentary and Notes on the Greek Text* (London: SPCK, 1955), 500.

[53]Cyril, *Commentary on John*, 294.

[54]Ibid., 282.

We have already made several passing references to Cyril of Alexandria's *Commentary on the Gospel of John*. Now is the time to think more deeply with Cyril in connection with the idea of Christ as prayer. The commentary is well known for its soteriological emphasis on the divinity of Christ.[55] Against the neo-Arians, Cyril would toe a distinctively Athanasian line, ratified at Nicaea, that if the Word is not fully divine then Christ cannot achieve salvation.

> The Only Begotten shone forth for us from the very essence of God the Father and had his Father completely in his own nature. ... Thus he who is God by nature is called and truly becomes the heavenly man. He is not a God-bearer, as some think, who have no detailed understanding of the depth of the mystery.[56]

But soteriology is not the sole concern in his commentary, and neither is the divinity of Christ. Although Cyril did not produce an independent treatise on the subject, he followed many in the early church of writing on prayer in the context of biblical commentary. His exegesis of Christ's prayer in John 17 is a case in point. The rigorously Christological analysis of prayer, which draws liberally on incarnational language, concepts and creedal categories, is considered by some to be 'one of the great patristic works on the theology of worship' and prayer.[57]

From what we know of Cyril already, it should not be surprising that his commentary on John 17 seeks to emphasize the divinity of Christ. 'He and the Father share all things in common, including their natural divinity and authority. We have one God, whom we worship as the holy and consubstantial Trinity.'[58] Thus, as Jesus Christ prays he prays *as* God and as fully divine he is the worthy recipient of our prayer. The strength of the emphasis Cyril places on the divinity of Christ has led many to call into question the adequacy of his Christology. John Macquarrie, for example, stands in a long line of those who accuse Cyril's Christology of 'undermining the humanity of Christ' and therefore of 'repeating in a slightly different

---

[55]See Daniel A. Keating, 'Divinization in Cyril: The Appropriation of Divine Life', in *The Theology of St Cyril of Alexandria: A Critical Appreciation*, ed. by Thomas G. Weinandy and Daniel A. Keating (London: T&T Clark, 2003), 149–85.

[56]Cyril, *Commentary on John*, 303–4.

[57]Torrance, *Theology in Reconciliation*, 177.

[58]Cyril, *Commentary on John*, 284.

form the heresy of Apollinarius'.[59] If Macquarrie is right, Cyril will prove a false ally in this chapter's concern with the (anti-Apollinarian) protection of the fully human reality of prayer.

However, staying true to our methodological commitment of attending to the often-overlooked doxological sources alongside the more explicitly doctrinal material, Cyril's analysis of Christ's prayer, as it unfolds in his exegetical work on Jesus' prayer in John 17, reveals a highly balanced Christology that is very much concerned with the complete humanity of Christ and its practical consequences for the Christian life of prayer. Although never discussing Apollinarianism directly, perhaps because by this time the early church was embroiled in new battles against new heresies (namely Nestorianism), the issue of the humanity of Christ raised by Apollinarianism remains very much in the background of his exegesis. For Cyril, whatever is appropriate to being human is appropriate to Jesus Christ. Because, as we have said, to be fully human is to pray, Cyril is resolute that – precisely by praying – Christ is fully human. Christ's prayer life, therefore, is frequently showcased by Cyril as the imitable model of our life of prayer. Moreover, his commentary on John 17 is shot through, as Torrance discovers, with the theme of the vicarious humanity of Christ. Summarizing Cyril, Torrance explains that 'it was precisely by becoming man that the Son of God became Priest, for it was through sharing our human nature and condition, taking over our creaturely and human habits, ... [for example,] in speech and worship, that Christ could act for us and in our place, offering prayer and worship to God the Father for mankind'.[60]

But what Cyril is really concerned with in his commentary on John 17 is neither the divinity nor the humanity of Christ's prayer in isolation from each other but rather the union of Christ's divine nature and human nature in the praying person of Jesus Christ. For Cyril as for John, the deepest reality of Jesus is to be 'one in God'. 'You, Father, are in me and I am in you' (Jn 17.21). In what would become classic Chalcedonian fashion, then, Cyril

---

[59]John Macquarrie, *Christology Revisited* (London: SCM Press, 1998), 50, 51. Others, however, have rightly problematized this reading of Cyril, arguing instead that the complete humanity of Christ is an indispensable element in his soteriological and liturgical thought. See Thomas G. Weinandy and Daniel A. Keating (eds), *The Theology of St Cyril of Alexandria: A Critical Appreciation* (London: T&T Clark, 2003).
[60]Torrance, *Theology in Reconciliation*, 171.

writes of John 17 that 'Christ addressed the heavenly Father in both a divine and a human way'.[61] The theme of the union of the divine and the human in the praying person of Christ takes us to the heart of what we mean by the notion of 'Christ as prayer'.

To cite once again Evagrius, prayer is 'conversation with God' (*On Prayer* 3). 'Conversation' is an immensely resourceful word to describe prayer as it carries the notion not only of dialogue and therefore of relationship with God, but also the theme of union, as we have noted in earlier chapters. Con-versation suggests the bringing together (*con*) of that which otherwise is in opposition (*versus*). If Evagrius is right then Christ not only models conversation but is the very definition of what it means for the divine and the human to converse, to be caught up in an exchange of love and mutual indwelling – or as John would say, to 'abide' with God. Jesus Christ, it can be said, is the true conversant. It is in this context of the union of Christ's divinity and humanity in the person of Christ that McCabe's notion of Christ as 'sheer prayer', cited above, makes most sense. Christ's prayer, he writes, is 'simply the showing forth, the visibility in human terms, in human history, of the relationship to the Father which constitutes the person who is Jesus'.[62] Jesus Christ is the pray-er and prayer itself – the very embodiment of what prayer, at its most profound level, is: union with God. Hence Cyril writes that Jesus Christ is here 'speaking [or "*conversing*"] in a divine and human way at the same time, since he was God and a human being in the same being'.[63]

Earlier we said that John 17 can be read as a 'double improvisation' on both the synoptic traditions and on the Pauline tradition of prayer. John's 'improvisation' on Pauline theology seemed so obvious to Cyril that he regularly drew on Pauline material (especially Romans 8 and its cognates) to interpret what was going on theologically in John 17. It is precisely through these Pauline lenses, then, that Cyril interprets the theme of 'union', which is critical to John 17 in terms of both the union the Son shares with the Father and the union that is extended by Jesus to God and the world. 'As you, Father, are in me and I am in you, may they also be in us' (Jn 17.21). God eternally wills to share God's 'oneness' with another,

---

[61]Cyril, *Commentary on John*, 278.

[62]McCabe, *God Matters*, 220.

[63]Cyril, *Commentary on John*, 282.

with us, in prayer. On one occasion of many, reading John through Pauline lenses, Cyril says:

> Indeed, our reconciliation to God through Christ the Savior could have been accomplished in no other way than through communion in the Spirit and sanctification. That which knits us together, as it were, and unites us to God is the Holy Spirit. When we receive the Spirit, we are made participants and sharers in the divine nature, and we receive the Father himself through the Son and in the Son. ... And what does Paul say about this? 'And because you are sons', he says, 'God has sent the Spirit of his Son into our heart, crying, "Abba! Father!"' implying that if we had remained without participation in the Spirit, we would never have known that God was in us at all, and that if we had not been enriched by the Spirit that puts us in the rank of sons, we would never have been sons of God at all.[64]

For Cyril (following John), this oneness is mediated Christologically and (following Paul) is achieved pneumatologically. 'No one could have union with God except through participation in the Holy Spirit.'[65] Torrance is alert to the pneumatological dimension of Cyril's understanding of participation in prayer. Citing his commentary on John, he writes:

> While it is through Christ that we have access to God the Father, that takes place *in one Spirit* (Eph. 2.18). ... It is then in pneumatological terms that Cyril understands the intimate union between us and Christ. ... Nothing of all this takes place, and we have no participation in God or in the vicarious activity of Christ, however, expect in and through the Spirit and his distinctive activity in uniting us to the Son and through him to the Father.[66]

In this sense, as we have said many times before, Christian prayer is not simply imitational (following the teaching and example of Christ) but incorporative (being taken up by the Holy Spirit into the prayer of Christ and thus into the union the Son shares with the Father). For Cyril, working from John,

---

[64]Ibid., 298.
[65]Ibid., 302.
[66]Torrance, *Theology in Reconciliation*, 182.

the pray-er's union with God is by way of incorporation into the complete humanity of Christ. 'Christ, then, yokes himself to us on account of his human nature.'[67] To utter prayer is to do so, as Calvin says, 'as from the [human] mouth of Christ himself' as we call upon God in the name of Jesus.

Indeed, a lot hinges on praying in the name of Jesus in the Gospel of John (see, Jn 14.13, 14.14, 15.16, 16.23). In common parlance, to act or speak in someone's name means acting or speaking on their behalf as if they were themselves present. When preachers, for example, begin their sermon with the words, 'May I speak in the name of the Father, Son, and Holy Spirit,' they are saying that their words, however clumsy, come to speak something of God's proclamation to the world. But by praying in the name of Jesus, John is not saying that the pray-er now speaks on behalf of Jesus but precisely the opposite. In prayer, Jesus speaks (prays) on behalf of the pray-er before God. 'That is what "in my name" means,' writes Cyril. 'We approach God the Father in no other way than through the Son. Through him "we have access by the one Spirit to the Father" (Eph. 2.18), as it is written.'[68] It is into the name, which makes known the very presence of God in the world, that the pray-er enters as they pray in the name of Jesus. As we pray in the name of Jesus, 'our stance in prayer', McCabe argues, 'is not simply, or even primarily, that of the creature before the creator but that of the Son before the Father'.[69]

In summary, if prayer is about union with God, as it is for Evagrius, then the Johannine emphasis on the union the Son shares with the Father makes Jesus Christ more than the pray-er or teacher of prayer, even the teacher of prayer par excellence. Jesus Christ is the very definition of prayer, 'sheer prayer', as McCabe puts it.

Prayer: Fully divine, fully human

At the end of the previous chapter, we raised the question of the relation between divine and human agency in prayer. We are now able to answer that question more fully using some of the Christological tools this chapter has made available. There has so far been a strong steer in this book to reconfigure prayer as principally a divine action, as practising God's

---

[67]Cyril, *Commentary on John*, 292.
[68]Ibid., 263.
[69]McCabe, *God Matters*, 220.

presence in us. This has been a deliberate move to shift the axis of prayer away from a simple human action onto the more richly perplexing practice of the divine into which the human pray-er is incorporated – what we called earlier a 'maximalist' understanding of prayer. While the primacy of the divine must be protected, this chapter, working from the humanity of Christ, has suggested that prayer is also importantly understood as genuinely human action. Jesus Christ teaches *us* to pray. If prayer is to avoid falling into something of an ethical Docetism, only ever 'appearing' but not really human, it is crucial that prayer is understood as genuinely and rightly human.

In 451 the Council of Chalcedon was convened to settle the question of the relation between the full divinity and the full humanity of the person of Jesus Christ. Although the council met a few years after the death of Cyril, his 'stamp on the Council's Creed is unmistakable' and to 'read the Chalcedonian Creed other than through the eyes of Cyril is to misread it'.[70] The Chalcedonian formula spoke of

> one and the same Christ, Son, Lord, Only-begotten, recognized in two natures, without confusion, without change, without division, without separation; the distinction of natures being in no way annulled by the union, but rather the characteristics of each nature being preserved and coming together to form one person and substance, not as parted or separated into two persons, but one and the same Son and Only-begotten God the Word, Lord Jesus Christ.

Drawing on the paradoxical logic of Chalcedon's hypostatic union, in which the two natures of Jesus Christ are perfectly one and yet remain without confusion, we can articulate something of the complexity of the relation between divine agency and human agency in the practice of prayer.

On the one hand, the logic of the creed rules out omni-causality in either agential direction: prayer cannot be reduced to either the work of the divine or the work of the human in (Nestorian) isolation from one another. Just as there can be no exclusively human activity posited in relation to God when it comes to prayer, God elects not to act alone in prayer, at least when

---

[70]Thomas G. Weinandy, 'Cyril and the Mystery of the Incarnation', in *The Theology of St Cyril of Alexandria: A Critical Appreciation,* ed. by Thomas G. Weinandy and Daniel A. Keating (London: T&T Clark, 2003), 23–54 (43).

the human priesthood of Christ's ongoing intercession is duly maintained. Instead, God and humanity converse in prayer 'without separation' or 'division' – they coincide and cohere. On the other hand, the Chalcedonian logic rules out the sublation of prayer into a (Eutychian) third, composite thing that is indifferentially divine and human. Instead, God and humanity converse in prayer in a fellowship of intimacy 'without confusion', 'without change' and without the transformation of one into the other. The agential 'distinction' is in 'no way annulled by the union'. Put together, we are left with the suggestive paradox that prayer is not to be understood as either divine or human, or even also divine and human, but fully divine and human in a way that defies resolution or easy description.[71] Cyril is clear that although 'consubstantiality in our case is not the same kind as that of the Father and God the Word',[72] prayer remains the work of 'double agency' – fully human, fully divine: this is the mystery of prayer.

Summary

This chapter has explored the Christology of prayer. It has suggested that a full-bodied Christology of prayer accounts for Jesus' activity as pray-er (the one who teaches us to pray and prays on our behalf) and the more demanding Christological notion that Jesus Christ is prayer itself (the very embodiment of what it means to pray: to participate in the divine life). This chapter has also spoken of the humanity of Christ. The praying activity of the person of Jesus, rooted in the humanity of Christ, represents what it means to be human in the fullest possible sense. As for Christ, so for us, being human means being in prayer. We are 'praying animals' as we said in the introduction to this book. The next chapter picks up where this chapter leaves off. That is, with the issue of the relation of divine and human agency in prayer as it plays out in one of the most pressing questions the practice of prayer raises: does God answer prayer?

---

[71]I am borrowing these terms and the application of the 'Chalcedonian logic' to describe the shape of the relation of divine and human agency, from George Hunsinger, *How to Read Karl Barth: The Shape of His Theology* (New York: Oxford University Press, 1993).
[72]Cyril, *Commentary on John*, 286–7.

CHAPTER 5
PETITION AND PROVIDENCE

Prayer can mean many things. For Evagrius, as we now know well, it meant 'conversation with God' (*On Prayer* 3). For others it might mean contemplation, thanksgiving, praise, intercession, meditation, attention, glorification and so on. According to Simon Tugwell, however, 'originally there can be no doubt whatsoever that words for "prayer" meant "petition"'.[1] If Tugwell is right, petitionary prayer – the prayers that ask God for this or that – is one of the earliest ways Christians practised prayer. Unlike some other theories of prayer in practice in the ancient world, the early Christians dared not only to petition God but had confidence that the unchangeable, immutable God would answer their petitions.

Christian theology affirms that God does not create the world and then back off but remains actively involved in worldly existence – actively drawing all things into God. The doctrine of providence is the doctrine that sets about describing what it means to speak theologically of God's involvement in creation, and its relation to petitionary prayer is the focus of this chapter.[2] At stake in the doctrine of providence are some of the most fundamental theological questions. In what ways is God active in the world? Can we be free, given the active presence of an omnipotent and omniscient God in the world? Is God responsible when things go wrong in the world? How does divine agency relate to human agency in the unfolding

---

[1]Simon Tugwell, 'Prayer, Humpty Dumpty and Thomas Aquinas', in *Language, Meaning and God*, ed. by Brian Davies (London: Chapman, 1987), 24–50 (24).
[2]For studies on the theme of providence and prayer, see Peter R. Baelz, *Prayer and Providence: A Background Study* (London: SCM, 1968) and *Does God Answer Prayer?* (London: Darton, Longman and Todd, 1982); H. H. Farmer, *The World and God: A Study of Prayer, Providence and Miracle in Christian Experience* (London: Nisbet, 1936); and Terrance Tiessen, *Providence and Prayer: How does God Work in the World?* (Downers Grove: InterVarsity Press, 2000); from a more biblical perspective, see David Crump, *Knocking on Heaven's Door: A New Testament Theology of Petitionary Prayer* (Grand Rapids: Baker Academic Press, 2006); and for a more philosophical analysis, see Scott A. Davison, *Petitionary Prayer: A Philosophical Investigation* (Oxford: Oxford University Press, 2017).

of history? A vast quantity of theological debate meriting extended discussion lies in the responses these questions have generated.[3] The particular interest of this chapter, however, has to be more prescribed. It can be summarized in the question many have asked of prayer down the ages: does God answer prayer?

From the very earliest theological reflections on prayer, petition has presented something of a providential conundrum. In the first half of the third century Origen, for example, rehearsed and responded to what appeared even then to be a series of firmly established objections to the practice of petitionary prayer (*De oratione* 5–7), the first of which reads:

> God knows all things before they come to be, and nothing that is established will first be known to Him when it is established, and so unknown to Him before that. Therefore, what use is it to offer prayer to One who knows what we need even before we pray? For our heavenly Father knows what we need before we ask Him (*De oratione* 5.2).

Indeed, Platonic philosophy, thick in the air of early Christianity, was abound with criticisms of petitionary prayer.

> Plato's Socrates sets the tone, by praying only for what is good for him …; but the theme continues, through Philo of Alexandria and Maximus of Tyre – with a fine satirical treatment by Lucian, in the *Icaromenippus* – to Plotinus, Porphyry and beyond. Any suggestion of bribery or constraint of the gods is to be rejected absolutely. The issue is further complicated in later times by the influence of the Stoic doctrine of determinism, which more or less require that rational prayer, such as a philosopher would indulge in, can only be for the acceptance of what is inevitable. In any case, it is not for us to decide what is good for us, and a benevolent God will not grant what we ask for in ignorance of our true good, any more than a good doctor will allow his patient's desires to determine his dietary prescriptions or other treatment.[4]

---

[3]For an admirably thorough treatment of the history of the doctrine of providence, see Mark W. Elliott, *Providence Perceived: Divine Action from a Human Point of View* (Berlin: De Gruyter, 2015).
[4]John Dillon and Andrei Timotin, 'Introduction', in *Platonic Theories of Prayer*, ed. by John Dillon and Andrei Timotin (Leiden: Brill, 2016), 1–6 (2).

Further objections to petitionary prayer are raised within the Christian tradition itself. If God is impassible can prayer 'move' God?[5] If the entirety of created reality is subject to a single, comprehensive divine 'plan' is there space for the freedom and spontaneity of prayer? If God is the unchangeable 'cause' of all things, the one who determines and effects created reality, does prayer change anything? In short: if all things fall within God's providential ordering of creation, what is the point of prayer?

These ancient questions have proved remarkably durable and became increasingly acute in the modern period during which many came to think that received forms of the doctrine of providence no longer offered satisfyingly cogent interpretations of the world.[6] For Kant, who banished God from intervening in the world, the clusters of objections to prayer stacked so high that prayer lost plausibility in relation to providence. He concluded that prayer in the modern age is a 'superstitious delusion (a fetish-making); for it only is the *declaring of a wish* to a being who has no need of any declaration regarding the inner disposition of the wisher, through which nothing is therefore accomplished nor is any of the duties incumbent on us as commands of God discharged; hence God is not really served'.[7] Feuerbach's reduction of prayer to monological therapy, already discussed, can be seen to push Kant's theory of prayer to its logical completion.[8]

In the light of these objections, as we will see towards the end of this chapter, some have set about reinterpreting the nature of divine providence. God's knowledge of the world might include the past and present but does not necessarily include the future, which remains open and worked out in collaboration with the petitions of the world. If God answers petitionary prayer, the efficacy of prayer, others believe, can be quantifiably measured

---

[5]Philip Clements-Jewery, *Intercessory Prayer: Modern Theology, Biblical Teaching and Philosophical Thought* (Aldershot: Ashgate, 2004) investigates the relation between the doctrine of impassiblity and the practice of petitionary prayer.

[6]Some of the twists and turns the doctrine took under the conditions of modernity are detailed in John Webster, 'Providence', in *Mapping Modern Theology: A Thematic and Historical Introduction*, ed. by Kelly M. Kapic and Bruce L. McCormack (Grand Rapids: Baker Academic, 2012), 203–26.

[7]Kant, *Religion within the Boundaries of Mere Reason*, 186. Kant appears to anticipate Kierkegaard's adage that 'prayer does not change God, but it changes him who prays'. See Søren Kierkegaard, *Upbuilding Discourses in Various Spirits* (Princeton: Princeton University Press, 1993), 22. For a fuller treatment of Kierkegaard's understanding of prayer, see J. Heywood Thomas, 'Kierkegaard on Prayer', *New Blackfriars*, 98.1077 (2017), 501–9.

[8]Feuerbach, *The Essence of Christianity*, 119–24.

(and hence finely tuned) under controlled scientific conditions.[9] Even if it could be 'proved' that God answers prayer in this way, further questions present themselves. Petitionary prayer has been questioned by others on the grounds that it assumes a problematic 'occasionalism': God is otherwise absent from the world except when prompted to intervene on the occasion of human prayer.[10] Under these conditions, prayer ends up covertly disabling – rather than enabling – genuine conversation between God and humanity. How, then, to navigate through this thorny territory?

On first thoughts, there are at least two equally uninviting routes on offer. One view is that God answers petitionary prayer and intervenes in the ordinary course of events to bring about something that otherwise would not have happened. Prayer here is answered because the future is not yet determined, which is to be worked out in covenantal dialogue with creation. Another view is that God does not answer prayer because all events are already absolutely determined. The point of prayer, according to the second option, must presumably lie somewhere other than petitioning the unchangeable God to change the unchangeable course of history. Prayer becomes about changing that which is changeable: the self, not God. In this chapter, we engage the writings of two of the most commanding figures in the Western theological canon who although stand apart on many matters both seek a way beyond these two options: Thomas Aquinas and Karl Barth.

The first section of this chapter explores Aquinas's understanding of the relation between prayer and providence in the light of his theory of causation and his doctrine of desire. The second section turns to Barth and his Christological thinking about prayer and providence to explore the difference Christology makes to the very framing of the question occupying this chapter. Then the final section explores with Kathryn Tanner a 'non-competitive' understanding of the divine–human relation. Here we encounter the *lex orandi* once again at work and discuss it in dialogue with the strange dialectics of divine difference and presence as experienced by John of the Cross.

---

[9]For example: Candy Gunther Brown, *Testing Prayer: Science and Healing* (Cambridge: Harvard University Press, 2012). For a critique of the efficacy-testing approach, see Vincent Brümmer, *What Are We Doing When We Pray? On Prayer and the Nature of Faith* (Aldershot: Ashgate, 2008; revised edn), 2–7.

[10]On this, see Eleonore Stump, 'Petitionary Prayer', *American Philosophical Quarterly*, 16.2 (1979), 81–91.

Thomas Aquinas: Causation and desire

Aquinas did not set about doing a 'spiritual theology' as a separate task to the undertaking of his theological and philosophical work.[11] Instead, he did theology in the fullest sense of the word: he did it on his knees. As a consequence, it is difficult to distinguish the theological from the spiritual in Thomas's writings. Whether he is writing about the attributes of God, the doctrine of the incarnation, the Trinity, or whatever doctrine is under examination, the end is the same: to change us spiritually. The meticulously ordered theo-logic pursued in his *Summa Theologiae*, and the scholastic method of disputation it enshrined, was understood by Thomas to be itself a contemplative exercise. It was integrally related to the wider spiritual project of the ordering of the self before God. Reading the *Summa*, therefore, like reading Evagrius's *On Prayer*, is to subject oneself to a process of 'manuduction' – being 'led-by-the-hand' into participation in God.[12] Hence, elsewhere in his writings Thomas says that 'for him who practices it, theology takes on the modality of prayer (*modus orationis*).[13] The *Summa Theologiae*, also written under the *modus orationis*, is best understood as 'both an exhortation to contemplation and an act of contemplation'.[14] Although all things relate to the life of

---

[11]My reading of Aquinas in this chapter owes much to the essays on the subject by three contemporary Dominicans: Brian Davies, Herbert McCabe and Simon Tugwell. In particular, see Brian Davies, *Thinking about God* (London: Geoffrey Chapman, 1985), 307–34; *The Thought of Thomas Aquinas* (Oxford: Clarendon Press, 1992), 158–84; 'Prayer', in *The Oxford Handbook of Aquinas*, ed. by Brian Davies and Eleonore Stump (Oxford: Oxford University Press, 2012), 467–74; the essays on prayer in Herbert McCabe's *God Matters*, 215–25 and *God Still Matters* (London: Continuum, 2002), 54–63, 64–75, and 215–18; and Simon Tugwell, *Prayer – Volume 1: Living with God* and *Prayer – Volume 2: Prayer in Practice* (Dublin: Veritas, 1974). Much of the background of Thomas's life of prayer, and in particular the centrality of the Lord's Prayer in his life of prayer, has been provided by Paul Murray, OP, *Praying with Confidence: Aquinas on the Lord's Prayer* (London: Burns and Oaks, 2010) and *Aquinas at Prayer: The Bible, Mysticism and Poetry* (London: Bloomsbury, 2013). For a collection of Aquinas's writings on prayer, see Thomas Aquinas, *Albert and Thomas: Selected Writings*, ed. and trans. by Simon Tugwell, CWS (New York: Paulist Press, 1988).

[12]Candler engages with the *Summa* at length in *Theology, Rhetoric, Manuduction*, 90–107.

[13]Cited in Torrell, *Saint Thomas Aquinas*, 17.

[14]Williams, 'Mystical Theology Redux', 56. See also, Timothy Radcliffe, 'Dominican Spirituality', in *The Cambridge Companion to the Summa Theologiae*, ed. by Philip McCosker and Denys Turner (Cambridge: Cambridge University Press, 2016), 23–33.

prayer in Aquinas's theology, he still includes in the second part of the *Summa* a dedicated discussion of the practice of prayer; and weighing in at seventeen articles, the question on prayer is the *Summa's* longest (*ST* 2a2æ, q.83).

At the time of writing this extensive exploration of prayer, it was becoming increasingly fashionable to sharpen a long standing distinction in Christian spirituality between contemplation and petition. Many of Thomas's contemporaries took contemplation to be the 'higher' prayer, the kind of prayer that the pray-er matures into when they have grown out of the spiritually less refined practice of petitioning of God. Contemplation was fast becoming the preserve of the elite, and petition downgraded to the uncouthly realm of the beginner.[15] Aquinas, swimming against these cultural tides, insists on a very precise understanding of prayer, which is offered without hesitation: prayer is the humble, everyday practice of petition – the practice of asking God for what we want.

There is something refreshing about Thomas's unfashionable defining of prayer as petition. Prayer is not about method, skill or technique. In fact, in the main section on prayer in the *Summa* there is little guidance on actually how to pray. Debunking any vestiges of spiritual elitism, he assumes that anyone can pray because praying means simply asking for things from God. Petitionary prayer is levelling. Anyone can call out to God, irrespective of spiritual maturity. The interest Thomas had in petitionary prayer, unusual as it was in his context, exposes a somewhat different side to this towering figure of Western philosophy and theology than is perhaps customary. Even at his most 'speculative' and technical, for which he is famed, here is someone very much in touch with the spiritual realities of the Christian life, as Robert Baron displays so well.[16]

Besides these pastoral reasons, Aquinas cites good authority for prioritizing petition. He sees himself tapping into a long tradition of interpreting the word '*oratio*' in terms of petition. 'In this present context', he explains, 'we are considering prayer as a request or petition; this is the primary meaning of prayer because as Augustine says, "prayer is a petition",

---

[15]On the shifting interpretation of the word '*oratio*', see Tugwell, 'Prayer, Humpty Dumpty and Thomas Aquinas' and in Tugwell's introduction in his CWS volume, *Albert and Thomas*, 271–9.

[16]Robert Barron, *Thomas Aquinas: Spiritual Master* (New York: Crossroad, 1996).

and as Damascene states, "to pray is to ask fittings things from God"" (*ST* 2a2æ, q.83, art.1). More than the good company Thomas keeps, he sees the origins of his prioritization of petition in the dominical teaching of Jesus Christ. When the disciples asked Jesus how to pray, he taught them a string of requests: the Lord's Prayer, which Aquinas fittingly dubs 'the best of all' prayers (*ST* 2a2æ, q.83, art.9).[17]

His refusal to budge from this strong identification of prayer as petition not only flew in the face of many of his medieval contemporaries but also forced Thomas into tackling head-on some perplexing doctrinal issues that might have been avoided had a more contemplative kind of prayer been prioritized in its place. In particular, it forced the question of the relation between petition and providence.

In the *Summa*, Thomas locates one of his two principal engagements with the doctrine of providence within his doctrine of God. Providence is part of the perfections of God (*ST* 1a, q.22, art.2). All that happens in the world, in order for it to happen, is known by God in God's perfection and eternity. Everything owes its existence to God. Aquinas is well aware of some of the concerns such a 'close' doctrine of providence presents to the practice of petitionary prayer. He rehearses these concerns in the form of a series of objections to one of the articles in his long treatment of prayer aptly titled: 'Is prayer useful?' The second of which reads accordingly:

> Through prayer the mind of him to whom we pray is changed so that he does what is requested. God's mind, however, is unchangeable and inflexible. … Therefore it is not fitting that we should pray to God (*ST* 2a2æ, q.83, art.2).

A similar series of objections are raised in a parallel discussion of the relation between petition and providence that took place a few years earlier in Book III of the *Summa contra Gentiles*, which was finished between 1259 and starting the *Summa Theologiae* in about 1266.[18] In the *Summa contra*

---

[17] For more on the Lord's Prayer in Thomas's life and work, see Murray, OP, *Praying with Confidence*.

[18] My engagement with *SCG* follows that of Brian Davies outlined in his reliably helpful, *Thomas Aquinas's Summa Contra Gentiles: A Guide and a Commentary* (Oxford: Oxford University Press, 2016), 244–69. Aquinas discusses the relation between prayer and providence in

Gentiles, he treats prayer within a discussion of providence (*SCG*, 3.95–96) and offers the following response to the objections:

> We should also keep in mind the fact that, just as the immutability of providence does not impose necessity on things that are foreseen, so also it does not suppress the value of prayer. For prayer is not established for the purpose of changing the eternal disposition of providence, since this is impossible, but so that a person may obtain from God the object which he desires.
>
> Indeed, it is appropriate for God to consent to the holy desires of a rational creature, not in the sense that our desires may move the immutable God, but that He, in His goodness, takes steps to accomplish these desired effects in a fitting way.
>
> So, it is proper for God, in accord with His goodness, to bring to a fitting conclusion the proper desires that are expressed by our prayers (*SCG*, 3.95.1–3).

In his responses, Aquinas is saying that the value of prayer is not 'suppressed' within the context of God's close providential involvement in the world. How can this be? How can Aquinas confess the absolute providence of God and still maintain genuine space for the freedom and spontaneity of petitionary prayer?

There are at least two threads to Thomas's defence of the compatibility of petition and providence alluded to above that are worth unpicking. The first involves the way Thomas sets prayer against the broader metaphysical backdrop of his understanding of causation. The second involves the way he seeks to reframe the very terms of the objections against petitionary prayer by repositioning prayer in the domain of desire. Both threads are discussed below, and in turn.

Prayer and causation

More than once in his investigation of prayer, Thomas points to his theory of causation (*ST* 2a2æ, q.83, art.1-2 and *SCG*, 3.96.8). Causation is the

---

Questions 95 and 96, which can be found in Part II of Book 3 of the University of Notre Dame edition translated by Vernon J. Bourke and published in 1975.

broad framework against which he organizes reflection on God and God's dealing with the world. His treatment is technical and complex.[19] In short, adapting the Aristotelian scheme of causation, Aquinas distinguishes between causation of two kinds: 'first' (or 'primary') causation, which concerns divine action; and 'secondary' causation, which concerns human action. Providence, as the action of the divine, falls under the first kind of causality and petition, as the action of the creature, under the second.

His theory of causation both sets the stage for his doctrine of providence and assumes an understanding of the world as radically permeated by the providential presence of God. As first cause, God causes all things into being. The fact that there is something rather than nothing is due to God bringing about all that is. Causation concerns more than the bringing about things into being, however. In bringing all things into existence, Aquinas says that God calls all things to an end; that is, into participation in God's own life. 'Hence everything that is real in any way whatsoever is bound to be directed by God to an end' (*ST* 1a, q.22, art.2). This 'end' will become significant shortly. Causation concerns the end as well as the beginning and, moreover, everything in between: the ongoing 'conserving' of all things in their existence and action.

> Just as God has not only given being to things when they first began to exist, and also causes being in them as long as they exist, conserving things in being. … So also has he not merely granted operative powers to them when they were originally created, but always causes these powers in things. Hence, if this divine influence were to cease, every operation would cease. Therefore, every operation of a thing is traced back to God as to its cause (*SCG*, 3.67.3).

Because God is the source of all that is not God, Aquinas would say that God's providential involvement in the world is comprehensive and constant. If all things are brought into existence by God, sustained in their existence by God (see *ST* 1a, q.104), and directed by God to an end, it makes complete sense, says Aquinas, to petition God for all things in

---

[19]For a fuller treatment, see Michael Rota, 'Causation', in *The Oxford Handbook of Aquinas*, ed. by Brian Davies and Eleonore Stump (Oxford: Oxford University Press, 2012), 104–14; and for Aquinas's relation to Aristotle, see Giles Emery and Matthew Levering, ed., *Aristotle in Aquinas's Theology* (Oxford: Oxford University Press, 2015).

prayer. His 'idea here is ridiculously simple', Brian Davies observes.[20] If God is the cause of all things, ask the cause of all things for all things. Although simple, the objection that such a tight providential ordering of all things is corrosive of the freedom and spontaneity of prayer remains live. After all, Thomas is quite clear that 'divine providence not only disposes what effects will take place, but also the manner in which they will take place, and which actions will cause them' (ST 2a2æ, q.83, art.2). If God's unchangeable providence determines the effects, the manner and the actions of all things then what comes of prayer?

This critical passage from Aquinas's Summa contra Gentiles, which is found a few chapters after the one previously cited, sheds further light on the issue:

> In every agent, in fact, there are two things to consider: namely, the thing itself that acts, and the power by which it acts. Fire, for instance, heats by means of heat. But the power of a lower agent depends on the power of the superior agent, according as the superior agent gives this power to the lower agent whereby it may act; or preserves it; or even applies it to the action, as the artisan applies an instrument to its proper effect, though he neither gives the form by which the instrument works, nor preserves it, but simply gives it motion. So, it is necessary for the action of a lower agent to result not only from the agent by its own power, but also from the power of all higher agents. ... And just as the lower agent is found immediately active, so also is the power of the primary agent found immediately in the production of the effect. For the power of the lower agent is not adequate to produce this effect of itself, but from the power of the next higher agent; and the power of the next one gets this ability from the power of the next higher one; and thus the power of the highest agent is discovered to be of itself productive of the effect, as an immediate cause (SCG, 3.70.5).

By distinguishing between two kinds of causality, indeed, two qualitatively different kinds of causality (again, this will become important later), God's primary causality works in such a way that does not displace but empowers

---

[20]Davies, 'Prayer', 470.

creaturely causality. As Davies explains in his instructive commentary on the text:

> What Aquinas means here is that created agents act and get things done even though their power to act derives from God working in them. For Aquinas, creatures are always secondary causes as they bring about effects. They are secondary, not primary, because all created activity derives from God. Yet Aquinas believes that secondary causes are genuine causes. They have power; so they act. Their power derives from God acting in them; so what they bring about by their power is also what God is bringing about while acting in them.[21]

For Aquinas, therefore, 'natural effects are attributed to God and to a natural agent' (*SCG*, 3.70.1). The one action proceeds from the two agents. Thus the 'same effect is not attributed to a natural cause and to divine power in such a way that it is partly done by God, and partly by the natural agent; rather, it is wholly done by both, according to a different way, just as the same effect is wholly attributed to the instrument and also wholly to the principal agent' (*SCG*, 3.70.8). The issues here are complex, as Aquinas readily admits, but may be illustrated by way of an analogy.

Imagine you are listening to one of Rachmaninoff's piano concertos. Rachmaninoff, as composer, Aquinas would say, 'does not only dispose what effects will take place' (the concerto itself) but also 'which actions will cause them' (which instruments will play what and when) and 'the manner in which the effects will take place' (the pitch, the notes and the rests, the signatures, the articulations and so on). Despite the comprehensive 'control' Rachmaninoff has over its sound, the concerto does not just 'happen', unilaterally travelling from score to ear. Instead, nothing short of a miracle, it is dependent upon a complex combination of causes: the conductor directing the score, the pianist, the orchestra, the technicians ensuring that audio levels are balanced and so on. In this analogy, the composer is the first cause and all else – the conductor, the musicians, the instruments – belong to the realm of secondary causation. Both kinds of causation 'cause' the concerto to happen, but in different ways.

A similar thing can be said of prayer. For Thomas, divine causality achieves its end by working through, rather than unilaterally upon,

---

[21]Davies, *Thomas Aquinas's Summa Contra Gentiles*, 247.

secondary causality. God's action in the world is meditated through creaturely causality just as Rachmaninoff's concerto is mediated through the actions of the conductor, the musicians, the technicians and so on. Indeed, for Thomas, God not only causes the whole process to work but as we have said sustains the integrity of each action in the complex web of causation. God sustains the musicians *as* musicians, enabling and empowering them in a way that protects their integrity and freedom. And so he writes that although 'God must be everywhere and in all things' (*SCG*, 3.68.1) it would be an 'error' to think 'that no creature has an active role in the production of natural effects' (*SCG*, 3.69.1).[22]

While God is not restricted to operating through creaturely causality in the same way that Rachmaninoff is (hence, Aquinas's retention of the category of miracles to cater for divine action by extraordinary means), God, who remains absolutely primary, has nevertheless determined to act in the world *through* ordinary means. 'And thus', Thomas concludes, 'secondary causes are not incompatible with providence; instead, they carry out the effect of providence. In this way, then, prayers are efficacious before God, yet they do not destroy the immutable order of divine providence, because this individual request that is granted to a certain petitioner falls under the order of divine providence' (*SCG*, 3.96.8).

Earlier we noted that 'the end' is significant for Thomas. Aquinas thinks that God is both the initiating cause and the final cause of all things. Put in terms of teleology, the end of all things is a good, he says (*SCG*, 3.16.4). And the highest good is union with God as a personal reality. Since prayer, and its gradual conforming of human selfhood to God, is ordered to God and has exactly this union with God as its end, prayer is not only placed 'under the order of providence' but providence is found at the very heart of prayer.

In short, Aquinas's theory of causation can be seen to provide a way of theorizing the inherent compatibility of prayer and providence, and thus how it might be that God answers petitions without being coerced or changed by them. Prayer is consistent with providence because as a form of secondary causality our petitions have been determined in the first place to effect the

---

[22]For an exploration of the doctrine of providence through the metaphor of the theatre, see Timothy J. Gorringe, *God's Theatre: A Theology of Providence* (London: SCM Press, 1991), and especially Chapter 6 on prayer.

cause of divine providence. 'For we do not petition in order to change the decree of divine providence, rather we pray in order to impetrate those things which God has determined would be obtained only through our prayers' (*ST* 2a2æ, q.83. art.2). Both our prayer and God's answer to prayer are part of what comes about by God's providence. Under these conditions, says Aquinas, it would be an error not to ask God for things. Just as it is absurd to say that there is no point in eating 'in order to be nourished' (*SCG*, 3.96.8), by the same token it is absurd to say that prayer has no role within providence: the two are entirely compatible.[23] As well as making sense of God's answering of prayer, his theory of causation is equally geared up to making sense of the reality that prayer is not always answered. Despite granting a metaphysical status to prayer, he does not suppose that all prayer must therefore be answered. In fact, his theory of causation strictly rules this out. There are some petitions that simply fall outside of providence. For example, if prayer is not teleologically ordered towards the good then petition, no matter how earnest, would work against divine providence and thus go unanswered. The key questions, for Aquinas, then become about discernment ('what is the good?') and formation ('how can prayer be ordered toward the good?'); and these questions take us to the theme of desire.

Prayer and desire

Aquinas's treatment of prayer in the *Summa* is one of great theological and spiritual subtlety. Yet it contains little about the mechanics of prayer and resists offering advice on formal techniques to help the pray-er deepen in relationship with God through prayer. His key interest concerns the more fundamental question of why we pray in the first place. Put differently, the interesting thing about prayer for Aquinas is not strictly speaking the relation it has with God's providence but the relation it has with desire and, crucially, with the formation of desire. For Aquinas, the 'purpose' of prayer

---

[23]A similar response is developed by C. S. Lewis. If the argument against prayer, he writes, 'is sound, surely it is argument not only against praying, but against doing anything whatever? ... Why wash your hands? If God intends them to be clean, they'll come clean without your washing them. If He doesn't, they'll remain dirty (as Lady Macbeth found) however much soap you use. Why ask for the salt? Why put on your boots? Why do anything?' See C. S. Lewis, *God in the Dock: Essays on Theology and Ethics*, ed. by Walter Hooper (Grand Rapids: William B. Eerdmans, 2014), 105.

'is so that a person may obtain the object which he desires' (*SCG*, 95.1). When right human desire and divine desire cohere, the tension between prayer and providence is resolved. For it is in this coherence that we ask for the things that God providentially desires of us.

But how do we come to desire the right things in prayer? In his commentary on the Lord's Prayer, and citing Rom. 8.26, Thomas admits that 'knowing what we ought to ask for is extremely difficult, as is knowing what we ought to desire'.[24] To a certain extent, the Lord's Prayer, he goes on to say, regulates what we ought to desire. 'In the Lord's Prayer we not only ask for all the things we can rightly desire, but also in the sequence that we ought to desire them, so that this prayer not only teaches us to ask for things, but also in what order we ought to desire them' (*ST* 2a2æ, q.83, art.9). The Lord's Prayer provides a model of what right desire looks like and gives working examples of the things for which we should be praying: the hallowing of the divine name, the coming of the kingdom, the forgiveness of sin – the things that God desires of us. But even with this clear guidance it may well be the case that we know deep down what we ought to be praying for (say, the coming of the kingdom) and yet what is really occupying our desire at the particular moment of prayer is for things quite different, even things that conceal a misshapen desire for power and pride (say, a brand new car). So in another of his famous definitions of prayer, Aquinas writes that prayer is the 'interpreter of our desire' (*ST* 2a2æ, q.83, art.9). By this he means that in praying we learn to 'read' our desires and to work out why we desire certain things and not others and, ultimately, how human desire can be aligned with divine desire.

To move from what he calls our 'animal desire' (the new car) to what we ought really to desire (the coming of the kingdom), Aquinas falls back on a broadly Augustinian account of the transformation of desire.[25] In prayer, our desire is both interpreted and transformed. Intriguingly, Thomas counsels against sidestepping our animal desire and taking up praying for something more holy instead. In his reply to the claim that we must not seek temporal things, Aquinas says that these 'are lawfully desired, not as our main and final goal but as helps towards eternal happiness' (*ST* 2a2æ, q.83, art.9). Praying for a new car is thus a means to an end. To access our true

---

[24]Aquinas, 'From the Lectures on St Matthew', in *Albert and Thomas: Selected Writings,* ed. and trans. by Simon Tugwell, CWS (New York: Paulist Press, 1988), 445–75 (455).
[25]On this, see Augustine 'Our Lord's Sermon on the Mount', 38.

desire (the 'desire from God') we must pray *more* fervently for what we want rather than what we think we should want because in this context of prayer the misshapen desire for power and pride that otherwise remains concealed is laid to bare. We pray for the things we immediately want not to normalize unchecked desire but to hand them over to God for their transformation. This is what it means to follow the way of the praying Christ who, in the Garden of Gethsemane, disclosed his true desire. 'In this fashion Christ's prayer was indeed the expression of his sensuous impulses to the degree that his prayer took on as it were the role of spokesman for the sensuous impulse, expressing its desires' (*ST* 3a, q.21, art.2). What is required, as Herbert McCabe explains, is an 'honesty' before God about what we want rather than what we think we should want.

> If we are honest enough to admit to our shabby infantile desires then the grace of God will grow in us, it will slowly to be revealed to us, precisely in the course of our prayer, that there are more important things that we truly do want. But this will not be some abstract recognition that we ought to want these things, we will really discover a desire for them in ourselves. But we must start where we are.[26]

In the crucible of prayer, human desire, rough as it is, is interpreted and shaped in the light of desire for God.

It would not be until late in life, however, in Thomas's commentary on Romans written during his last years in Naples (1272–3), that his theory of the interpretation of desire would gain greater pneumatological articulation. In dialogue with Romans 8, Thomas concludes that the Holy Spirit 'causes right desires in us'.[27] It is through the Spirit's work in the pray-er that human desire is set on a slow journey of transformation until it reaches true desire: when human desire and divine desire complexly 'converse', in the Evagrian sense of the word, when the spiritual groan of which Paul speaks in Romans 8 is silenced and when the conflict between providence and prayer is finally settled.

---

[26]McCabe, *God Matters*, 224. McCabe speaks of the importance of 'praying for what we *want*, and not for what we just think we *ought* to want' in his chapter on prayer in *God, Christ and Us*, ed. by Brian Davies (London: Continuum, 2005), 103–8 (105).

[27]Aquinas, 'From the Commentary on Romans', in *Albert and Thomas: Selected Writings*, ed. and trans. by Simon Tugwell, CWS (New York: Paulist Press, 1988), 520–3 (522).

To recap, Aquinas's reply to the objection that prayer is 'useless' is mounted on the following logic: right prayer follows right desire; right desire is a gift from God; right desire is divine desire which by definition falls within the scope of God's eternal providence. 'The nearer certain things are to their mover, the more efficaciously do they follow the influence of the mover' (*SCG*, 95.4). This logic might not prove fully satisfying. Some have argued that Aquinas merely sidesteps the problem. In terms of causation, of course God answers prayer because God has determined the prayer and the divine response to prayer in the first place. In terms of desire, Aquinas neutralizes the tension by narrating a shift from prayer changing God to prayer changing the pray-er. Again, some see here a doctrinal sleight of hand. Of course prayer is part of God's providential activity in the world, but only the right kind of prayer that follows the right kind of desire – which is God's desire in the first place. There is a further piece of Aquinas's argument that clarifies some of the assumptions that underlies the air of dissatisfaction, which we will tackle shortly. In the meantime, it is instructive to feed into our discussion a theologian who like Thomas was deeply invested in the question of the relation between prayer and providence but charts different routes through this perplexing doctrinal ground.

Karl Barth's Christology of prayer

Karl Barth, like Thomas Aquinas, is best understood as a spiritual writer. Like Thomas, Barth nowhere writes an independent spiritual theology. Spirituality is elegently integrated within his broader theological under-taking. From the first pages of his monumental *Church Dogmatics* to his swansong lectures of the 1960s, Barth remained committed to a theological methodology that was deliberately rooted in prayer.

> The first and basic act of theological work is *prayer*. … Theological work does not merely begin with prayer and is not merely accompanied by it; in its totality it is peculiar and characteristic of theology that it can be performed only in the act of prayer. In view of the danger to which theology is exposed and to the hope that is enclosed within its work, it is natural that without prayer there can be no theological work. We should keep in mind the fact that prayer, as such, is work; in fact, very hard work, although in its execution the hands are most fittingly not moved but folded. Where theology is concerned, the rule

Ora et labora! is valid under all circumstances – pray and work! And the gist of this rule is not merely that *orare*, although it should be the beginning, would afterward be only incidental to the execution of the *laborare*. The rule means, moreover, that the *laborare* itself, and as such, is essentially an *orare*. Work must be that sort of act that has the manner and meaning of a prayer in all its dimensions, relationships, and movements.[28]

Like Thomas, Barth integrated dedicated treatments of prayer into his magnum opus, locating the most important in his doctrine of providence, in his ethics of creation and in his ethics of reconciliation.[29] And like Thomas, Christian doctrine for Barth has a transformative potential: he believed that you will be a different kind of person if you believe in this or that doctrine – it will change your life.

Throughout these sections of the *Church Dogmatics*, Barth rivals even Aquinas's insatiable prioritization of petition. As was Aquinas, Barth was writing in an intellectual culture in which petitionary prayer had fallen out of theological fashion.[30] Barth is adamant however that prayer necessarily acquires the character of petition. 'The only possible status of the creature in this matter is that of one who asks' (*CD* III/3, 274). Echoing Aquinas again, Barth appeals – interestingly via Romans 8 – to a broadly Augustinian theory of the transformation of desire to describe the process through which human asking is brought into 'correspondence' with divine

---

[28]Barth, *Evangelical Theology*, 160. For engagements with Barth's theology of prayer, see Cocksworth, *Karl Barth on Prayer*; Eberhard Jüngel, 'Invocation of God as the Ethical Ground of Christian Action: Introductory Remarks on the Posthumous Fragments of Karl Barth's Ethics of the Doctrine of Reconciliation', in *Theological Essays I* (Edinburgh: T&T Clark, 1989), 154–72; John C. McDowell, '"Openness to the World": Karl Barth's Evangelical Theology of Christ as the Pray-er', *Modern Theology*, 25.2 (2009), 253–83; and John Webster, *Barth's Ethics of Reconciliation* (Cambridge: Cambridge University Press, 1995).

[29]*CD* III/3, 265–8; *CD* III/4, 87–115; and all of *ChrL*.

[30]In *The Life of Prayer in a World of Science: Protestants, Prayer, and American Culture, 1870-1930* (Oxford: Oxford University Press, 2000), Rick Ostrander charts the history of the gradual pushing of petitionary prayer out of the theological realm as beginning with Schleiermacher. For Schleiermacher's writings on prayer, see 'Prayer in the Name of Christ', in *The Christian Faith*, 668–75; 'On Prayer in Jesus' Name' (Sermon on Jn 16.23), in *Servant of the Word: Selected Sermons of Friedrich Schleiermacher* (Philadelphia: Fortress Press, 1987), 169–80; and 'The Power of Prayer in Relation to Outward Circumstances' (Sermon on Matt. 26.36-46), in *Selected Sermons of Schleiermacher* (New York: Funk and Wagnalls, 1890), 38–51. For Barth's critique of Schleiermacher's reduction of prayer to 'self-help', see *ChrL*, 103.

desire (*ChrL*, 106–7). In further agreement with Aquinas, Barth sees no contradiction in affirming the universal nature of God's providential action in the world and the full spontaneity of human prayer.

Although Barth seems to be aware of the 'arguments against the permissibility and possibility of asking in prayer', unlike Aquinas, he is reluctant to give them much of an airing and is fundamentally unconcerned about constructing anything like a systematic response to them. He simply heads the objections off from the outset as false – even 'impious' (*CD* III/4, 96) – and concedes to the mystery of prayer, which is no less mysterious, he thinks, than the incarnation itself (*ChrL*, 89). Indeed, it is precisely in the domain of Christology that Barth's refusal to engage in debates around prayer's efficacy gains clarity – as we shall see shortly. Although Barth can be seen to utilize the categories of causation, he finds them more problematic than does Aquinas. Instead, his approach to the doctrine of providence is via the classical threefold division found often but not exclusively in the Reformed tradition, which he interprets christologically.[31]

Christian theologians down the ages have looked to the threefold action of God's conservation of creation (*conservatio*), God's concurrence with creation (*concursus*) and God's governance of creation (*gubernatio*) to shape the doctrine of providence. All that is not God depends on some way or another on the animating agency of God to sustain its existence, accompany its history and draw all activity towards perfect happiness. It is in this doctrinal context of providence that Barth locates one of his principal treatments of prayer. Alongside faith and obedience, prayer (by which he means petition) comprises the 'attitude' of the Christian under the providential 'lordship of God' (*CD* III/3, 239–88). Of the threefold division of providence, the divine accompaniment (*concursus Dei*) proves the most helpful to Barth in resourcing his understanding of the role of petition within God's providential ordering of creation. The *concursus Dei* literally means the 'concurrence', the coming together of the activity of God with the activity of the creature. It undergirds all that Barth says about 'the lordship of God in relation to the free and autonomous activity of the creature'

---

[31]Barth is ultimately suspicious of the language of 'cause', fearing that it produces a 'featureless' doctrine of God, preferring instead the more covenantal language of 'partners', which Barth explicates throughout his doctrine of election. For Barth's critique of the language of causation, see *CD* III/3, 98.

(*CD* III/3, 90) in general and the relation between petition and providence in particular.[32]

Like Aquinas, in his account of the *concursus*, Barth has a strong sense of God's unequivocally 'sovereign' action in the world. God's 'activity determines our activity even to its most intimate depths, even to its most direct origins' (*CD* III/3, 132) so that 'nothing can be done except the will of God' (*CD* III/3, 113). God precedes, accompanies and follows creaturely action. It could be assumed that the extent of God's 'universal lordship' leaves little space for the freedom of human action. After all Barth writes that God 'co-operates with it, preceding, accompanying and following all its being and activity, so that all the activity of the creature is primarily and simultaneously and subsequently His own activity' (*CD* III/3, 105). Yet Barth works hard throughout his doctrine of providence and elsewhere to ensure that divine agency does not overwhelm the full reality of human action. Alongside the activity of God, he affirms a valid place for the creature. The divine accompaniment 'affirms and recognizes and respects the autonomous actuality and therefore the autonomous activity of the creature as such. He does not play the part of a tyrant towards it' (*CD* III/3, 92). The key ethical category Barth deploys throughout his doctrine of providence, therefore, is 'partnership'. The creator and the creature work in the world as partners – united by grace. 'Because the community asks', Barth writes, 'God finds in the world and has in it a partner' (*CD* III/3, 279–80). In asking, the community responds to its election in Christ with a 'yes' to acting with and alongside God's concursive grace in faith, obedience and prayer.

There are several intriguing parallels between Aquinas and Barth regarding their shared affirmation of the compatibility of prayer and providence. But there are also significant differences. One point of difference concerns their respective christologies of prayer. In terms of his main treatment of prayer (in *ST* 2a2æ, q.83), despite being the longest chapter in the *Summa*, Aquinas says little about the specific role of Jesus Christ in prayer. When Christology does feature in his analysis, Aquinas is invariably concerned with either Christ's

---

[32]See Paul T. Nimmo, *Being in Action: The Theological Shape of Barth's Ethical Vision* (London: T&T Clark, 2007), 118–30. The divine *concursus* is of central significance for Barth's understanding of prayer, on this, see Christopher C. Green, *Karl Barth on Divine Providence, Evil, and the Angels* (London: T&T Clark, 2011), 58–91. For a more general treatment of the *concursus*, see Charles M. Wood, *The Question of Providence* (Louisville: Westminster John Knox Press, 2008).

own prayer life or his teaching on prayer.[33] In either case, the Christological emphasis seems to fall mostly on the level of instruction. Our practice of prayer is undertaken in imitation of Christ, following his example and teaching. Jesus Christ models right prayer through his practice and his teaching, which culminates for Thomas in the giving of the Lord's Prayer. As Corey Barnes argues, 'Thomas Aquinas believed that Jesus Christ provided a model (*exemplum*) for prayer.'[34] For Barnes, the 'full force' of Christ as the *exemplum* for prayer is not felt, however, until Aquinas returns to the theme of prayer sometime later in the *Summa* in a discussion of 'Christ's Prayer' (*ST* 3a, q.21). Here 'the exemplary force of Christ's prayer' takes centre stage.[35] Aquinas's treatment of 'Christ's Prayer' is placed within a broader discussion of Christ in relation to the Father. There, Aquinas speaks of how Christ models the perfect human relation to the Father through his prayer life. 'Christ prayed in order to instruct humanity. Christ's prayer shows that he is from the Father and provides a model (*exemplum*) for praying' – modelling, among other things, right desire.[36] To pray well, then, means to pray (and therefore to desire) more like Christ. And by imitating Christ in this way the pray-er is guaranteed of God's answer to prayer. 'The fulfillment of prayer depends upon which will the prayer manifests. Christ's deliberative will (will as reason) conformed perfectly to the divine will in all things; every prayer manifesting Christ's deliberative will was heard.'[37] To return to our musical analogy, under these conditions to pray means to follow the direction of Jesus Christ who takes on, as it were, the role of the conductor who teaches the concerto of prayer.

Herein lies the interesting rub between our two theologians. Like Aquinas, Barth is alert to the exemplary nature of Christ's prayer. For Barth, because we cannot pray as we ought, we need to be taught how to pray. Christ teaches us how to pray – in word and deed – and we follow Christ's example by praying the petitions of the Lord's Prayer. 'The Gospels tell us

---

[33]See respectively, *ST* 2a2æ, q.83, art.10 and *ST* 2a2æ, q.83, art.12 for some examples.

[34]Corey Barnes, 'Thomas Aquinas on Christ's Prayer', in *A History of Prayer: The First to the Fifteenth Century,* ed. by Roy Hammerling (Leiden: Brill, 2008), 319–35 (319). Barnes's reading of Aquinas is substantiated by Jean-Pierre Torrell who also argues that 'a Christological exemplarity is always present in the mind of Master Thomas'. See Jean-Pierre Torrell, *Christ and Spirituality in St. Thomas Aquinas* (Washington: The Catholic University of America Press, 2011), 102.

[35]Barnes, 'Thomas Aquinas on Christ's Prayer', 320.

[36]Ibid., 331.

[37]Ibid., 333.

that He taught His disciples to pray, and that He did so by repeating a prayer with them, by being their Leader in prayer. This fact is of decisive practical importance for the meaning and character of Christian prayer' (*CD* III/3, 274). In addition to this 'exemplary' dimension there is a further aspect of Barth's Christology of prayer that is not so readily emphasized in the specific sections on prayer in Aquinas's writings.[38] The 'exemplarism' that Barnes finds dominating Aquinas's Christology of prayer can be complemented by a more explicit sense of the 'vicarious' character of the prayer of Christ as presented by Barth. Citing more than once Calvin's notion that we pray 'by His mouth' (*CD* III/4, 94, 108; *ChrL*, 105), Barth is led to conclude that 'this means that He, Jesus Christ, is really and properly the One who prays' (*CD* III/4, 94). 'He was human asking' (*CD* III/3, 274–5). For Barth, our asking is bound up with Christ's asking who stands before the Father as our 'Representative and Substitute' (*CD* III/3, 276). Our petition, consequently, 'is a repetition of His petition, … enclosed in His asking' (*CD* III/3, 277). And thus, for Barth, Jesus Christ is not only the teacher of the concerto of prayer but manifestly prays himself.

These two distinct dimensions of Barth's Christology of prayer – the exemplary and the vicarious – do not pull in opposite directions but are two sides of the same Christological coin. As John Webster explains:

> Thus Barth can write that Jesus Christ 'founded calling on God the Father – and made it binding on his people – by doing it first himself, and in so doing giving a prior example of what he demanded of them, or rather, demanding it of them by himself doing it. He took them up into the movement of his own prayer.' Here the two modes are brought together: Christ's invocation is both vicarious ('he took them up into the movement') and that which enables and elicits further invocation ('demanding it of them by doing it').[39]

In other words, the complexity of Barth's Christologically driven reading of prayer means that he can affirm that prayer is at once fully human ('as

---

[38]A more comprehensive sense of participation in Christ, however, is discussed elsewhere by Aquinas. On this see, Rik Van Nieuwenhove, 'The Saving Work of Christ', in *The Oxford Handbook of Aquinas*, ed. by Brian Davies and Eleonore Stump (Oxford: Oxford University Press, 2012), 436–47.

[39]Webster, *Barth's Ethics of Reconciliation*, 185 – citing *ChrL*, 64.

the primal and basic form of the whole Christian ethos') and fully divine ('by Jesus Christ and through his Spirit they have been taken up into *his* invocation of God').[40]

With this complex Christology of prayer in hand Barth is unfazed by questions of the compatibility of divine providence and the practice of petitionary prayer. The answer to the question, 'How can we so boldly and unquestioningly take the content of our human asking into our hope in God, into the very will of God Himself?' (*CD* III/4, 107), is found, characteristically for Barth, in Jesus Christ.

> Now if the Son asks Him, how can the Father possibly fail to hear Him? How can His asking fail to be accompanied by hearing? And how, then, can the Father fail to hear and answer those whom His Son calls His own, who are together with His Son His children, who ask Him in company with His Son, with whom and for whom the Son asks? How can there be even the smallest interval between asking and hearing? As Jesus Christ asks, and we with Him, God has already made Himself the Guarantor that our requests will be heard. Indeed, He has already heard them (*CD* III/4, 108).[41]

Because it is Jesus Christ who asks, God cannot fail to hear our prayer: God 'has *already* heard' us, Barth says. There is one further, even more curious Christological move Barth makes which is worth discussing further as it explains why he takes the divine answering of prayer as given.

Barth sees Jesus Christ as not only the 'true pray-er', the one who models right prayer and right desire, and not even the 'true asker', into whose asking our asking is incorporated and affirmed. But for Barth, being Barth, Jesus Christ is also the 'answer' to our prayer.

> Of all the things that are needed by man, and needed in such a way that he can receive them only from God, that only God can give them to him, there is one great gift. And to all the true and legitimate requests

---

[40]*ChrL*, 89 and 100.

[41]By arguing that because of Christ's praying activity 'it is always God who prays to God', Balthasar reaches a similar Christological settlement to the problem of petitionary prayer in Hans Urs von Balthasar, *Theo-Drama: Theological Dramatic Theory - Volume 2: Dramatis Personae: Man in God* (San Francisco: Ignatius Press, 1990), 292–302 (300). Indeed, for Balthasar, there is 'a trinitarian certainty that prayer is answered', 301.

that are directed necessarily to God, there is one great answer. This one divine gift and answer is Jesus Christ. (*CD* III/3, 271)

Jesus Christ as fully God and fully human is both the (human) asker and the (divine) answer to prayer. 'For however difficult it may sound', Barth writes, 'the hearing really precedes the asking' (*CD* III/3, 270). This does not mean that God has already answered our every prayer, such that human freedom is rendered null and void, but that in Christ God has 'elected' to be in covenantal communion with humanity. Our election in Christ comes with the confidence that God is irrevocably committed to hearing and answering our prayer and to working with us in genuine partnership.

In this Christological context, the question of prayer's compatibility with divine providence is somewhat subverted. According to Barth's theological methodology, to consider the relation between prayer and providence one needs to look no further than Jesus Christ. For Barth, as with all other matters, there can be no talk of the matter of the relation between divine and human agency in abstraction from the concrete conditions of the event of divine and human relationship in the person of Jesus Christ. As Robert Leigh explains: 'In the final resort, the only evidence the church need trust to prove the simultaneous facts of God's causal control over history and the authenticity of creaturely history is that in Jesus Christ God willed to become and actually became a genuine creature, thereby establishing a real covenant with two real partners.'[42] It is here in Jesus Christ that true human freedom is discovered. 'God is "omnipotent in the freedom of His creatures", rather than omnipotent in competition with, or opposition to, that freedom.'[43]

For Barth, questions over the efficacy of prayer not only are less problematic when versed in Christology but are rendered the wrong questions to ask in the first place. God answers prayer because God in Christ is the one praying. 'God is the Father of Jesus Christ, and that very man Jesus Christ has prayed, and he is praying still. Such is the foundation of our prayer in Jesus Christ. It is as if God himself has pledged to answer our request because all our prayers are summed up in Jesus Christ; God

---

[42]Robert Leigh, *Freedom and Flourishing: Being, Act, and Knowledge in Karl Barth's Church Dogmatics* (Eugene: Cascade Books, 2017), 95–6. See, *CD* III/3, 105–6.
[43]John Webster, *Barth's Moral Theology: Human Action in Barth's Thought* (London: T&T Clark, 2004), 105 – citing *CD* II/1, 598.

cannot fail to answer, since it is Jesus Christ who prays.'[44] As with Aquinas so too with Barth: a lot hangs on his understanding of the 'non-competitive' relation between divine and human agency, mentioned already in passing and now to be discussed more fully.

Between petition and providence, there is no competition

As we have seen, Aquinas sees no incompatibility between providence and prayer because God, as first cause, works non-coercively within and through rather than upon creaturely causality. Prayer is about the interpretation and then transformation of human desire into the likeness of divine desire. And for Barth, as we have also seen, prayer and providence are compatible because the 'concursive' operation of God, again non-coercively, precedes, accompanies and follows human agency so closely that in our prayer God 'hears his own voice' – the voice of the praying Son, whom God cannot fail to answer. In both cases, prayer is no longer in conflict with the providential will of God but becomes its paradigmatic human expression.

There is a streak within modern theology that remains unconvinced by these kinds of constructions of the divine–human relationship. Aquinas and Barth have both borne the brunt of similar accusations of producing a doctrine of providence that is little more than determinism and an account of human freedom that is more apparent than real.[45] In Thomistic terms, creaturely causality cannot avoid being a conduit for divine causality. God unilaterally pulls the strings on a frivolous marionette show that lacks any meaningful possibility for the human to have acted otherwise. Barth's overwhelming sense of divine sovereignty cannot but obliterate human freedom giving only the illusion that human prayer 'exerts an influence upon God's action, even upon his existence' but in reality God remains 'Lord' and the creature operates submissively 'under' God's rule.[46] Prayer is really about receiving from God that which God has already determined to give. In either agential setup, so the criticisms run, a providential situation

---

[44]Barth, *Prayer*, 14.

[45]For some critiques of Aquinas and Barth on this issue, see Paul Fiddes, *Participating in God: A Pastoral Doctrine of the Trinity* (London: Darton, Longman and Todd, 2000), 121–4; Brümmer, *What Are We Doing When We Pray?* 59; and Clements-Jewery, *Intercessory Prayer*, 96.

[46]Barth, *Prayer*, 13.

arises in which as divine sovereignty increases, human freedom must, by implication, decrease. The two are mutually exclusive.

One way of getting around the perceived lack of human spontaneity and self-determination that some have detected in classical configurations of the divine–human relation has been to rework the notion of divine providence. A contemporary example of this reworking can be seen in 'open theism' which has been prominent in some strands of North American evangelicalism over the past few decades.[47] Blending the metaphysics of process thought with post-Calvinist theology,[48] open theism seeks to recover the so-called 'relational' God of the Bible. Fed up with the deterministic implications of the unrestricted sovereignty of the God of 'classical theism' (in which Barth and Aquinas are implicated), open theism speaks of 'limiting' divine power. Its aims are twofold: first, to recover the biblical God of compassion, love and responsiveness from what they would see as 'hellenistic distortions', thereby correcting false turns in the development of the doctrine of God; and second, to recover a biblical theology of prayer, untainted by alien philosophy, that protects the full reality of human freedom. On the latter, John Sanders cites a litany of prayers in the Bible that God answered as evidence for the answering of prayer today.

> For instance, God removed certain plagues at the request of Moses (Ex. 8.13, 31). When God told Moses that he was going to destroy the people and start over again with Moses, Moses cited reasons why God should not follow through with this plan. God changed his mind to accommodate Moses' desires (Ex. 32.10-14). When God announced to King Hezekiah through the prophet Isaiah that he would die very soon, Hezekiah prayed and gave God reasons why he should let him live longer. Because of his prayer God sent Isaiah back to Hezekiah to inform him that God had changed his mind and would grant his request (2 Kgs 20.1-6). If Moses and Hezekiah had not prayed to God about these matters, biblical history would have been different.[49]

---

[47]A representative example of the doctrine of providence in open theism relating specifically to prayer is John Sanders, *The God Who Risks: A Theology of Divine Providence* (Downers Grove: InterVarsity Press, 1998), 277–84.

[48]For an account of prayer from a process perspective, see Marjorie Hewitt Suchocki, *In God's Presence: Theological Reflections on Prayer* (St Louis: Chalice Press, 1996).

[49]Sanders, *The God Who Risks*, 280. It is suggestive that of the many biblical characters open theism tends to cite, Jesus is not one of them. It could be said, then, that what open theism lacks

Providence here is not about causation or unrestricted sovereignty. Instead God works by way of persuasion, lure and under a degree of 'risk' to bring about a contingently 'open' future in 'genuine give-and-take dynamics'.[50] Feeding this agential setup into our musical analogy, the composer may have an overall idea of shape of the concerto, but its exact score remains unfinished. It is produced in creative interaction with all involved in its actualization. Open theism rejects the thesis of 'classical theism' in order to safeguard its antithesis. Put differently, it produces a mirror image of exactly that which it rejects: divine sovereignty must now *decrease* for human freedom to increase and, by implication, for petitionary prayer to make a difference.

There are others, however, who see at risk here a category mistake in both the criticisms of 'classical theism' and the relational model developed by the likes of open theism to stand in its place. By this they mean that divine agency and human agency have been forced into a false opposition. Kathryn Tanner has diagnosed and denounced the root of the category mistake as an issue of 'competition', and considers it to be a particularly modern problem – this will become important later.[51] God and the world

---

is a developed Christology of prayer, along the lines discussed in Chapter 4, that 'maximizes' prayer as more than simply human action.

[50]Sanders, *The God Who Risks*, 71. Fiddes utilizes the process category of 'persuasion' and integrates it with a trinitarian theology of participation in his 'relational' account of intercession, in which 'our asking draws us into the dance of divine perichoresis', *Participating in God*, 139.

[51]Kathryn Tanner, *God and Creation in Christian Theology: Tyranny or Empowerment* (Oxford: Blackwell, 1998). Similarly 'non-contrastive' accounts of the action of God and creatures can be found in David B. Burrell, *Freedom and Creation in Three Traditions* (Notre Dame: University of Notre Dame Press, 1993) and Frances Young, *God's Presence: A Contemporary Recapitulation of Early Christianity* (Cambridge: Cambridge University Press, 2013), which utilizes the sophisticated dialectics of early Christian theology to develop an account of divine action in the world that seeks to hold together the 'otherness and the providential presence of God' (397). Despite disagreeing elsewhere, the non-competitive agential setup found in the classical tradition bears interesting connections with some feminist theologies that are similarly seeking an understanding of the divine–human relationship that reaches beyond competitive constraints. According to Sallie McFague, notions of agency based on the competitive pursuit of power 'over-against' others runs the risk of reifying patriarchal patterns of domination and reinforcing 'feminized' states of submission. In place of a 'scarcity' model of power, in which there is only so much agency to go around, is a redescription of divine agency as non-competitive, relational and non-coercive and as that which fulfils rather than forces human agency as the primary animator of action. See Sallie McFague, *Models of God: Theology for an Ecological, Nuclear Age* (Philadelphia: Fortress Press 1987), 63.

are catapulted on a collision course that culminates in a competitively zero-sum standoff. On this sliding-scale of agency, the more of one necessarily implies the less of the other: the more God is immutable the less meaningful human prayer can be; and the more meaningful human prayer is the less God can be immutable. But what cannot be accommodated is both. Modifying 'broken' patterns of discourse about God and creation in modern Christian thought, Tanner seeks to redeploy an account of the divine transcendence, basic to classical accounts of creation and providence, to present an alternative agential configuration in which divine agency transcends rather than competes with human agency. Because God is 'other', God and humanity do not cancel each other in an 'either/or' competition for space. Jeremy Begbie explains this non-competitive understanding of agency through another musical analogy. Suppose one of the musicians in the orchestra of the Rachmaninoff concerto plays two notes on a violin, 'it makes no sense to think of the strings as in competition, or simply "allowing" each other room to vibrate – the lower string enhances, brings to life the upper strings, frees it to be itself, neither compromising its own integrity nor that of the upper strings.'[52] Divine agency and human agency, providence and petition – like two strings on a bow – do not compete with but enhance each other.

Thinking of the relationship of the two causalities in a non-competitive way renders the choice between divine providence and human freedom a false one. Just as it would be odd to think that the more Rachmaninoff composes his concerto the less space there is for the orchestra to be 'orchestra', theological thinking about providence shaped by a non-competitive reading of agency makes it similarly odd to think that the more God is 'God' the less of a place there can be for the full reality of human agency expressed in petitionary prayer. This would be to compare like with like, which would be a categorical error. Working from Aquinas, McCabe clarifies the fruit of this kind of non-binary reasoning when he writes:

> If I fill up a basket with apples and oranges, the more apples there are, the less room there is for oranges, and vice versa. The apples and oranges compete for the available space. But apples and God do not compete for available space. ... We do not say that the more apples

---

[52]Jeremy S. Begbie, 'Through Music: Sound Mix', in *Beholding the Glory: Incarnation Through the Arts,* ed. by Jeremy S. Begbie (London: Darton, Longman and Todd, 2000), 138–54 (146).

there are in the basket the less room there is for God. The presence of God does not leave less room for the apples. On the contrary, it is because of the presence of God that the apples are there at all. We can say, 'There is nothing here except an apple', just *because* God is there too. The apple is not moved to one side by God. It is where it is because of God.[53]

Barth likewise draws on an underlying doctrine of divine difference in his construction of the God–world relationship to say that between 'the sovereignty of God and the freedom of the creature there is no contradiction. The freedom of its activity does not exclude but includes the fact that it is controlled by God' (*CD* III/3, 166).

For Tanner, this non-competitive logic is the agential outworking of the doctrine of creation out of nothing. Similarly, by treating providence within the doctrine of creation, Barth identifies the God who provides with the God who creates out of nothing. Because 'the control of God is transcendent' (*CD* III/3, 165), there is a radical discontinuity between divine action and human action. Divine and human agencies 'are not merely not alike, or not similar, but subjects which in their absolute antithesis cannot even be compared' (*CD* III/3, 102). Here Barth is adumbrating a Thomistic axiom: 'God is not a genus' (*ST* 1a, q.3, art.5). Whatever can be said of God, 'God is not an inhabitant of the universe, not a thing or a kind of thing',[54] who behaves as other things behave only in a bigger and better way, competing with other things of the world for a finite amount of agential space. The God who creates out of nothing is 'wholly other', as Barth said, utterly unlike any other thing; not a thing but the creator of all things, the one who stands before and beyond all things. Applying this non-competitive logic onto prayer, God's answering of prayer is sui generis, of its own kind.

It is on this basis that Barth engages the notion of the divine immutability, which classically concerns the unchangeable character of the divine will and historically has been something of a stumbling block when it comes to petitionary prayer. For Barth, God's immutability should not be uncritically identified with a theological determinism that makes a scandal of human freedom. Instead, the immutability of God functions

---

[53] Herbert McCabe, *Faith within Reason* (London: Continuum, 2007), 73–4.
[54] McCabe, *God Matters*, 6.

as part of a package of negative 'attributes' (though Barth offers important qualifications of that term) associated with the divine transcendence that seeks to clarify God's involvement in the world precisely by insisting on the difference between the agency of God and other agencies. By calling God 'immutable' Barth was not saying that God is closed to the prayers of the world but was making an iconoclastic statement about who this God 'is': God is unchangeable yet, because of God's election in Christ, God is changed by prayer. The decks are being cleared here to avoid confusing God's immutability with that of an 'immovable idol' (CD III/4, 109). Hence the series of qualifications Barth offers to explain how God's immutability does not imply 'immovability':

> God is not free and immutable in the sense that He is the prisoner
> of His own resolve and will and action, that He must always be alone
> as the Lord of all things and of all occurrence. He is not alone in
> His trinitarian being, and He is not alone in relation to creatures.
> He is free and immutable as the living God, as the God who wills to
> converse with the creature, and to allow Himself to be determined
> by it in this relationship. His sovereignty is so great that it embraces
> both the possibility, and, as it is exercised, the actuality, that the
> creature can actively be present and co-operate in His overruling
> (CD III/3, 285).

The question, then, that the doctrine of the divine immutability considers is not whether or not God can be changed by prayer, but how God can 'converse with the creature' in deep responsiveness and reciprocity. It is because God is immutable that God can accompany human agency in such a way that 'embraces', as he says, both divine sovereignty and the authenticity and spontaneity of human cooperation.

The logic of this 'double agency' complicates any attempt to draw clearly demarcated lines of agency describing where divine causality ends and creaturely causality begins. As Aquinas says, providence is not 'partly done by God, and partly by the natural agent; rather, it is wholly done by both, according to a different way' (SCG, 3.70.8). And as Barth says, 'To describe the *concursus divinus* we cannot use the mathematical picture of two parallel lines' (CD III/3, 133). 'We have to understand the activity of God and that of the creature as a single action' (CD III/3, 132). Unravelling secondary causation from its context in first causality, in this sense, does not consummate human autonomy but signals the self-defeating end of being. Augustine had a word for the construal of human freedom as total self-determination: he called it 'sin'.[55] Viewed from this non-competitive perspective, we have reached a place where we can say that the human agent perplexingly is never freer and never closer to divine providence than when in prayer.

The doctrine of providence and the 'law of prayer'

As we draw this chapter to a close, it is worth reflecting on the way the *lex orandi* has behaved in this investigation of petition and providence. On one level, the doctrine of providence (the *lex credendi*) can be seen to regulate the practice of petitionary prayer. In order for belief and practice to hang together, the practice of petition must express something of the doctrine of God. So, in the case of open theism, as discussed above, the doctrine of God shapes how petitionary prayer is understood. Because, they say, God works by persuasion rather than coercion, accounts of petitionary prayer must reflect the doctrinal commitment that God is open to change. Petition, it must follow, changes God. Or in the case of 'double agency', however petition is understood it must proceed on the basis that God's ways in the world are not on the same plane as human beings and acting. The doctrine of creation out of nothing, as Tanner demonstrates, directs a way beyond the compatibility issues that have come to frustrate the relation between providence and human freedom in modern theology to make better sense of what we are up to when we petition God. What makes divine providence and creaturely petition compatible is precisely and perplexingly their incompatibility. In either case, if the practice of petitionary prayer needs to be modified by whatever controlling doctrinal logic so be it because in order to get prayer right the doctrine of providence needs to be right first.

But on another level, it has become apparent once again, and true to form, that prayer (the *lex orandi*) radicalizes the doctrine of God. In Chapter 3 we saw that the practice of prayer daringly pushed the doctrine of God into new, uncharted areas: the experience of God in prayer made God strange, *trinitarianly* strange. In this chapter, prayer has performed a similar role in terms of the doctrine of providence. In the world of late antiquity, consumed as it was by Platonic thought, petitionary prayer

---

[55] Alistair McFadyen, *Bound to Sin: Abuse, Holocaust and the Christian Doctrine of Sin* (Cambridge: Cambridge University Press, 2000), 167.

was the stuff of fools. The cultural despisers of prayer went 'as far as the rejection of petitionary prayer altogether'.[56] But in this foolishness, the Christian wisdom of prayer is found. As we have seen with Barth, prayer changes, *really* changes the unchangeable, utterly immutable God. It is this kind of supple, and admittedly perplexing, dialectic that contemporary theologies of prayer urgently need to recover. Indeed, it could be said that it is precisely this kind of dialectic that is missing from open theism's theory of prayer. Open theism presents an easy option. It makes a great deal of sense to say that because God answers prayer God cannot be immutable. It is significantly messier, more doctrinally complex, perplexing even to say that in prayer divine immutability and human freedom increase in equal and not inverse proportion. The prerogative of the *lex orandi*, as we said in Chapter 3, is to defer to the strange.

Pushing the radicalizing logic of the *lex orandi* further, it could arguably be said that this kind of dialectic is not simply worked out doctrinally and then applied to the practice of prayer, but is itself more complicatedly the product of prayer. If nothing else, what is disclosed in the strangeness of prayer is the experience of the otherness of God. It is precisely this experience of otherness that the doctrine of creation out of nothing, to which the doctrine of providence often is closely linked, seeks to make sense of. In prayer, we encounter the God who is unfathomably unlike us.[57] To take a classical example, the experience John of the Cross sets out to explicate in *The Dark Night*, of the 'actual felt absence of consolation, the sense of God as distant, rejecting, as hostile', could be described in terms of an experience of divine difference.[58] What John experienced was not

---

[56]See Gilles Dorival, 'Modes of Prayer in the Hellenic Tradition', in *Platonic Theories of Prayer*, ed. by John Dillon and Andrei Timotin (Leiden: Brill, 2016), 26–45 (26).

[57]It is perhaps appropriate at this point to note that the practice of prayer has also been put to creative theological work in other areas of the doctrine of creation. In *The Blue Sapphire of the Mind: Notes for a Contemplative Ecology* (New York: Oxford University Press, 2012), which lifts its title from Evagrius's concept of the 'blue sapphire', Douglas Christie seeks to recover the contemplative practices of the monastic traditions to recover a deep ecological awareness lost in modern conceptions of the self. Precisely as a contemplative issue, the current ecological crisis might only be met satisfactorily by a contemplative response: in prayer we relearn our creatureliness, reshape our desires and attitudes to the rest of creation and reconnect with the land and to the non-human animals with whom we share the land. Rom. 8.22-24, with its vivid description of 'the whole of creation … groaning' with us 'while we wait for adoption', might again prove resourceful.

[58]Williams, *The Wound of Knowledge*, 170; see John of the Cross, 'The Dark Night', in *John of the Cross: Selected Writings*, ed. Kieran Kavanaugh, CWS (New York: Paulist Press, 1987),

so much God's presence as God's otherness. Similarly, as we saw in our engagement with Evagrius in Chapter 1, if the logic of imageless prayer is permitted to run its course fully, the more one prays the more one is confronted with the difficult fact that God's activity in the world, precisely as God's, is an 'imageless' mystery. This is why images of the world bear no resemblance to God's ways in the world and are better left behind in the contemplative ascent into the divine. Perhaps the doctrinal confession that God is not a thing of the world but, as the creator who creates *ex nihilo*, stands unfathomably before and beyond all things emerges out of and seeks to make sense of experiences of God in prayer such as these.

The doctrine of creation out of nothing speaks of the divine difference, the absolute otherness of God from all that is not God. But the divine difference should not be confused with God's absolute absense from the world. It should not be confused, for that matter, with anything worldly. The divine difference, as a result of the experience of God in prayer, renders any contrast with creaturely agency acutely ineffective. In the matrix of contemplation, and the kinds of practices of 'dispossession' it inculcates, prayer unsettles the steady stream of desire that dupes us into thinking that this God is 'one of us' who behaves and acts in the world as we do – only Bigger and Better. In his brief but programmatic investigation of the doctrine of creation and its relation to the practice of contemplative prayer, Brian Robinette argues precisely this. 'Contemplative prayer helps us to gain a lived sense that God is not a "Big Other" against whom we must strive in the search for identity.'[59] These contrasts – God as Bigger, Larger, More Powerful – fall away as one knuckles down to the hard slog of prayer. Contrastive pairs like otherness and immanence, presence and absence, providence and petition fall away in prayer to make space for the strangeness of what is God's. A confession of the divine difference is not, then, an end in itself but, just as the doctrine of providence is classically linked to the doctrine of creation, creation out nothing sets up a more profound sense of divine presence in the world than is otherwise possible. Precisely because God is 'other' from the world, God is *more* intimately present in the world.

162–209.

[59]Brian Robinette, 'Undergoing Something from Nothing: The Doctrine of Creation as a Contemplative Insight', in *The Practice of the Presence of God: Theology as a Way of Life*, ed. by Martin Laird and Sheelah Treflé Hidden (London: Routledge, 2017), 17–28 (19).

What is sometimes experienced in prayer as a deep sense of the absolute otherness of God could oddly and equally be described as a profound feeling of divine presence. This experience of divine presence, as we said above, does not competitively overwhelm the self: the more God is involved in the world does not mean the less space there is for human identity in the way that more oranges necessarily implies fewer apples. Prayer does not adhere to these dynamics. It has its own logic, and abides by it. In prayer, God can be experienced as fully present *and* fully other; and in prayer, the more of God does not equate to the less of me. These admittedly strange dialectics, which have their grounding in the doctrine of creation, are not easily explained or described but make most sense in the domain of prayer as they are felt in contemplation. Moreover, the dialectics inherent to the doctrine of creation remain somewhat in the abstract until belief and practice are reconnected, and that work of reconnection falls on the *lex orandi*. In this sense, the doctrine of creation *ex nihilo* displays doctrinally the 'internal logic of prayer'.[60] Once again, God's action in the world is more perplexing, a good deal odder when viewed through the lens of prayer and its peculiar interplay of divine presence and absence.

Earlier we noted the importance of Tanner's argument that competition between God and the world is a distinctively modern problem, and perhaps this is why. That the increasing competition between God and the world neatly maps onto the progressive detachment of theology from prayer that seemed to occur over the same historical period is not coincidental. If the scholarly consensus explored in Chapter 2 is anything to go by then around the same time theologians stopped seeing prayer as central to the theological task, modern theology and its 'prayer-denying' intellectual culture drifted from that which until then had been utterly fundamental: God is not the same as anything else. In losing God's otherness, the very otherness felt most acutely in prayer, God could either be sovereign or creatures free but no longer both. It might be that the intensification of opposition between God and the world and indeed the 'domestication of transcendence', to borrow a term from William Placher, that is characteristic of much of modernity can be understood as a symptom of modern theology's loss of prayer.[61]

---

[60]On this, see Susannah Ticciati, *A New Apophaticism: Augustine and the Redemption of Signs* (Leiden: Brill, 2013), 98.
[61]William C. Placher, *The Domestication of Transcendence: How Modern Thinking about God Went Wrong* (Louisville: Westmister John Knox Press, 1996).

Summary

Katherine Sonderegger, in the first volume of her systematic theology – a systematic vision richly rooted in prayer – writes this:

> All too often the 'problem of prayer' – its place within the doctrine of Divine Omnipotence – finds itself reduced to a technical debate over 'divine answer' in prayer, as though the problem dogmaticians face in this doctrine can be exhausted by a close study of the divine response to human petition. To be sure, that problem cannot be waived away with the back of a hand! But the deeper reality that prayer exemplifies … moves beyond such worries. The central reality we must face here is the *exchange*, the living *commerce* between an Almighty God and His frail creature, the one who cries out to Him day and night.[62]

To an extent, this chapter has been chasing a red herring. The point of the doctrine of providence is not to determine whether and how God answers prayer. The doctrine of providence's principal purpose is to help Christians 'read' the world as permeated by grace and to see the self as known and loved by God. Prayer is about, as Sonderegger says, '*exchange*, the living *commerce*' between us and God. It is about covenantal partnership, as Barth says, or as 'conversation', as Evagrius has it. Read through the lens of prayer, the doctrine of providence functions as a piece of practical theology to help the pray-er realize that God is not along way off, but is involved deeply in the complete course of creaturely existence. Perhaps more than any other practice of prayer, petitionary prayer builds up a sense of the profound intimacy of the divine–human relation that the doctrine of providence assumes. When we pray, we are assured that our prayers are heard and indeed answered by God. It functions to set human existence in the context of working with and alongside divine agency for the realization of the petition for the coming of the kingdom of God. As Jon Sobrino writes in a brilliant discussion of Jesus' prayer practices, 'Mere appeals to God are useless; they must embody and go hand in hand with real life practice.'[63] It is appropriate, then, that we turn in the final chapter of this book to the political dimensions of prayer in the Christian life.

---

[62]Sonderegger, *Systematic Theology – Volume 1*, 291–2.
[63]Sobrino, *Christology at the Crossroads*, 149.

CHAPTER 6
THE CHRISTIAN LIFE AND THE
POLITICS OF PRAYER

In the early church, just as the law of prayer was necessarily connected to the law of belief, the *lex orandi* was also connected to the *lex agendi* – the law of action that governed the Christian life. So, when Origen responded to those questioning whether prayer is worth the bother he says look at the effects of prayer, on the regenerated mind and on the transformed behaviour of those who pray as they live out the Christian life (*De oratione* 8.2). Prayer changes the way we see and act in the world. When Gregory of Nyssa preached on the Lord's Prayer he spoke of prayer as the 'radical call to seek justice and social involvement in the lives of the needy rather than a mental practice divorced from life. In the end, … life without prayer ultimately leads to social disorder and chaos.'[1] Prayer is social, and so it is political. And if *leitourgia* (from which we derive the word 'liturgy') can also be translated as 'public service', then as *leitourgia* prayer is not simply generative of political action, priming and driving our ways in the world, but is inherently political.[2] In fact, as Graham Ward argues, prayer 'is the *most* political act any Christian can engage in'.[3] The question, then, is not whether, but how prayer is political.

In what follows, we investigate the 'integral' relation between prayer and the Christian life as it emerges in two different configurations: first, in the strand of contemporary Christian ethics known as 'ecclesial ethics', and what might be called its 'counter-politics' of prayer; and second, in the

---

[1]Hammerling, 'Introduction: Prayer – A Simply Complicated Scholarly Problem', 17; see Gregory of Nyssa, *The Lord's Prayer*, 21–84.

[2]For a valuable articulation of the 'inherent' link between prayer and the political life, see Matthew John Paul Tan, 'Christian Prayer as Political Theory', *Politics, Religion and Ideology*, 15.3 (2014), 1–14.

[3]Graham Ward, *The Politics of Discipleship: Becoming Postmaterial Citizens* (London: SCM Press, 2009), 281 – emphasis added.

praxis-rich spirituality of Latin American liberation theologies.[4] Taking cues from feminist and liberationist theologies, the third section of this chapter returns full circle to where this book began – to the posture of kneeling – to say something about what the praying body might indicate about the political complexion of prayer. The concluding section of the book thus recommends a shift in body posture: from kneeling to being upstanding, adopting the ancient and revolutionary posture of the 'orans'.

On the integrity of prayer and politics (I): prayer in the 'ecclesial turn'

Not all would agree that the integration of prayer and politics is a good thing. Let politics be politics and prayer be prayer, some might say. Stanley Hauerwas and Samuel Wells, two of the central figures in the strand of Christian ethics known as 'ecclesial ethics', explain that for much of the modern period it was felt that the two rightly and properly belonged apart. 'For a certain view of ethics – perhaps a dominant one within the academy over recent generations – this is just as it should be. The assumption has been made (or the aspiration has been held) that ethics is something *more* than worship – that it is broader, or deeper, or more objective, or more significant.'[5] One result of the progressive detachment of ethics from

---

[4]There are, of course, many other theologians for whom prayer is inherently political. The name of Johann Baptist Metz springs immediately to mind. See Johann Baptist Metz, *Faith in History and Society: Toward a Practical Fundamental Theology* (New York: Crossroad, 2007) and Karl Rahner and Johann Baptist Metz, *The Courage to Pray* (New York: Crossroad, 1981). Dorothee Sölle (about whom, more later), like Metz, has written extensively on the political shape of prayer as part of a wider project of reinstating the political import of the Christian message. In particular, see her 'political evensong', which seeks to re-politicize the church via the liturgy, and her interpretation of Mary and Martha, in which she argues for the integration of contemplation and action. See Dorothee Sölle, *Against the Wind: Memoir of a Radical Christian* (Minneapolis: Augsburg Fortress, 1999), 37–40 and *The Window of Vulnerability: A Political Spirituality* (Minneapolis: Fortress Press, 1990), 93–6. We have mentioned in passing Thomas Merton once before, in connection with his refusal to make firm distinctions between the work of theology and prayer. We can cite him again in this context for his famous querying of a too-simple distinction between contemplation and action. For example, see the late essay 'Contemplation in a World of Action', in the book of the same title, in which Merton develops the idea in terms of a 'certain depth of disciplined experience' as 'necessary ground for fruitful action'. See Thomas Merton, *Contemplation in a World of Action* (New York: Doubleday, 1971), 158.
[5]Stanley Hauerwas and Samuel Wells, 'Christian Ethics as Informed Prayer', in *The Blackwell Companion to Christian Ethics*, ed. by Stanley Hauerwas and Samuel Wells (Oxford: Wiley-

the life of prayer, they say, is the privatization of the church's liturgy: the political nature of prayer is kept behind closed (church) doors. Christian ethics has then to look elsewhere, outside the church and its practices, for its ethical sources and frameworks. The overriding aim of ecclesial ethics is to challenge exactly this separation of ethics and worship by recovering, among other things, the politics of prayer. In this section, we draw largely from *The Blackwell Companion to Christian Ethics*, edited by Hauerwas and Wells, the architects of ecclesial ethics who at the time of writing were based at Duke Divinity School. Now in its second edition, this flagship volume represents the most sustained experiment to date in thinking through the implications of this important but not uncontroversial strand of Christian ethics.

As its name suggests, ecclesial ethics is a way of doing Christian ethics that begins *from* the church. Rather than looking outside the church, ecclesial ethics turns back to the church, to its 'story' and practices, to articulate a distinctive theological ethic. The various strands of ecclesial ethics, diverse as they are, rally around the shared claim that the church's primary political activity is to be the church: confidently, unapologetically and in sharp discontinuity from the competing politics of the world.

> Ecclesial ethics is a call for a renewal of the visibility of the church and for an emphasis on the distinctiveness of Christian ethics, particularly in relation to the person of Jesus. Such a distinctive ethics may have something to offer those beyond the church – but that is not to be taken for granted; nor is it healthy to limit reflection about what is right for Christians to what can be expected of or legislated for everybody. Ecclesial ethics is less about the decisions everyone takes and more about the distinctive character of those making the decisions.[6]

The primary emphasis on formation of character ecclesial ethics to reposition the practices of the church at the very centre of ethical, and therefore political, reflection. Ecclesial practices embody the Christian story. And as the church community performs the Christian story in its practices, character is shaped and formed. Hence Hauerwas's co-authored primer in Christianity (which betrays many of the marks of the ecclesial

---

Blackwell, 2011; 2nd edn), 3–12 (4).
[6]Samuel Wells and Ben Quash, *Introducing Christian Ethics* (Oxford: Blackwell, 2017), 113.

turn) is intentional about beginning 'not with moral problems and ethical dilemmas', but 'with prayer. First learn to say these words, learn to pray in this way, learn to have your life bent in this direction. Then you will know how to live. Christians, like Jews, know no strong distinction between our worship and our ethics. Our ethics is a by-product of our worship.'[7] When isolated from the character-forming practices of the church, Christian ethics loses its way. It becomes principally about 'what this or that historical figure said about this or that moral problem', preoccupied with the moment of 'decision' (what I am to do in this particular, often 'hard case' ethical situation) and no longer able to access the richly political resources the church has to offer.[8] What is also lost is any meaningful sense of the 'public' dimension of ecclesial practices. Prayer is confined to the private sphere, hidden from public view, kept 'out of the fabricated realm of the "political"'.[9]

When ecclesial ethics speak of 'ecclesial practices' it tends to mean 'the liturgy', by which it means the Eucharist – which for ecclesial ethics summarizes the whole Christian story.[10] Our focus in this chapter is on the one hand more specific than the liturgy: it focuses on the single liturgical practice of prayer. On the other hand, because the Eucharist will likely happen in a context set apart from the rest of community life, the focus on prayer is also broader in scope.

> [Prayer] is a truly catholic form of worship. Not only is it shared by all denominations, including non-sacramental Christian churches such as the Salvation Army, but all Christian communities in all parts of the world, from the very origins of the church have also practiced it. Moreover, … it is not restricted to occasions of gathered worship but can be said in all times and in all places.[11]

---

[7]William H. Willimon and Stanley Hauerwas, *Lord, Teach Us: Lord's Prayer and the Christian Life* (Nashville: Abingdon Press, 1996), 47.

[8]Stanley Hauerwas and Samuel Wells, 'Why Christian Ethics was Invented', in *The Blackwell Companion to Christian Ethics*, ed. by Stanley Hauerwas and Samuel Wells (Oxford: Blackwell, 2011; 2nd edn), 28–38 (34).

[9]William T. Cavanaugh, *Torture and the Eucharist: Theology, Politics, and the Body of Christ* (Oxford: Blackwell, 1998), 9.

[10]*The Blackwell Companion to Christian Ethics* is structured around the four fold movement of the liturgy: meeting, listening, communing and sending.

[11]Luke Bretherton, *Christianity and Contemporary Politics: The Conditions and Possibilities of Faithful Witness* (Chichester: Wiley-Blackwell, 2010), 144–5.

Because prayer happens as much on the streets and in everyday life as inside the church, prayer is better positioned to resist the 'sectarian temptation' that many worry is the risk of Hauerwas's project.[12] Yet in agreement with the approach of ecclesial ethics, we might say that there is something about prayer that does provide a deep and distinctive formation. And indeed, there is something for us to learn from the definition of practices offered by ecclesial ethics. Ecclesial ethics is fundamentally concerned with *communal* practices, for community is the place where we learn the language (what to say) and the significance (what all this means) of the liturgy, whereas the practice of prayer is at constant risk of appearing 'individualistic'. Prayer can very easily become about my experience of God, my desires, my wants, my needs. If the political import of prayer is to be recovered then we need to be clear from the start that prayer is more than the sum of my self-propelled action, even my personal experience of incorporation into the life of the divine. The prayer 'Abba! Father!' is 'much more than merely personal – this is the cry of whole cosmos itself'.[13]

But what makes prayer political? Ecclesial ethics would want to avoid the idea that prayer becomes political as it is 'applied' to our political lives. The assumption here is that to be 'political' means to leave the (by implication, non-political) realm of worship. For ecclesial ethics, prayer *is* political. In and of itself, prayer enacts something political. More specifically, according to Luke Bretherton, 'in prayer we discover alternative repertories or scripts for envisioning the world to those of the dominant hegemony'.[14] This sums up well the basic claim of ecclesial ethics: the church and its practices, based as they are on the unique politics of God, contain a 'counter-politics' to the identity-constituting beliefs of surrounding culture that pull against the ethical agent's distinctively Christian formation.

To give a concrete example, Bretherton considers prayer's role in shaping an alternative politic of hospitality in the contemporary political context of

---

[12]The critique often levied against Hauerwas is that his ecclesial approach to Christian ethics ends up promoting a withdrawal from the world into the cloisters of the church; a charge, it should be said, that he persistently refutes. For his refutation, see Stanley Hauerwas, 'A Christian Critique of Christian America', in *The Hauerwas Reader*, ed. by John Berkman and Michael Cartwright (Durham: Duke University Press, 2001), 459–80 (477) and for coverage of the debate, see Nigel Biggar, 'Is Stanley Hauerwas Sectarian?' in *Faithfulness and Fortitude: In Conversation with the Theological Ethics of Stanley Hauerwas*, ed. by Mark Nation and Samuel Wells (Edinburgh: T&T Clark, 2000), 142–60.

[13]Willimon and Hauerwas, *Lord, Teach Us*, 38.

[14]Bretherton, *Christianity and Contemporary Politics*, 145.

the refugee crisis. He says, 'In the Lord's Prayer, the church as a body hears and performs the world as a place that is open to the transformative love of God and the neighbor.'[15] In prayer, the pray-er penitentially unlearns the practices of self-interest shaped by the dominant hegemony and relearns a participatory communion with God and the neighbour shaped by the radical hospitality of the liturgy. A narrative of inclusion and embrace forged in prayer replaces a narrative of exclusion and rejection encountered outside of the context of prayer. Thus 'prayer', Bretherton concludes, is 'preparation for meeting refugees as neighbors. For in prayer we move from the local and particular to the universal, we turn out from self to God and thence to neighbor.'[16] In this example the asymmetrical ordering that is characteristic of ecclesial ethics is at work: the way we relate to God in prayer becomes second nature (it becomes habitual) thereby ordering the way we relate to the other as neighbour. The more one prays, the more one inhabits this alternative Christian ethic of hospitality until it becomes habitual.

There are many other ways that the 'alternative grammar' of prayer, practised over time and in community, enacts a new kind of counter-politics to the world. The remainder of this section takes the petitions of the Lord's Prayer as a guide and draws them into dialogue with theologians who self-identify as ecclesial ethicists and others, like Bretherton, who broadly sympathize with the project, to explore more fully what happens to prayer when caught up in the ecclesial turn.

Praying 'Our Father' in the broad context of ecclesial ethics comes to be about disrupting the central axis of modern politics: the individualism of the political subject. To the self-as-individual assumed by much of modern politics,[17] the self uncovered in prayer is a person-in-relation. When we gather in prayer, Willimon and Hauerwas say, with those 'who ought – by the world's standards – to be perfect strangers', we 'call them "sister", "brother"', and call upon God as *Our* Father.[18] Similarly, the politics of class that bind communities to unjust social divisions are overcome by the possibility of a new form of solidarity bound to the familial relations of

---

[15]Ibid.

[16]Ibid., 144.

[17]This theme is explored outside of ecclesial ethics in Tan, 'Christian Prayer as Political Theory', 1–14.

[18]Willimon and Hauerwas, *Lord, Teach Us*, 32.

being the children of God. Bretherton terms the new relations conceived in prayer 'doxological relations'.[19]

Related to this, by praying 'your kingdom come' the pray-er learns and lives an alternative script for conceiving the bounded territory of the nation state. The petition generates a new kind of citizenship, established in Christ, of solidarity, equality and inclusion. Those who have been or are still excluded from community life under existing notions of citizenship are now included – women, children, the elderly, those living in poverty, those who have been criminalized – regardless of gender, sexuality, nationality, age, history and ethnicity. In those gathered to pray, Emmanuel Katongole argues, 'a new unique community is being constituted in a manner that both challenges, and offers a concrete alternative to, the story of race and racism'.[20] Prayer both rejects the narrative of exclusion drawn by the nation state and binds one another, friend and stranger, into an alternative common social space sustained by the grace of God.

Praying 'on earth as in heaven', as a practice of receptivity, is transgressive of the underpinning ideals of capitalism and its construction of market-led ultimate goods: labour, time and productivity. To modernity's commodification of time, and the conflation of labour with 'productivity', prayer (as *labora*) is an 'absolute waste of time', as McCabe would say.[21] It is 'hopelessly uneconomical' in the context of the working week, which perhaps is why prayer looks so utterly out of place in the modern workplace.[22] It does not produce anything useful. The point of prayer, as we said at the beginning of this book, is prayer itself – and nothing more. Encoded into prayer, then, is an alternative logic that refuses to bow to the powers of the capitalist agenda and throws a spanner into its mechanisms of production. The more we inhabit the peculiar time and rhythm of prayer, what the church calls the 'daily office', the more 'this

---

[19]Luke Bretherton, 'Class, Hierarchy, and Christian Social Order', in *The Blackwell Companion to Christian Ethics*, ed. by Stanley Hauerwas and Samuel Wells (Oxford: Blackwell, 2011; 2nd edn), 329–43 (342).

[20]Emmanuel Katongole, 'Greeting: Beyond Racial Reconciliation', in *The Blackwell Companion to Christian Ethics*, ed. by Stanley Hauerwas and Samuel Wells (Oxford: Blackwell, 2011; 2nd edn), 70–83 (75).

[21]McCabe, *God Matters*, 224.

[22]Michael Hanby, 'Interceding: Giving Grief to Management', in *The Blackwell Companion to Christian Ethics*, ed. by Stanley Hauerwas and Samuel Wells (Oxford: Blackwell, 2011; 2nd edn), 251–63 (262).

prayer claims our time, the more profoundly we are shaped by it'.[23] As a consequence, 'liturgy forms the worshiping soul and Christians, as Christ's body, in quite a different shape than does the discipline of the market'.[24] The dominant culture of management techniques is similarly 'challenged by Christian practices of intercession, which are in some ways their opposite because they are about acknowledging our dependency and limits, and are not just about the efficient use of power. … In management terms, intercession (like worship more generally) is profligate with time – and in particular it "squanders" time on those who often seem least likely to have a productive future – the disabled, the elderly, the dying.'[25] To those deemed outsiders by (or redundant to) the capitalist agenda, prayer says you are a part of a politics of a different kind: the kingdom of God on earth as it is in heaven.

Praying 'give us today our daily bread' offers an alternative script for determining our deepest desires and needs. It is about what happens when the political imagination is weaned off the idols that keep desire tethered to the promise of self-sufficiency and freed to structure one's life around prayer's alternative logic of dependency on another. It is to acknowledge that to be human means to be a 'burden' on God and others for the basics of life.[26] By petitioning God for our daily bread, bread is broken open and exposed for what it is: daily gift. In praying the fourth petition our behaviour towards the consumption and production of food is reordered and starts to change. Our training in consumerism is undone. From praying for our daily bread, we start to source, buy, eat and consume resources differently.

Relatedly, the kind of agential logic that we have said underpins prayer overflows into what Kathryn Tanner describes as an 'economy of grace', in which society is reordered around the graced themes of non-competitive relations (first experienced in prayer), freely given gifts, unconditional giving and an economy of reception. All this stands in stark comparison with the competitive logic of the capitalist, monetary economy.[27] The notion of scarce resources – on which much of political life turns – is unseated

---

[23]Hanby, 'Interceding', 259.

[24]Ibid.

[25]Wells and Quash, *Introducing Christian Ethics*, 261.

[26]Stanley Hauerwas and Brian Brock, *Beginnings: Interrogating Hauerwas*, ed. by Kevin Hagarden (London: T&T Clark, 2017), 99.

[27]See Kathryn Tanner, *Economy of Grace* (Minneapolis: Augsburg Press, 2005).

according to the sheer generosity of God's abundant 'gift' of prayer, which gives without exclusion.

Praying to 'forgive us our sins as we forgive those who sin against us' shapes alternative understandings of juridical punishment along the lines John Berkman has explored.[28] Recognizing both the individual and corporate dimension of both sin and reconciliation, the petition of forgiveness 'is in stark contrast to much of what is currently thought to justify punishment'.[29] Under the alternative of prayer, '"capital punishment" undermines the realization of the reformative or restorative aspects of the practice of reconciliation, to which any theologically defensible form of retributive justice must be ordered'.[30]

Finally, and more generally, as we pray without words and listen to God in the silence of prayer we learn to listen well to others. As Ward writes, 'For it is only in prayer that the discipline of listening is developed.'[31] Without prayer the voice of the other falls on closed ears.

In each of the cases above, prayer presents alternative social arrangements, priorities and orientations to the kind of formation prized by consumerist desire that dominates contemporary scripts. In this sense, the most political thing the church can do is to be (and thus 'practice' as) the church – to hold firm to its core beliefs and practices as peaceable alternatives to the status quo. 'Instead of being motives or causes for effective social work on the part of Christian people, these liturgies *are* our effective social work. For if the church *is* rather than *has* a social ethic, these actions are our most important social witness.'[32] Prayer, on this basis, is 'thus the most significantly political – the most "ethical" – thing that Christians do'.[33]

The ecclesial turn makes one thing paradigmatically clear: prayer is political. It not only generates political action but is itself political. The internal logic of prayer ripples out from the church into the world and restructures common life as it moves. The same claim of prayer is made by

---

[28]John Berkman, 'Being Reconciled; Penitence, Punishment, and Worship', in *The Blackwell Companion to Christian Ethics*, ed. by Stanley Hauerwas and Samuel Wells (Oxford: Blackwell, 2011; 2nd edn), 97–111.

[29]Berkman, 'Being Reconciled', 107.

[30]Ibid., 108.

[31]Ward, *The Politics of Discipleship*, 280.

[32]Stanley Hauerwas, *The Peaceable Kingdom: A Primer in Christian Ethics* (Notre Dame: University of Notre Dame Press, 1984), 108.

[33]Hauerwas and Wells, 'Christian Ethics as Informed Prayer', 6.

Latin American liberation theologies – but for different reasons. Whereas ecclesial ethics sees in the practices of the church an alternative politics to those that govern the structures of the world, liberation theology, the subject of the next section, sees in prayer a means of challenging those structures and overcoming them.

On the integrity of prayer and politics (II): *'Contemplativus in liberatione'*

It is the contention of this book that theology is possible not despite of prayer but because of it. Previous chapters have cited ancient examples of the integrity of prayer and theology (found supremely in Evagrius) and detected various 'turns to prayer' in contemporary theological discourse that renew the systematic task with the ancient rigour of prayer. At the beginning of this book, we said that although much of modern systematic theology would benefit from this kind of *ressourcement*, there are some branches of Christian theology that are already embodying the kind of theological integrity to which this book is reaching. An example of this habitable Christian wisdom about the theological importance of prayer is Latin American liberation theologies.

As the Jesuit theologian Jon Sobrino explains, liberation theology has always treated prayer 'not merely [as] a dimension of theology, … [but as] an integral dimension of the whole of theology'.[34] The experience of prayer, and more specifically the doxology of those living in poverty, is understood as the indispensable source of all theological work. Because of this, Gustavo Gutiérrez, the Peruvian priest and theologian, has lamented the methodological divisions in modern theology that pull theology and prayer in opposite directions and concludes, in agreement with Sobrino, that prayer 'constitutes a permanent dimension of theology'.[35]

Just as theology is inseparable from prayer, another characteristic mark of liberation theology is its understanding of the inseparability of prayer and political action. It should come as no surprise, then, that some of the most influential shapers of liberation theology have written on the intersection of spirituality, politics and theology. Some of the most important contributions

---

[34]Sobrino, *Spirituality of Liberation*, 49.
[35]Gustavo Gutiérrez, *A Theology of Liberation: History, Politics, and Salvation* (London: SCM Press, 1985), 5; for his account of the breakdown of the relation, see Gutiérrez, *We Drink from Our Own Wells*, 35–8.

include the justly celebrated *We Drink from Our Own Wells: The Spiritual Journey of a People* by Gutiérrez and Sobrino's *Spirituality of Liberation: Toward Political Holiness*.[36] Although the theme of prayer features in these now classic expressions of liberation spirituality, Gutiérrez and Sobrino are chiefly concerned with articulating the political shape of the general category of 'spirituality'. The Brazilian Franciscan Leonardo Boff, however, attends more specifically to the political particularities of prayer and for this reason is our main dialogue partner. In what follows, we draw from two key texts of Boff's on prayer. The first is an article on prayer and politics in which he coins the phrase that we have taken as the subtitle of this section: '*contemplativus in liberatione*' (which can be translated as 'contemplation in liberative activity'); the second, is his petition-by-petition interpretation of the Lord's Prayer: *The Lord's Prayer: The Prayer of Integral Liberation*, which to date is the single complete investigation of the Lord's Prayer from the perspective of liberation theology.[37]

It seems helpful to begin by examining what Boff and others mean by the term '*contemplativus in liberatione*'. Pedro Casaldáliga and José María Vigil offer this explanation of its background:

> Earlier movements of spirituality experienced God primarily in the desert (anchorites, the desert Fathers ...), in prayer and monastic work (*ora et labora*, prayer and work), in study and prayer for preaching (*contemptla aliss tradiere*, passing on what is contemplated to others), in apostolic activity (*contemplativus in actione*, contemplatives in action). We believed that today, in creative fidelity to this living tradition, we are called to live contemplation in liberative activity (*contemplativus in liberatione*), decoding surroundings made up of grace and sin, light and shade, justice and injustice, peace and violence, discovering in this historical process of liberation the presence of the Wind that blows where it will, uncovering and trying to build salvation history in the one history, finding salvation in liberation.[38]

---

[36]For a compilation of his spiritual writings, see Gustavo Gutiérrez, *Spiritual Writings* (Maryknoll: Orbis Books, 2011).

[37]Leonardo Boff, 'Spirituality and Politics', in *Liberation Theology: An Introductory Reader*, ed. by Curt Cadorette, Marie Giblin, Marilyn J. Legge and Mary H. Snyder (Maryknoll: Orbis Books, 1992), 236–43 – note that despite its title the focus of the article is very much prayer; and *The Lord's Prayer: A Prayer of Integral Liberation* (Maryknoll: Orbis Books, 1983).

[38]Pedro Casaldáliga and José María Vigil, *The Spirituality of Liberation* (Kent: Burns and Oats, 1994), 103.

To be more specific, there are least three core features of what it means to be 'called to live contemplation in liberative activity'.

First, in a basic sense, 'to live contemplation in liberative activity' is about being committed to liberation, and therefore to those living in poverty. As we said above, a defining mark of theologies of liberation is that they take as their point of dogmatic departure the prayer experiences of the poor and the oppressed. For in the cries and laments of the poor is to be heard the voice of the divine. 'God has burst upon our continent like an erupting volcano,' Boff writes, and 'has prioritized the poor as the sacrament of this self-communication.'[39] As the Brazilian liberation theologian and activist Cláudio Carvalhaes puts it: 'The law of prayer (*lex orandi*) is born out of the law of life (*lex vivendi*), the daily life of the poor, as it gives shape to their joys, concerns, and beliefs (*lex credendi*). The task for theologians is to attend to the *lex orandi-vivendi-credendi* of the poor, listening to their prayers and learning with them how to properly pray.'[40] Immediately we can identify a difference in approach between ecclesial ethics and the way of liberation theology. In our earlier canvassing of ecclesial ethics, we saw that prayer is recognized as a political practice because, for example, it is in listening to God in prayer that we learn to listen to the other. Within ecclesial ethics there is a ripple effect that moves from the church, and its distinctive set of counter-political practices, and into the world. 'It is only in prayer that the discipline of listening is developed,' we have heard Ward say.[41] The formative practices of church shape the people of the church who in turn shape the world for the coming of the kingdom. But for Boff, liberation theology moves in precisely the opposite direction. Liberation theology says that it is in listening to others in the world (which means the world of poverty) that we learn to listen well to God in prayer.

Second, 'to live contemplation in liberative activity' is about being committed to the praxis of liberation. For Boff, it is not enough simply to verbalize prayer. It is not enough to think that contemplation is 'reserved to the sacred space of prayer or to the sacrosanct enclosure of church

---

[39] Boff, 'Spirituality and Politics', 237.
[40] Cláudio Carvalhaes, 'Praying with the World at Heart', *Dialog: A Journal of Theology*, 52.4 (2013), 313–20 (315).
[41] Ward, *The Politics of Discipleship*, 280. I owe this point to Al Barrett and his work on 'radically receptive' ecclesiology and missional practice.

or monastery'.[42] In order for prayer to count as true prayer, it must go hand in hand with concrete praxis and more specifically with the kind of 'political, social, historical, transforming action' that revolts against the violent structures of oppression operating in the world today.[43] We will say something about what the praxis of liberation, inspired by prayer, looks like shortly. Third, 'to live contemplation in liberative activity' is about understanding prayer and liberation as mutually informing. Andrew Prevot says it well when he writes that 'doxology can be true in the fullest sense only if it is liberative, and liberation can be true in the fullest sense only if it is doxological'.[44] This means seeing the practice of contemplative prayer as integral to the struggle for liberation. Prayer is the 'wellspring of strength' for liberation without which the struggle for a just world is unsustainable.[45] But it also means seeing liberation as integral to the practice of prayer. We cannot pray as we ought as long as the structures of injustice remain oppressively intact. The liberation of the oppressed, in short, is a doxological as well as a social priority.

Boff is aware that he is outlining a 'new way' of seeking contemplation.[46] Within the politically charged arena of liberation spirituality, contemplative prayer is less the receptive practice of waiting on the divine and more the active response against structures of injustice undertaken in active solidarity with those suffering under the conditions of poverty. Here 'passion for God … [and] passion for the impoverished' deepen in equal proportion.[47] 'The God who says to us in our prayer, "Come," also says in the same prayer, "Go." The God who calls us into the divine union also calls us to make a commitment to liberation.'[48] While Evagrius, and countless other spiritual writers, drew on the metaphor of ascent to describe the movement of prayer, Sobrino turns this staple trope on its head by speaking of prayer in terms of a 'descent'. This descent, he says, is about 'going down into the world of poverty and the poor, a stripping of the self; the ascesis necessary in order to denounce and unmask oppression, to have historical patience and solidarity

---

[42]Boff, 'Spirituality and Politics', 240.
[43]Ibid., 238.
[44]Prevot, *Thinking Prayer*, 221. My engagement with liberation theology owes a great deal to Prevot who explores the politics of liberation in *Thinking Prayer*, 218–79.
[45]Boff, 'Spirituality and Politics', 240.
[46]Ibid., 237.
[47]Ibid., 238.
[48]Ibid., 240.

with the poor'.[49] The 'place of God' of which Evagrius spoke is discovered in the slums, the place of poverty. 'One is truly with the Lord when among the poor, when committed to struggle against poverty,' Boff writes echoing many other liberation theologians.[50] This new perspective on contemplation problematizes the ease with which we have appealed in this book to the category of 'dispossession' to describe the shape of contemplative prayer. What does it mean to speak of 'dispossession' for those who are in many ways already dispossessed? There is an unnamed privilege associated with being able to be dispossessed in the first place, to kneel in prayer, to close one's eyes in contemplation, to intercede for the 'other' who stands in need. Gutiérrez worries that the term can become a way for 'those in power ... to make the dispossessed an easier prey for the machinery of oppression'.[51] In place of a contemplative dispossession of the already dispossessed and disenfranchised, liberation theology speaks confidently of the political and spiritual 'empowerment' that comes through prayer.

Turning now to his commentary on the petitions of the Lord's Prayer, Boff reads the Lord's Prayer as a prayer of 'integral liberation'. For Boff, Jesus teaches us to pray for liberation. The disciples asked Jesus to teach them to pray, and he said 'pray, then, like this' and prayed a prayer of liberation. True prayer means praying for the coming of the kingdom in which the poor are liberated, the hungry are fed, the vulnerable are protected from the evil of structures of poverty and so on. In another sense, the Lord's Prayer functions for Boff as a diagnostic tool. The structures of poverty become utterly and starkly incompatible with the structures of peace articulated in the Lord's Prayer. The more one prays the petitions of the Lord's Prayer, the starker this dissonance appears and the more alive the question of social justice becomes. And the dissonance between the way of the Lord's Prayer and the way of the world's mechanisms of oppression is overcome not through prayer alone but, as we have said, through the 'synthesis' of prayer and liberative praxis.[52] Additionally, the Lord's Prayer provides what might be called 'contemplative scripts' that further help to articulate the struggle

---

[49]Sobrino, *Spirituality of Liberation*, 82.
[50]Leonardo Boff, 'The Need for Political Saints: From a Spirituality of Liberation to the Practice of Liberation', *CrossCurrents*, 30.4 (1980), 369–76 (373).
[51]Gutiérrez, *We Drink from Our Own Wells*, 10.
[52]Boff, 'Spirituality and Politics', 238.

for liberation, the problem of poverty itself and the hope of liberation. Let us consider these 'contemplative scripts' in a bit more detail.

As part of the broader process of 'conscientization', the Lord's Prayer provides the poor with a 'new awareness of their situation of exploitation and marginalization' and therefore with a framework to articulate the struggle for liberation.[53] Gutiérrez develops this notion in dialogue with the Carmelite spirituality of John of the Cross, whom we have encountered more than once in this book. But for Gutiérrez, John's 'dark night of the soul' becomes the 'dark night of injustice'. John's experience of abandonment by God is extended to include the agony of poverty, the experience of solitude and affliction, the sense of profound injustice. The language of prayer, and particularly the prayers of lament that echo throughout the long nights of poverty, gives voice to those who have been silenced by the gag of oppression. And just as John's experience of abandonment was articulated in terms of a paradoxical presence of God, so too Gutiérrez reiterates that foundation stone of liberation theology: the experience of the poor is an experience of the divine. 'John of the Cross speaks of the "frightful night" through which one must pass, but he also says that the desert is "the more delightful, savorous, and loving, the deeper, vaster, and more solitary it is." Such is the twofold experience of the Christian who wishes to be faithful to the Lord even in the blackest depths of "the dark night of injustice".'[54] Thus the 'song of the poor', as Gutiérrez says, is at once a song of lament and of hope in liberation from oppression.

The Lord's Prayer also provides a language, or a 'script', for speaking of the problem of poverty itself. For Boff, the Lord's Prayer even gives it a name: it is the 'evil' from which we petition God to be delivered. In his analysis of the final petition of the Lord's Prayer Boff has no apparent interest in speaking metaphysically of evil, interpreting evil through established frameworks (whether Augustinian, Irenaean or other), 'spiritualizing' evil or describing evil in the abstract. Not once does he vocalize theodicy questions. His chief concern is with narrating the embodiment of evil in the 'historical sense'.[55] That is, as evil is experienced in the actual lives of the poor and the oppressed.

---

[53]Gutiérrez, *We Drink from Our Own Wells*, 21. For further analysis of the process of 'conscientization', see Ada María Isasi-Díaz, 'Solidarity: Love of Neighbor in the 1980s', in *Lift Every Voice: Constructing Christian Theologies from the Underside*, ed. by Susan Brooks Thistlethwaite and Mary Potter Engel (San Francisco: Harper and Row, 1990), 31–40.
[54]Gutiérrez, *We Drink from Our Own Wells*, 131.
[55]Boff, *The Lord's Prayer*, 111.

His aim is 'to get beyond the pictures [of evil] and, so far as possible, to identify the realities and ideas pertaining to them'.[56] One of the realities of evil, for Boff, is that evil is the work of human hands, 'created by the sins of human beings'.[57] Sins do 'not die with the persons who committed them but have been perpetuated by actions that survived their perpetuates in the form of institutions, prejudices, moral and legal standards, and social customs'.[58] Evil is a structural, 'dynamic thing' that constructs a self-perpetuating system of oppression. Under these conditions,

> the evil one who offends God and debases human persons appears in the form of a collective selfishness embodied in an elitist, exclusivist social system that has no solidarity with the great multitudes of the poor. He has a name; he is the Capitalism of private property and the Capitalism of the state. In the name of money, privileges, and the reinforcement of governmental structures he holds men and women in terror. Many of them are imprisoned, tortured, and killed. Two-thirds of the population are held prisoner under the yoke of a legion of demons: hunger, sickness, disintegration of the family, and a shortage of housing, schools, and hospitals. This evil one has his ways of tempting; he slyly creeps into our minds and makes the heart insensitive to those structural inequities that he has created.[59]

An immediately striking feature of Boff's interpretation of the final petition of the Lord's Prayer is its sheer descriptiveness. He spends more time on this petition than any other, explicating the historical reality of evil in vivid, descriptive detail. This is for a very deliberate reason. By naming the injustice of poverty for what it is: evil, the pray-er's attention is refocused from questions around the origins of evil and onto a politics of resistance. By knowing what evil looks like, the pray-er is empowered to act against it. Through an ethic of concrete liberative praxis, the destructive powers of the world are acted against to bring about what Boff calls a 'global, grass-roots restructuring of reality'.[60] Key to Boff's

---

[56]Ibid., 115.
[57]Ibid., 111.
[58]Ibid., 111–12.
[59]Ibid., 119.
[60]Ibid., 16.

interpretation of the Lord's Prayer, then, is that whatever else evil is, it cannot claim the final word. The final word is hope. And for Boff hope means prayer; active hope that out of 'the heart of darkness bursts a liberating ray of light'.[61]

Finally, then, the Lord's Prayer articulates an agenda for structural change. 'In this respect, one can rightly interpret the Our Father as a series of supplications which, taken together, express a desire for everything that the fullness of liberation entails.'[62] Or as Gutiérrez says, the 'song of hope' sung in prayer is a song for a new society in which 'the poor, the afflicted, and those who have been denied justice are the primary benefactors'.[63] The Lord's Prayer also has a name for this new society: it is the kingdom of God. 'To pray "Thy kingdom come" is to activate the most radical hopes of the heart, so that it will not succumb to the continual brutality of the present absurdities that occur at the personal and social level.'[64]

In a moment, we will explore the theme of the body as it relates to the politics of prayer. For Gutiérrez, the bodily posture of prayer is not that of kneeling, which is too passive a posture for the *contemplativus in liberatione*. Instead it is that of 'walking'.[65] For Boff, this means walking in solidarity with the poor and the oppressed and along 'the paths that lead us toward justice, truth, and fellowship, overcoming the forces of selfishness and oppressive power'.[66] Carvalhaes goes one step further. The body is most political not when walking alongside others but when released into dance!

> To the *ora et labora* we must add *et saltare*, which is the Latin word for dance. Unless we learn to dance we would not be able to pray and work. By dancing we learn to live the fullness of life, for there is no life or religion without dancing. … To pray, work, and dance. And back again. To pray, work, and dance with our knees, hands, and our hips as well. Tear added to the sweat of our bodies: prayers in the flesh as much as in our hearts and souls; fully committed to God, to the

---

[61]Ibid., 23.

[62]Prevot, *Thinking Prayer*, 242.

[63]Boff, *The Lord's Prayer*, 15.

[64]Ibid., 61.

[65]For his account of 'walking according to the Spirit', see Gutiérrez, *We Drink from Our Own Wells*, 54–71.

[66]Boff, *The Lord's Prayer*, 119.

well-being of our sisters and brothers, especially to the poor, to the world, and to the joy of life.[67]

In either dancing or walking, the principal liberative praxis that resists oppression and stands directly counter to the solitude experienced in the 'long nights of injustice' is that of solidarity – of standing together, walking alongside, dancing and, above all, being with the oppressed. For Gutiérrez, 'it is impossible to separate solidarity with the poor and prayer'.[68]

The mention of solidarity as a praxis of liberation relates to the work of Ada María Isasi-Díaz, the Cuban activist theologian, and her rich restructuring of the second petition of the Lord's Prayer according to a liberationist logic.[69] The solidarity, which Isasi-Díaz argues must replace charity as an appropriate response to the structures of injustice and oppression, is what it means to pray for the coming of God's *kin*-dom. 'The word kin-dom makes it clear that when the fullness of God becomes a day-to-day reality in the world at large, we will all be sisters and brothers – kin to each other.'[70] The implementation of the kin-dom of God involves strategies of solidarity to establish the centrality of mutuality and a new order of relationships 'opposed to any and all forms of domination'.[71] Intriguingly, Isasi-Díaz identifies the first stage of the unfolding of the kin-dom as 'dialogue', conversation with the oppressed – which, as we have said, is a category of prayer.

Boff concludes his treatment of the Lord's Prayer with the word 'Amen'. The 'Amen', he says, is a political statement for it is offered in doxological gratitude to the God who is irrevocably committed to the liberation of the poor. Liberation is not simply a matter of social justice. Set to prayer and sealed by the Amen of the Lord's Prayer, liberation is nothing other than God's 'ultimate intention'.[72] Of course, within liberation theology there is little place for 'bystanders; otherwise the kingdom of God would be unhuman and an imposition'.[73] But liberation, ultimately, is divine gift. To

---

[67]Carvalhaes, 'Praying with World at Heart', 319–20.

[68]Gutiérrez, *A Theology of Liberation*, xxxii.

[69]Isasi-Díaz, 'Solidarity: Love of Neighbor in the 1980s', 32. See also, Ada María Isasi-Díaz, 'Kin-dom of God: A Mujerista Proposal', in *In Our Own Voices – Latino/a Renditions of Theology*, ed. by Benjamin Valentín (Maryknoll: Orbis Books, 2010), 171–90.

[70]Isasi Díaz, 'Solidarity: Love of Neighbor in the 1980s', 33.

[71]Ibid., 35.

[72]Boff, *The Lord's Prayer*, 54.

[73]Ibid., 15.

pray the Lord's Prayer is to pray for decisive divine action that 'God the Father [may] intervene, eschatologically, and put an end to what violates the divine order'.[74] In establishing justice, alleviating poverty, revolting against the structures of disorder, the pray-er is incorporated into the coming of God's kin-dom.

Prayer and the politically 'charged' body

In this third section of the chapter, we change tack somewhat. We have discussed two different configurations of the prayer–politics relation and have arrived at the same conclusion: prayer is inherently political. The focus now turns to the intersection of prayer, the political and the body (and its posture). In dialogue with Melanie May and Graham Ward, we see that the body is receptive to the political as well as actively political. From there we attempt to diversify the body's role in prayer working from Gabriel Bunge's classic study on prayer in the early church and the more recent work by James K. A. Smith on the intersection of the body, prayer and formation. Borrowing insights from feminist and post colonial theology, we discuss how the body at prayer, left unchecked, also has the potential to (de-)form us in ways that perpetuate rather than subvert political relations of dominance and power, and in ways that several of the thinkers already discussed in this book might not fully see. A response: to recover, via Dorothee Sölle's doxologically charged linking of prayer and resistance, the revolutionary posture of the 'orans', which we discuss in the concluding section of this book.

Melanie May's *A Body Knows* presents a vivid turn to the body as the site of theological engagement.[75] For May, who is writing from a feminist perspective and in the genre of 'doxological theopoetics',[76] speaks of the realization that we do not merely have bodies, we *are* our bodies. As such, knowing (and praying) happens through our bodies as well as our minds. The 'body is an active knower', she says.[77] In one of the poetic interludes that structures *A Body Knows*, curiously entitled 'Standing', May speaks of

---

[74]Ibid., 43.

[75]Melanie A. May, *A Body Knows: A Theopoetics of Death and Resurrection* (New York: Continuum, 1995).

[76]'To say theology is doxology also affirms my experience and women's experience to be a source of theological knowledge', May, *A Body Knows*, 23.

[77]May, *A Body Knows*, 102.

the ways images of the word 'inhabit me', 'words move through me', events 'stumble into memory'.[78] The body, for May, is 'a textured web of physical, mental, social, affective, sexual connections with persons and places and times'.[79] As such, the body is political. Albeit from a different perspective, in *The Politics of Discipleship*, Graham Ward presents a similarly subtle theory of how the political realm implicates the knowing body. For Ward, the relation between prayer and politics, and indeed between the private and the public, hinges on the body. The body, he says, cannot be imperviously sealed off from the world. In agreement with May's premise that the body is an 'active knower', he argues that 'the body has a knowledge into which we have only oblique insight'.[80] As much as we are caught up in the world, the world – 'that vast network of relationships of which we are part, the complex corporations onto which our bodies are mapped' – is caught up in us. Because of this 'deep inhabitation' of the world, the world's events and narratives are absorbed into the body. And as they move through us we are shaped and formed by them, often in unarticulated ways and at a level below the fully conscious. The world's events reach us through various sources including 'the media, present circumstances, the hearing of other people's stories'. However they reach us, the 'political' is imprinted biologically on our, as it were, now 'charged' praying bodies as they are 'filtered through our ensouled flesh'.[81] The political does not simply come and go but leaves a permanent impression on our bodies.

When it comes to prayer and its agential complexities, the events of the world that have been absorbed through the porosity of 'our ensouled flesh' are not only presented to God as petition and intercession but absorbed into the life of the divine in a more complicatedly bodily way. So Ward:

> That miraculous escape we read about in the newspaper that bring us joy, those gangs of teenage girls and boys congregating at the corner shop late at night that cause us to fear and move us to pity, those scenes of carnage on the news in the wake of a bomb attack that cause us to shudder at the violence and grieve with the shell-shocked – all

---

[78]Ibid., 93–6.
[79]Ibid., 103.
[80]Ward, *The Politics of Discipleship*, 281.
[81]Ibid., 281.

these events pass through us and change us. And as we dwell in Christ and he in us, then they pass through Christ also. This is what I mean by praying: that deep inhabitation of the world, its flesh and its spirit, that stirs a contemplation and a reading of the signs of the times that is more profound than we can ever apprehend or appreciate.[82]

In a sense, Ward is narrating an outworking of the kind of Christology of prayer we encountered in previous chapters. If prayer is more than an exclusively individual action – that which I do before God – but an 'incorporation' into the corporate prayer of the praying Son in the fullest sense of that word, then incorporation concerns not just my prayer being swept up into the life of the divine but the sweeping up of my body into the body of Christ. Add to the embodied nature of prayer Ward's notion that the body is animated by the world and its events, what is being complicated here is the idea that prayer can be an exclusively private affair. Whenever I go into my room and shut the door and pray in secret (Mt. 6.6), my praying body has been already shaped by the world and its narratives in such a way that these events cannot but flow through my praying body into my petitions and therefore into the praying body of Christ. May's and Ward's theories of the political saturating the praying body and therefore the body of Christ support this chapter's overall claim that prayer is not simply political but as an embodied practice is *inherently* political – unavoidably receptive of the political. The praying body, as we are now to explore in the final pages of this book, is both receptive of the political and also actively political.

In his classic study on prayer in the patristic tradition, Gabriel Bunge uncovers a rich theology of the body that once characterized both the Eastern and Western traditions of Christian prayer.[83] In an illustrated manuscript of the 'Nine Ways of Prayer of Saint Dominic', which is one of the founding documents of Dominican spirituality, Bunge sees prayer being expressed physically in a variety of ways: 'deep bows, prostrations (*venia*), genuflections, standing, praying with hands outstretched in the form of a cross, meditating while sitting'.[84] In what becomes a persuasive corpus of liturgical, biblical and textual evidence, he proceeds to demonstrate that the

---

[82]Ibid.
[83]Gabriel Bunge, *Earthen Vessels: The Practice of Personal Prayer According to the Patristic Tradition* (San Francisco: Ignatius Press, 1996).
[84]Bunge, *Earthen Vessels*, 139.

body played a central role in the shaping of the pray-er's orientation to God and the world. Body posture, direction, breathing, the use of a rosary and incense to stimulate the bodily senses of smell and touch, the movement of the lips, the laying of hands, the rhythm of words, gesturing, bowing, hand-clasping, the closing of eyes, the signing of oneself, the finger gestures of the benediction (which, of course, encode particular Christological perspectives), the denial of the body through abstinence of all sorts – all of these practices of prayer implicate the body and form the self before God.[85] I said above that he 'uncovers' these traditions of the body because for Bunge 'this entire wealth of bodily expressions has been lost bit by bit … until in modern times, only kneeling remained'.[86] The pray-er has become a 'sedentary creature' bound to the now near-ubiquitous pew-kneeler.[87]

In a different way, James K. A. Smith shares Bunge's lament about the ambiguity much of Western Christianity has towards the body. In his 'cultural liturgies' project, which consists of three volumes,[88] Smith suggests that contemporary Christianity, and especially a particular strand of Reformed Protestantism, has too uncritically absorbed a hyper-rationalistic picture of the human sketched by modernity. These strands 'tend to foster an overly intellectualist account of what it means to be or to become Christian'.[89] The result is that Christian formation has become largely an 'intellectual project' preoccupied with the acquisition of information that reduces human beings

---

[85]On body posture and prayer in the early church, see Andrew Louth, 'The Body in Western Catholic Christianity', in *Religion and the Body*, ed. by Sarah Coakley (Cambridge: Cambridge University Press, 1997), 111–30 and Reidar Hvalvik, 'Nonverbal Aspects of Early Christian Prayer and the Question of Identity', in *Early Christian Prayer and Identity Formation*, ed. by Reidar Hvalvik and Karl Olav Sandnes (Tübingen: Mohr Siebeck, 2014), 57–90.

[86]Bunge, *Earthen Vessels*, 139.

[87]Ibid., 141. According to McGuckin, the liturgical culture developed somewhat differently in the Eastern Orthodox tradition in which it remains 'important to synthesize the physical acts with the sentiment of the intellectual worship contained within the words: and both (that is the physical reverence and the intellectual prayer) are themselves important only in so far as they serve to bring the human soul into a conscious attentiveness towards God. Orthodox spiritual traditions are generally geared to this threefold understanding of the task of prayer: the harmonization into a single sounded note of the body, the mind, and the heart (*kardia*)'. See McGuckin, *The Orthodox Church*, 349.

[88]James K. A. Smith, *Desiring the Kingdom: Worship, Worldview, and Cultural Formation* (Grand Rapids: Baker Academic, 2009), *Imagining the Kingdom: How Worship Works* (Grand Rapids: Baker Academic, 2013) and *Awaiting the King: Reforming Public Theology* (Grand Rapids: Baker Academic, 2017). The final instalment, which has direct links with this chapter's themes, was published after the completion of this manuscript.

[89]Smith, *Desiring the Kingdom*, 42.

to little more that 'brains on sticks': 'mammoth heads that dwarf an almost non-existent body'.[90] To counter this trajectory within modern Protestantism, Smith seeks to 're-think thinking' in such a way that unhooks Protestant theology's fixation on epistemic matters – such as doctrines, ideas and beliefs – by bulking up the pray-er with a renewed emphasis on the body. Understood not as Cartesian 'thinking things' but as embodied 'praying animals', Smith charts a course back to a fuller bodied understanding of prayer.

> We are not primarily *homo rationale* or *homo faber* or *homo eco-nomicus*; we are not even generically *homo religiosis*. We are more concretely *homo liturgicus*; humans are those animals that are religious animals not because we are primarily believing animals but because we are liturgical animals – embodied, practicing creatures.[91]

Christian formation, which is his central concern, 'is not didactic; it is kinaesthetic', in which the movement of the body is intrinsically related to the ways we think, pray and act in the world.[92]

Generally speaking, for Smith, liturgy falls into one of two categories: good liturgy and bad liturgy. In a captivating rhetorical flourish that begins his cultural liturgies project, drawing on Charles Taylor's notion of the 'social imaginary', Smith offers a description of the shopping mall as an environment of 'rival liturgy', saturated by formative counter-rituals to those of Christianity.[93] These so-called 'secular liturgies', 'too, recruit our unconscious drives and desires through embodied stories that fuel our imagination and thus ultimately govern our action'.[94] In either the church or the shopping mall, we are formed kinaesthetically; through the things we do as much as the things we believe in. Not unlike ecclesial ethics, true formation is the reserve of the liturgy of the church alone.

As discussed above, a similar reclaiming of prayer as an embodied practice can be found in much of Christian feminist writings on prayer.[95] However, unlike Smith, in addition to the formative potential of the

---

90 Ibid., 43.
91 Ibid., 40.
92 Ibid., 96.
93 Ibid., 19–27.
94 Smith, *Imagining the Kingdom*, 15.
95 For an introduction to feminist interpretations of the body, see Lisa Isherwood and Elizabeth Stuart, *Introducing Body Theology* (Sheffield: Sheffield Academic Press, 1998).

embodied practice of prayer many feminist theologians (such as Marjorie Procter-Smith and Nicola Slee) and postcolonial liberation theologians (such as Cláudio Carvalhaes and Nancy Pereira Cardoso) are also alert to the possibility that prayer can be de-formative as well as formative.

Exploring the complex intersection of politics, body posture, gender, ethnicity and prayer in the context of North America, Lauren F. Winner argues that our knowledge of kneeling is 'formed by countless cultural cues, biblical and extra-biblical'.[96] One such cultural narrative, she continues, is that of the 'kneeling slave'. As Winner narrates, on the rare occasions that black slaves have been the subjects of public art, they were invariably depicted on their knees. The enslaved took on the posture of kneeling in reverent submission before their slave masters. As the anti-slavery movement gathered pace, the depiction of the kneeling slave remained unchanged. For example, an iconic image of the abolition movement was by Josiah Wedgwood, which was adopted by the American Anti-Slave Society and depicts a black slave petitioning a white slave master for his freedom – on his knees. Although the relationship of master and slave has shifted to 'giver and receiver', the unmodified body posture continued to conceal a paradigm of power that subordinates one to the mastery of the other. Even post-abolition, the posture of the now-liberated slave continued to be that of kneeling. In Thomas Ball's 1867 'Freedman's Memorial', in Washington, DC, which was commissioned to mark the abolition of slavery passed by Congress just a few years earlier, a black man, shirtless and shackled, is knelt at the feet of Abraham Lincoln, the 'Great Emancipator'. The kneeling man is no longer posturing obedience to the superiority of the white master or petitioning him for his freedom, but the oppressive power dynamics are nevertheless maintained: the freed slave is immortalized in a position of eternal thanksgiving to the benevolent slave master-come-liberator for the gift of his new-found freedom. Here, the body has been scripted into a violent quasi-liturgy precisely through the liturgy of prayer. The practice of kneeling looks, as Winner concludes, rather different when situated in this history and context.

---

[96]Lauren F. Winner, 'Interceding: Standing, Kneeling, and Gender', in *The Blackwell Companion to Christian Ethics*, ed. by Stanley Hauerwas and Samuel Wells (Oxford: Blackwell, 2011; 2nd edn), 264–76 (274).

The postcolonial theologian Cláudio Carvalhaes is also attentive to the de-formative potential of the posture of kneeling. He says this of kneeling in prayer in the context of Latin America:

> Our evangelisation in Latin America, both from Roman Catholicism and Protestantism, taught us to be careful, suspicious and even hateful of our bodies. We learned that there was a proper (read civilised) way of moving, believing, acting, singing, looking, gesturing and touching within the worshiping space and in the world. Silently, the Christian evangelization targeted first of all, our knees. They were taken from our own control and educated by priests and pastors to behave accordingly. Put in another way, through a powerful and continuous catechesis, we were/are taught that we were/are to learn three main things: to control our knees, to internalise a proper code of behaviour and to be happy with it.[97]

Being forced into kneeling in prayer in this way, he explains, is a mechanism of control. The liturgy functions to train pray-ers in particular habits of body that repeat, even learn by rote, the oppressive structures of power that are geared up to maintain the colonialist logic of the status quo. Drawing on the Brazilian theologian Nancy Pereira Cardoso, Carvalhaes thus calls for the 'de-evangelization of our knees'. By this Cardoso speaks of liberation by reclaiming ownership of one's knees, of kneeling but only 'when it is time and willed' as part of an ethic of empowerment rather than enforcement.[98]

Feminist theologians have long argued that the posture of the body in prayer is dangerously, though subtly, effective in forming our relationship with others as well as our relationship with God. In her seminal study of feminist prayer, *Praying with Our Eyes Open*, Marjorie Procter-Smith argues that

> Some of the conventional postures of prayer, especially the posture of the heads bowed and eyes closed (to say nothing of prostrations),

---

[97]Cláudio Carvalhaes, '"Gimme de kneebone bent": Liturgics, Dance, Resistance and a Hermeneutics of the Knees', *Studies in World Christianity*, 14.1 (2008), 1–18 (2).

[98]See Nancy Pereira Cardoso, 'De-Evangelization of the Knees: Epistemology, Osteoporosis, and Affliction', in *Liturgy in Postcolonial Perspectives: Only One is Holy*, ed. by Cláudio Carvalhaes (New York: Palgrave, 2015), 119–23 (122).

duplicates the posture of submission before an absolute monarch. Bowing and kneeling have their roots and echoes in the power relationships between master and servant or slave. To bow or prostrate one's self is to make one's self completely physically vulnerable, unable to defend one's self. To bow the head is to bare the neck, inviting the ruler before whom one bows to cut off one's head if it pleases him to do so.[99]

The gestural vocabulary of prayer (bowing before the almighty, praying with closed eyes and indeed kneeling) may, therefore, conceal troubling 'relations of dominance', which are similarly problematic in their maintenance of potentially oppressive protocols of submission as the names that are used to call upon God in prayer – Father, King, Lord, Almighty.[100] Left unchecked, as Procter-Smith argues, a posture signalling dependent vulnerability, such as kneeling before God, could valorize relations of dominance and submission before others in the political realm.

Through these examples, it is possible that a liturgy of violence could be perpetuated precisely by prayer and its posturing in a way that reinforces social divisions, re-inscribes the very narratives of oppression it seeks to oppose and debilitates the pray-er's ability to resist coercive structures of power. Kneeling in prayer might well be part of the problem not the solution to the injustices of the world.

A theology undertaken on the knees might also be interpreted as a form of political passivity, of keeping eyes closed to unjust structures of power. In her poem, 'Praying Like a Woman', Nicola Slee recommends instead that

> we must pray with our eyes wide open, refusing to see nothing of what is hidden, secret – blatant lies.
> We must pray with heads held high refusing to bow in obsequiousness to prelate, priest, or pope.[101]

---

[99]See Marjorie Procter-Smith, *Praying with Our Eyes Open: Engendering Feminist Liturgical Prayer* (Nashville: Abingdon Press, 1995), 78.

[100]Procter-Smith, *Praying with Our Eyes Open*, 71–88. According to Musa W. Dube Shomanah, gender research has revealed that 'the metaphorical use of male language to represent realms of power does in fact reinforce the exclusion and subordination of women in society'. See Dube Shomanah, 'Praying the Lord's Prayer in a Global Economic Era', 444.

[101]Nicola Slee, *Praying Like a Woman* (London: SPCK, 2004), 1.

The mention of prayer's refusal to acquiesce 'blatant lies' has similarities with Dorothee Sölle's account of prayer as an exercise in 'truth-telling'. The language of prayer and particularly that of lament, Sölle says, is the 'language that at least says what the situation is'.[102] Prayer describes the shape of reality for what it is without recourse to falsehood or sugar-coating. But for Sölle truth-telling is only one aspect of the politics of prayer. The Christian life of prayer is also about 'resistance'. As Slee implies in her poem and Cardoso through her notion of the 'de-evangelization' of the knees, just as the body has been a site of oppression the praying body can also be a site of resistance to those forces of oppression.

Summary: Recovering the 'orans'

In dialogue with the writings of Evagrius, this book began by commending the posture of kneeling. The true theologian is the one who kneels in prayer, Evagrius would say; or would he? If we accept Bunge's thesis, literally speaking, the posture of kneeling in prayer is not one Evagrius would have immediately recognized. 'The only bodily posture Evagrius appears to know of at all in his famous *153 Chapters on Prayer* is "standing during prayer"'.[103] Evagrius stood for prayer not out of choice but out of fear for his safety.

> 91. If you are intent on praying, make yourself ready for the demons' onslaughts and boldly endure their lashes – for they will come upon you suddenly like ferocious animals and harm your whole body.

> 106. It has come to our attention that the Evil One so attacked one of the saints who was praying that, as he was raising his hands, the Evil One changed into the shape of a lion. Raising his front paws upright, he sank his claws into both of the fighter's thighs from either side and did not let go until he lowered his hands – but he never lowered them even a little before he had completed his usual prayers.

---

[102]Dorothee Sölle, *Suffering* (Philadelphia: Fortress Press, 1975), 74. See the appendix for further resources on the theology and practice of lament.
[103]Bunge, *Earthen Vessels*, 144.

For Evagrius it was vitally important that he remained upstanding, with eyes peeled and ready to face head-on whatever demonic attacks might come his way. The prowling demons sought to divert him from this position of reverent standing before God. They weighed down his mind and therefore his body with the thoughts, images and concepts that dragged him to his knees into a posture of vulnerability and ultimately away from the ascent of prayer. Kneeling was a mark of enforced subscription into a system of (demonic) oppression, whereas standing was about resistance.

Although we began on our knees, we end this book with an exhortation to shift the posture of our praying bodies from kneeling to standing and then to walking (and dancing!) in solidarity with others. We end, in other words, with a call to adopt the ancient, revolutionary attitude of the 'orans'. As recorded in early Christian iconography (in the Catacombs of Priscilla in Rome, for example) and elsewhere in early patristic literature (in treatises on prayer by Clement, Origen, Tertullian and Cyprian, for example), Evagrius was not alone in being upstanding as he prayed. The standing posture of the orans seemed to be the dominant prayer posture in early Christian practices of prayer. Canon 20 issued by the Council of Nicaea in the fourth century went so far as to decree against kneeling on Sundays and through the season of the Pentecost because it was felt to be too inconsistent with resurrection joy. 'To the intent that all things may be uniformly observed everywhere (in every parish), it seems good to the holy Synod that prayer be made to God standing.'[104] In the orans, the pray-er would be at 'full stretch': upstanding, face-to-face with God, even on tip-toes, with hands extended, palms outwards and 'eyes wide open' (as described in 1 Tim. 2.8 and elsewhere). As Origen writes, here the pray-er 'should not doubt that the position with the hands outstretched and the eyes lifted up is to be preferred before all others, because it bears in prayer the image of characteristics befitting the soul and applies it to the body' (*De oratione* 31.2).[105]

---

[104]'The First Ecumenical Council', in *The Seven Ecumenical Councils*, NPNF, series 2, vol. 14 (Edinburgh: T&T Clark, 1980), 1–56 (42). Even by the time Origen was writing, there was also an established practice that determined the directional position of the orans – to the orient, the East. Apart from during the confessing of sins, the pray-er must 'stand at prayer' and face East, 'since this is a symbolic expression of the soul's looking for the rising of the true Light' (*De oratione* 32).

[105]In a curious turn of liturgical events, a version of the orans has been rediscovered within contemporary Pentecostal traditions of prayer that – and not without political import –

But more than posturing delight in resurrection hope, the orans is a political posture. The Roman Catacombs were used as the meeting places for early Christians to pray and worship in safety from persecution. The early Christian pray-er would wear on the body a posture that stands up to institutions of oppression, injustice and persecution. Many centuries later, Dorothee Sölle, who combined prayer and the political in a unique way, is helpfully explicit in describing prayer in terms of active, political 'resistance' to oppression. Putting her body on the line, she took to the streets to protest nuclear armament, environmental destruction, patriarchal domination, capitalism, totalitarianism, militarism and many other issues that frustrate the flourishing of common life. In the introduction to *The Silent Cry: Mysticism and Resistance*, Sölle reflects on the choice between mysticism and resistance that had troubled her throughout her life. The choice between the two, she now realizes, is a false one: her lifelong political struggle was her prayer.[106] Elsewhere, she says that 'to pray is to revolt. The one who prays is not saying, that's the way it is and that's that! The one who prays is saying, that's the way it is, but it should not be that way!'[107] This emphasis on revolt against disorder sets Sölle's theory of prayer in a decidedly active and unavoidably political trajectory. In addition to public practices of protest, as discussed in her other writings, prayer's resistance takes shape in the doxological practices of sharing, patience, community-building and other everyday practices that work towards the peace of the kingdom/kin-dom of God. Interestingly, in his ethics of reconciliation, Barth also invokes the language of 'revolt' to describe the attitude of prayer. 'Christians are summoned', he writes, 'to a simultaneous and related revolt, and therefore to entry into a conflict' (*ChrL*, 206). And 'the decisive action of their revolt against disorder, which, correctly understood, includes within itself all others, is their calling upon God in the second petition of the Lord's Prayer: "Thy kingdom come"' (*ChrL*, 212). The German word, typically rendered in English as 'revolt', can translate more literally as 'up-stand' (*Aufstand*). The revolutionary posture of 'revolt' and resistance, for both

---

likewise 'wear with the body' the joy that is becoming to the soul.
[106]Dorothee Sölle, *The Silent Cry: Mysticism and Resistance* (Minneapolis: Fortress Press, 2001), 5–6.
[107]Dorothee Sölle, *Not Just Yes and Amen: Christians with a Cause* (Philadelphia: Fortress Press, 1985), 40.

Sölle and Barth, is nothing less than the ancient upstanding posture of the orans.

Prayer is revolutionary. As Christians stand before God in prayer, they stand for the flourishing of common life. This means standing against violence and injustice, standing up to the demons of oppression, standing alongside those who otherwise walk the precarious path of oppression alone and asking others to stand alongside them in times of need. And it is here, in this revolutionary posture of standing, that we end this book on prayer.

APPENDIX:
ANNOTATED BIBLIOGRAPHY OF SELECTED SOURCES ON PRAYER

The purpose of this bibliography is to provide an annotated list of sources on prayer. The subheadings do not generally follow the chapters of the book, although there are some exceptions. The list is selective, and makes no claims to be comprehensive. It restricts itself to English speaking scholarship and, when possible, to theological treatments of prayer rather than collections of prayers themselves – although again, there are some exceptions.

A history of prayer

Where available, I have suggested volumes in the Classics of Western Spirituality series, as these volumes present the material in an accessible form and often with substantive introductions.

ACW	Ancient Christian Writers
ANF	The Ante-Nicene Fathers: Translations of the Writings of the Fathers down to A.D. 325
CWS	Classics of Western Spirituality
FC	Fathers of the Church
LCC	Library of Christian Classics
NPNF	A Select Library of the Nicene and Post-Nicene Fathers of the Christian Church

Primary text readers

For one of the few primary text readers on prayer, see Matthew Levering (ed.), *On Prayer and Contemplation: Classic and Contemporary Texts*

(Oxford: Rowman & Littlefield, 2005), which includes extracts from patristic, medieval and some modern (Roman Catholic) theologians.

Evagrius of Ponticus

For primary texts relevant to theme of prayer in the Evagrian corpus, see Augustine Casiday (trans.), *Evagrius Ponticus* (London: Routledge, 2006); Robert E. Sinkewicz (trans.), *Evagrius of Pontus: The Greek Ascetic Corpus* (Oxford: Oxford University Press, 2006); John Bamberger (trans.), *Evagrius Ponticus: The Praktikos; Chapters on Prayer* (Kalamazoo: Cistercian Publications, 1981), each of which contains helpful introductions to the texts and to the figure of Evagrius. In terms of secondary literature, there is now more than ever. Augustine Casiday, *Reconstructing the Theology of Evagrius Ponticus: Beyond Heresy* (Cambridge: Cambridge University Press, 2013) is a detailed analysis of the historical reception of Evagrius's writings, focusing in particular on the charges of heresy. Other secondary literature investigating Evagrius's understanding of prayer and its relation to theology include William Harmless, *Desert Christians: An Introduction to the Literature of Early Monasticism* (Oxford: Oxford University Press, 2006), 311–71, which features a useful glossary of Evagrian terminology; Luke Dysinger, *Psalmody and Prayer in the Writings of Evagrius Ponticus* (Oxford: Oxford University Press, 2005); David W. Fagerberg, 'Prayer as Theology', in *A History of Prayer: The First to the Fifteenth Century*, ed. by Roy Hammerling (Leiden: Brill, 2008), 117–36; and Columba Stewart, 'Imageless Prayer and the Theological Vision of Evagrius Ponticus', in *A History of Prayer: The First to the Fifteenth Century*, ed. by Roy Hammerling (Leiden: Brill, 2008), 137–66.

Early Christianity

In the Greek tradition, one of the earliest treatments of Christian prayer is by Clement of Alexandria and occurs in Book 7 of his 'Stromata', see *Hermes, Tatian, Athenagoras, Theophilus, and Clement of Alexandria*, ANF, vol. 2 (Edinburgh: T&T Clark, 1994), 532–37. Origen's influential document on prayer, which (unlike many other ante-Nicene treatments) goes beyond an interpretation of the Lord's Prayer, is published as 'On Prayer', in *Origen: An Exhortation to Martyrdom, Prayer and Selected Works*, trans. by Rowan E. Greer, CWS (New York: Paulist Press, 1979), 41–79. Gregory of Nyssa's homilies on the Lord's Prayer, notable for their reference to the 'spirit petition', are published as *The Lord's Prayer, The Beatitudes*, ACW, vol. 18 (London: Longman, 1954), 21–84. John Chrysostom also preached on the subject, see *Saint Chrysostom: Homilies on the Gospel of Saint Matthew*, NPNF, series 1, vol. 10 (Edinburgh: T&T Clark, 1980), 134–7. In his commentary on the Gospel of Luke can be found Cyril of Alexandria's interpretation of the Lord's Prayer, *St Cyril of Alexandria: Commentary on the Gospel of Luke* (Oxford: Oxford University Press, 1859), 297–320. And Maximus the Confessor's commentary on the Lord's Prayer is published as 'Commentary on the Our Father', in *Maximus Confessor: Selected Writings*, trans. by George C. Berthold, CWS (New York: Paulist Press, 1985), 99–125. Prayer also received considerable attention in the Latin tradition. For Tertullian's famous treatise, see 'On Prayer', in *Tertullian*, ANF, vol. 3 (Edinburgh: T&T Clark, 1997), 681–91. This early document on prayer consists of a full interpretation of the Lord's Prayer followed by instruction on several diverse issues relating to prayer – from whether Christians should wash their hands before prayer, to the role of women in prayer and the use of the psalms in public prayer. Although Cyprian of Carthage follows Tertullian in many ways, Cyprian's later treatise on prayer is addressed directly to catechumens, 'On the Lord's Prayer (Treatise IV)', in *Hippolytus, Cyprian, Caius, Novatian*, ANF, vol. 5 (Edinburgh: T&T Clark, 1995), 447–57. Ambrose writes on prayer within his treatise on the sacraments published in *Theological and Dogmatic Works*, FC, vol. 44 (Washington: The Catholic University of America Press, 1963), 314–8, 322–8. Prayer features in several of Augustine's writings, including his famed commentary on the Sermon on the Mount and in particular 'Sermon 6' in *St Augustine: Sermon on the Mount, Harmony of the Gospels, Homilies on the Gospels*, NPNF, series 1, vol. 6 (Edinburgh: T&T Clark, 1996), 274–89. He also explicates the petitions of the Lord's Prayer in the context of his anti-Pelagian writing, see 'On the Gift of Perseverance', in *St Augustine: Writings against the Pelagians*, NPNF, series 1, vol. 5 (Edinburgh: T&T Clark, 1997), 525–9; 'Enchiridion', in *St Augustine: On the Holy Trinity, Doctrinal Treatises, Moral Treatises*, NPNF, series 1, vol. 3 (Edinburgh: T&T Clark, 1997), 237–76; 'On Nature and Grace', in *St Augustine: Writings against the Pelagians*, 121–51; and in 'Letter 130 to Proba', in *St Augustine: Prolegomena, Life and Work, Confessions, Letters*, NPNF, series 1, vol. 1 (Edinburgh: T&T Clark, 2001), 459–69. Two further contributions from the Latin tradition include Peter Chrysologus's series of homilies on the Lord's Prayer (Sermons 67–72), published in *St Peter Chrysologus: Sermons - Volume 2*, FC, vol. 17 (Washington: The Catholic University of America Press, 2004), 274–96 and Caesarius of Arles's sermons 35: On the Lord's Prayer and Love of Enemies', in *Caesarius of Arles: Sermons - Volume 1*, FC, vol. 31 (Washington: The Catholic University of America Press, 1956), 171–5; 'Sermon 144: On Prayer, Repentance, and the Ninivites', 'Sermon 147: An Explanation of the Lord's Prayer'; and 'Sermon 148: On Prayer', in *Caesarius of Arles: Sermons - Volume 2*, FC, vol. 47 (Washington: The Catholic University of America Press, 1964), 300–3, 311–15, 315–19. John Cassian, sitting as he does between the East and West, helps to mediate some of the insights on prayer from the Eastern to the Western Christian world. This mediation comes in the form of 'conversations' (or 'conferences') among pray-ers on the topic of prayer. The ninth and tenth concern the Lord's Prayer, see John Cassian, *Conferences*, trans. by Colm Luibheid, CWS (New York: Paulist Press, 1985), 101–24 and 125–40.

Medieval

For a collection of Anselm of Canterbury's game-changing approach to prayer, see *The Prayers and Meditations of St Anselm with the Proslogion*, ed. by Benedicta Ward (London: Penguin, 1973). For a collection of prayers by Hildegard of Bingen, see *Prayers of Hildegard of Bingen* (Cincinnati: St Anthony Messenger Press, 2003). The key texts in Thomas include *Summa contra Gentiles: Book III - Providence, Part 2* (Notre Dame: University of Notre Dame, 1975), chapters 95–6; his analysis of prayer in 3a, q.21 of volume 50 and the major treatment of prayer in 2a2æ, q.83 of volume of 39 of *Summa Theologiae* (London: Blackfriars, 1964). An extensive collection of Thomas's writings on prayer, including commentaries and lectures on the topic, can be found in *Albert and Thomas: Selected Writings*, ed. by Simon Tugwell, CWS (New York: Paulist Press, 1998), 363–523. For the founding documents on prayer in the Dominican tradition, see 'The Nine Ways of Prayer of St Dominic' and 'William Peraldus' Sermon on Prayer', in *Early Dominicans: Selected Writings*, ed by Simon Tugwell, CWS (New York: Paulist Press, 1982), 94–103 and 163–79 respectively. Julian of Norwich's theology of prayer is integrated in her 'Showings', see Julian of Norwich, *Showings*, trans. by Edmund Colledge and James Walsh, CWS (New York: Paulist Press, 1978); and Catherine of Siena's 'The Dialogue' is shot through with prayer, see *The Dialogue*, trans. by Suzanne Noffke (New York: Paulist Press, 1980).

Reformation

In terms of the Lutheran strand of the Reformation tradition, Martin Luther wrote a great deal on prayer, connecting prayer often with the theme of 'obedience'. For an extensive collection of his writings on prayer see *Luther's Spirituality*, ed. and trans. by Philip D. W. Krey and Peter D. S. Krey, CWS (New York: Paulist Press, 2007), 183–251, which includes commentaries, extracts from the Large Catechism, the Lord's Prayer and of course his famous letter about 'A Simple Way to Pray' to his barber, Peter. Philip Melanchthon's treatise 'On Prayer' and a selection of his own prayers can be found in *Early Protestant Spirituality*, ed. and trans. by Scott H. Hendrix, CWS (New York: Paulist Press, 2009), 210–20. In terms of the Reformed tradition, see Heinrich Bullinger, 'Of Adoring or Worshipping, of Invocating or Calling Upon, and of Serving the Only, Living, True, and Everlasting God', in *The Decades of H. Bullinger* (Cambridge: Cambridge University Press, 1851). John Calvin famously devoted one of the longest chapters of the *Institutes* (Book III, Chapter 20) to the subject of prayer, which includes a profound analysis of the theme of mediation and an exploration of the Lord's Prayer, and can be found here: *Institutes of the Christian Religion*, LCC (Louisville: Westminster John Knox Press, 1960), 850–920. The chapter has been republished in abbreviated form as part of the CWS volume alongside some of Calvin's own prayers, *John Calvin: Writings on Pastoral Piety*, ed. and trans. by Elsie Anne McKee, CWS (New York: Paulist Press, 2001), 195–245. For John Knox's investigation of prayer, see 'A Treatise on Prayer, or, a Confession, and Declaration of Prayers', in *Selected Writings of John Knox: Public Epistles, Treatises, and Expositions to the Year 1559*, ed. by Kevin Reed (Dallas: Presbyterian Heritage Publications, 1995). In terms of the Roman Catholic tradition of this period, Teresa of Ávila's heady writings on prayer can be found in *The Way of Perfection* in *The Collected Works of St Teresa of Ávila – Volume 2* (Washington: Institute of Carmelite Studies, 1980), 76–186 – there she devotes some sixteen chapters to an exploration of the Lord's Prayer (chapters 27–42). The writings of John of the Cross on his experience of prayer can be found in *John of the Cross: Selected Writings*, ed. by Kieran Kavanaugh, CWS (New York: Paulist Press, 1987) and Ignatius of Loyola's *Spiritual Exercises*, the founding document of Ignatian prayer, is published in *Ignatius of Loyola: The Spiritual Exercises and Selected Works*, ed. by George E. Ganss, CWS (New York: Paulist Press, 1991).

APPENDIX

Early modern

Richard Hooker has a series of chapters on prayer in *Of the Laws of Ecclesiastical Polity* published as *The Folger Library Edition of the Works of Richard Hooker - Volume 2* (London: The Belknap Press of Harvard University Press, 1977), Book 5. Jacob Arminius, founder of the Arminianism movement bearing name, explores prayer in his treatise 'On Prayer' published in *The Works of James Arminius - Volume 2* (Grand Rapids: Baker Books House, 1986). For a Puritan perspective, see Richard Baxter, 'Chapter 23', in *The Practical Works of Richard Baxter - Volume 4* (London: Paternoster, 1847), 483–92. One of the few book-length treatments of prayer from this period is Matthew Henry, *A Method of Prayer* published in *The Complete Works of Matthew Henry: Treatises, Sermons, and Tracts - Volume 2* (Grand Rapids: Baker Books, 1979). George Whitefield's sermon on 1 Thess. 5.25 is also worthy of note, see 'Intercession', in *Sermons of George Whitefield* (Peabody: Hendrickson, 2009), 292–300.

Modern theology

For Kant's critique of prayer as 'monological', see *Religion within the Boundaries of Mere Reason and Other Writings* (Cambridge: Cambridge University Press, 1998), 182–8. Ludwig Feuerbach takes a similar stance in *The Essence of Christianity* (Cambridge: Cambridge University Press, 2011), 119–24. For Kierkegaard on prayer, T. H. Croxall's *Meditations from Kierkegaard* (London: James Nisbet and Company Ltd., 1955) features a collection of prayers as well as homilies and meditations on the subject. One year later, P. Le Fèvre published another collection of Kierkegaard's prayers as *The Prayers of Kierkegaard* (Chicago: University of Chicago Press, 1956). There is a section on prayer in Schleiermacher's *Glaubenslehre*: 'Prayer in the Name of Christ', in *The Christian Faith* (London: T&T Clark, 1999), 668–75, and two further sermons on the topic published as: 'On Prayer in Jesus' Name' (Sermon on Jn 16.23), in *Servant of the Word: Selected Sermons of Friedrich Schleiermacher* (Philadelphia: Fortress Press, 1987), 169–80 and 'The Power of Prayer in Relation to Outward Circumstances' (Sermon on Mt. 26.36-46), in *Selected Sermons of Schleiermacher* (New York: Funk and Wagnalls, 1890), 38–51. The key sections on prayer in Karl Barth's writings can be found in his doctrine of providence - *Church Dogmatics*, III/3 (Edinburgh: T&T Clark, 1960), 265–88; in his ethics of creation - *Church Dogmatics*, III/4 (Edinburgh: T&T Clark, 1961), III/4, 87–115; in his ethics of reconciliation, which is structured around the petitions of the Lord's Prayer and under the controlling concept of invocation and published as *The Christian Life: Church Dogmatics IV/4 - Lecture Fragments* (Edinburgh: T&T Clark, 1981); in chapter 14 of *Evangelical Theology: An Introduction* (London: Collins, 1965), in which he discusses the relation between prayer and theology; and in his late 1940s seminars on the Lord's Prayer in dialogue with Reformation thought, *Prayer: 50th Anniversary Edition* (Louisville: Westminster John Knox Press, 2002). Paul Tillich discusses the 'paradox of prayer' in dialogue with Romans 8 in *The New Being: As Love, Freedom, Fulfilment* (London: SCM, 1956), 135–8. One of Emil Brunner's significant engagements with prayer occurs in his *Dogmatics - Volume 3: The Christian Doctrine of the Church, Faith and the Consummation* (Philadelphia: Westminster Press, 1962), 324–35. *The Content of Faith: The Best of Karl Rahner's Theological Writings* (New York: Crossroads, 1992) has several of Karl Rahner's writings on the theme of prayer and in particular two essays on the practice of petitionary prayer – see, *The Content of Faith*, 513–18 and 518–20; additionally, Rahner has an important essay entitled 'Some Theses on Prayer "In the Name of the Church"', in *Theological Investigations - Volume 5: Later Writings* (London: Darton, Longman and Todd, 1966), 419–38. Rahner also produced more popular works on prayer, including *The Need and the Blessing of Prayer* (Collegeville: The Liturgical Press, 1997) and *Happiness through Prayer* (Dublin: Clonmore and Reynolds, 1958). Yves Congar considers prayer in *Jesus Christ* (London: Geoffrey Chapman, 1968), 86–106. Hans Urs von Balthasar has a book-length treatment of prayer published as *Prayer* (San Francisco: Ignatius Press, 1986). He also explored prayer in 'Beyond Contemplation and Action?', in *Explorations in Theology - Volume 4: Spirit and Institution* (San Francisco: Ignatius Press, 1995), 302–7; 'Toward a Theology of Christian Prayer', *Communio*, 12 (1985), 245–57 and 'Christian Prayer', *Communio*, 5 (1978), 15–22. In addition, see 'The Victory of Prayer', in *Glory of the Lord - Volume 2: Studies in Theological Style - Clerical Styles* (Edinburgh: T&T Clark, 1984); 253–9; 'Spirit and Prayer', in *Theo-Logic: Theological Logical Theory - Volume 3: The Spirit of Truth* (San Francisco: Ignatius Press, 2005), 369–76; and 'Theology and Sanctity', in *Explorations in Theology - Volume 1: The Word Made Flesh* (San Francisco: Ignatius Press, 1989), 181–209. Adrienne von Speyr's strangely mystical and Christologically disciplined meditation on prayer, from which Balthasar readily draws, is published as *The World of Prayer* (San Francisco: Ignatius Press, 1985). Dietrich Bonhoeffer is another prayer-soaked theologian of the twentieth century. His handbook on prayer written for the Finkenwalde community, *Life Together*, is a classic example of the 'integrity' of prayer and theology, published as *Life Together, Prayerbook of the Bible*, Dietrich Bonhoeffer Works 5 (Minneapolis: Fortress Press, 2005). The *Prayerbook of the Bible* is also a significant work on prayer and reveals the centrality of the psalmody in Bonhoeffer's prayer life. Simone Weil includes a short but punchy petition-by-petition interpretation of the Lord's Prayer in *Waiting for God* (New York: G. P. Putnam's Sons, 1951). Thomas Merton wrote extensively on prayer. A mere sample from his vast theological output on the topic includes *Seeds of Contemplation* (New York: New Directions, 1949); *New Seeds of Contemplation* (London: Burns and Oates, 1962); *Contemplative Prayer* (New York: Herder and Herder, 1969); *What is Contemplation?* (Springfield: Templegate, 1978) and *Contemplation in a World of Action* (Garden City: Doubleday, 1971). For a classic treatment of prayer in the tradition of *ressourcement* with aims to develop the connection between contemplation and the mission of Christian life, see Jean Daniélou, *Prayer: The Mission of the Church* (Grand Rapids: William B. Eerdmans, 1996). For one of Jürgen Moltmann's explorations of prayer, see *The Source of Life: The Holy Spirit and the Theology of Life* (Minneapolis: Fortress Press, 1997), 125–45. Wolfhart Pannenberg, *Systematic Theology – Volume 3* (Grand Rapids: William B. Eerdmans, 1998), 202–11, is a richly pneumatological and eschatological reading of prayer. Dorothee Sölle has written extensively on prayer, including *Against the Wind: Memoir of a Radical Christian* (Minneapolis: Augsburg Fortress Press, 1999), 37–40; *The Window of Vulnerability: A Political Spirituality* (Minneapolis: Fortress Press, 1990), 93–6; and *On Earth as in Heaven: A Theology of Sharing* (Louisville: Westminster John Knox Press, 1993). Prayer is discussed by Robert W. Jenson in 'Some Platitudes about Prayer', *Dialog*, 9.1 (1970), 60–6; 'The Praying Animal', *Zygon*, 18.3 (1983), 311–25; and is worked out more systematically in *Systematic Theology – Volume 2: The Works of God* (Oxford: Oxford University Press, 1999), 58–61 and 184–5. Marjorie Hewitt Suchocki considers prayer through the lens of process theology in *In God's Presence: Theological Reflections on Prayer* (St Louis: Chalice Press, 1996). In terms of the modern Eastern Orthodox tradition, Andrew Louth explores prayer in several chapters of *Introducing Eastern Orthodox Theology* (London: SPCK, 2013) – including chapters on Christology and the doctrine of the Trinity, and throughout *Theology and Spirituality* (Oxford: Fairacres Publications, 1976). As we mentioned in Chapter 4, a strong Christology of prayer is developed in Sergius Bulgakov, *The Comforter* (Grand Rapids: William B.

Eerdmans, 2004), 371–2 and 374–6. For a profound meditation on the idea of 'God as prayer', see Kallistos Ware, *The Orthodox Way* (Crestwood: St Vladimir's Seminary Press, 1979), 105–32. And for an example of the Orthodox commitment to thinking theology through prayer, see Vladimir Lossky, *The Mystical Theology of the Eastern Church* (Crestwood: St Vladimir's Seminary Press, 1976). There is some helpful introductory material on prayer in John Anthony McGuckin, *The Orthodox Church: An Introduction to its History, Doctrine, and Spiritual Culture* (Oxford: Wiley-Blackwell, 2010). Finally, see *The Art of Prayer: An Orthodox Anthology* (London: Faber and Faber, 1997), complied by Igumen of Valamo Khariton, for a selection of writings on prayer from Greek and Russian sources, including the Philokalia.

Secondary literature

For a secondary source that explores the historical traditions of prayer in Platonic thought, see the fine set of essays edited by John Dillon and Andrei Timotin, *Platonic Theories of Prayer* (Leiden: Brill, 2016). For a study on prayer in the early church, see Paul E. Bradshaw, *Daily Prayer in the Early Church* (New York: Oxford University Press, 1982). Carol Harrison explores prayer under the category of 'listening' in chapter 6 of *The Art of Listening in the Early Church* (Oxford: Oxford University Press, 2013). Roy Hammerling (ed.), *A History of Prayer: The First to the Fifteenth Century* (Leiden: Brill, 2008) presents a wealth of highly informative material covering much of the patristic and medieval traditions. Gabriel Bunge covers the early material admirably in his classic *Earthen Vessels: The Practice of Personal Prayer According to the Patristic Tradition* (San Francisco: Ignatius Press, 2002). Mark Kiley (ed.), *Prayer from Alexander to Constantine: A Critical Anthology* (London: Routledge, 1997) is an extensive historical investigation of the prayer traditions and practices of the early church. And Santha Bhattacharji and Dominic Mattos (eds), *Prayer and Thought in Monastic Tradition: Essays in Honour of Benedicta Ward* (London: Bloomsbury, 2014) is a stimulating collection of essays devoted to the theme of prayer in the medieval period. *The Tradition of Catholic Prayer* (Collegeville: Liturgical Press, 2007), edited by the monks of Saint Meinrad, is less scholarly than Hammerling's volume and covers a broader history and set of themes but is helpfully accessible. Timothy J. Johnson (ed.), *Franciscans at Prayer* (Leiden: Brill, 2007) is unrivalled in its depth and scholarship of the period it investigates. Josef Andreas Jungmann, *Christian Prayer Through the*

APPENDIX

Centuries (London: SPCK, 2007) explores the history of prayer from its beginnings to the modern age, this time from a more liturgical perspective.

Prayer in the Bible

Oscar Cullmann, *Prayer in the New Testament* (Minneapolis: Fortress Press, 1995) is a classic treatment of the doctrine and practice of prayer in the New Testament, exploring themes such as the difficulties of praying, objections to prayer and prayer in the Synoptic Gospels, Pauline material and in John. Richard N. Longenecker (ed.), *Into God's Presence: Prayer in the New Testament* (Grand Rapids: William B. Eerdmans, 2009) covers the theme of prayer in the New Testament (and includes chapters on the Jewish tradition and an exploration of Jesus at prayer) by scholars from a wide range of confessional backgrounds. David Crump, *Jesus the Intercessor: Prayer and Christology in Luke-Acts* (Tübingen: Mohr Siebeck, 1992) is a thorough exploration of the centrality of intercession in the Lukan tradition. For a detailed exegetical study on the communal and individual dimensions of intercession, this time in dialogue with the Pauline tradition, see Gordon P. Wiles, *Paul's Intercessory Prayers: The Significance of the Intercessory Prayer Passages in the Letters of St Paul* (Cambridge: Cambridge University Press, 1974). Mathias Nygaard, *Prayer in the Gospels: A Theological Exegesis of the Ideal Pray-er* (Leiden: Brill, 2012) develops an 'anthropology of prayer' in dialogue with the prayer materials in the Gospels. Marianus Pale Hera offers an exegesis of prayer in John 17, as it relates to the person of Jesus and Christian discipleship, in *Christology and Discipleship in John 17* (Tübingen: Mohr Siebeck, 2013). For a collection of essays on prayer that reflects a more evangelical perspective exploring the 'biblical theology of prayer' as well as perspectives on prayer outside of contemporary evangelicalism (in Hinduism, Buddhism, Islam and Roman Catholicism), see D. A. Carson, *Teach Us to Pray: Prayer in the Bible and the World* (Grand Rapids: Baker, 1990). For a dedicated treatment of prayer in the Hebrew Bible, see Samuel E. Balentine, *Prayer in the Hebrew Bible: The Drama of Divine-Human Dialogue* (Minneapolis: Fortress Press, 1993); similarly, Walter Brueggemann has produced several collections of prayers drawing from the prayer traditions of the Old Testament and, particularly, the psalmody, including *Praying the Psalms: Engaging Scripture and the Life of the Spirit* (Eugene: Wipf and Stock, 2007; 2nd edn), *Great Prayers of the Old Testament* (Louisville: Westminster John Knox Press, 2008) and *Prayers for a Privileged People* (Nashville: Abingdon Press, 2008).

The Lord's Prayer

As mentioned in Chapter 4, the Lord's Prayer has received considerable scholarly attention. The following is a selection of some of the most significant. Nicholas Ayo, *The Lord's Prayer: A Survey Theological and Literary* (Oxford: Rowman and Littlefield, 2003), which includes primary text extracts from Cyprian, Gregory of Nyssa, Maximus the Confessor, Aquinas, Origen, Teresa of Ávila, Simone Weil, Augustine and Leonardo Boff, as well as an extensive bibliography of further reading on the Lord's Prayer. Roy Hammerling has written helpfully on the history of the prayer, *The Lord's Prayer in the Early Church: The Pearl of Great Price* (New York: Palgrave, 2010) and in particular on its development in the early church. Ernst Lohmeyer, *The Lord's Prayer* (London: Collins, 1965) is a canonical treatment of the topic first published in German in 1952 that draws out the eschatological and communal nature of the text. Kenneth W. Stevenson's *The Lord's Prayer: A Text in Tradition* (London: SCM Press, 2004) gives a fairly comprehensive account of the prayer through the ages. His more popular *Abba, Father: Understanding and Using the Lord's Prayer* (Norwich: Canterbury Press, 2000) is similarly reliable. N. T. Wright, *The Lord and His Prayer* (Grand Rapids: William B. Eerdmans, 1996) is a petition-by-petition analysis of the Lord's Prayer that integrates pastoral reflection and analysis of the historical context of the Lord's Prayer. Evelyn Underhill, the twentieth-century Anglican divine, wrote prolifically on the topic of prayer. For her reflections on the Lord's Prayer, see *Abba: Meditations Based on the Lord's Prayer* (London: Longmans, Green and Co., 1940) and *Prayer in Modern Life* (Oxford: Mowbray, 1930). The German Lutheran New Testament scholar Joachim Jeremias has written two short but important studies on prayer published as *The Lord's Prayer* (Philadelphia: Fortress Press, 1964) and *Abba: The Prayers of Jesus* (Philadelphia: Fortress Press, 1978). William H. Willimon and Stanley Hauerwas provide a co-authored example of what the Lord's Prayer looks like when caught up in the 'ecclesial turn', as referenced in Chapter 6: *Lord, Teach Us: The Lord's Prayer and the Christian Life* (Nashville: Abingdon Press, 1996). For a feminist engagement, see Helen Hull Hitchcock (ed.), *The Politics of Prayer: Feminist Language and the Worship of God* (San Francisco: Ignatius Press, 1992), 209–28; for postcolonial readings of the Lord's Prayer that comment on both the positive and negative consequences of the popularity of the Lord's Prayer, see Musa W. Dube Shomanah, 'Praying the Lord's Prayer in a Global Economic Era', *The Ecumenical Review*, 49.4 (1997), 439–50 and Bénézet

Bujo, *The Impact of the Our Father on Everyday Life: Meditations of an African Theologian* (Nairobi: Paulines, 2002); and for a treatment of prayer from the perspective of Latin American liberation theology, see Leonardo Boff's classic *The Lord's Prayer: A Prayer of Integral Liberation* (Maryknoll: Orbis Books, 1983).

Prayer and theology

Mark A. McIntosh, *Mystical Theology: The Integrity of Spirituality and Theology* (Oxford: Wiley-Blackwell, 1998) is an insightful investigation of the relationship between prayer and theology as it is worked out in the traditions of mystical theology. His chapter in the *Modern Theologians* ('Theology and Spirituality', in *The Modern Theologians: An Introduction to Christian Theology Since 1918*, ed. by David F. Ford and Rachel Muers (Oxford: Wiley-Blackwell, 2005; 3rd edn), 392–407) discusses what happened to this 'integrity' in the modern period and presents Simone Weil and Hans Urs von Balthasar as examples of modern theologians who break with the conventions of the time. For a great example of what theology looks like when shot through with prayer, see McIntosh's *Mysteries of Faith* (Chicago: Cowley, 2000). Unlike many other introductions to Christian theology, which too infrequently integrate prayer and doctrine, McIntosh's *Divine Teaching: An Introduction to Christian Theology* (Oxford: Wiley-Blackwell, 2007) is a valuable alternative. Martin Laird and Sheelah Treflé Hidde (eds), *The Practice of the Presence of God: Theology as a Way of Life* (London: Routledge, 2017) is an edited collection of essays exploring the integrity of prayer and theology on several levels, from several perspectives – Roman Catholic, Methodist, Anglican and Orthodox. Sarah Coakley has written extensively on the methodological rerouting of theology through prayer culminating in the first volume of her systematic theology, *God, Sexuality, and the Self: An Essay 'On the Trinity'* (Cambridge: Cambridge University Press, 2012). Other relevant works include her *Powers and Submissions: Spirituality, Philosophy and Gender* (Oxford: Blackwell, 2002); *Praying for England: Priestly Presence in Contemporary Culture*, ed. with Samuel Wells (London: Continuum, 2008); *The Spiritual Senses: Perceiving God in Western Christianity*, ed. with Paul L. Gavrilyuk (Cambridge: Cambridge University Press, 2012); and *For God's Sake: Re-Imagining Priesthood and Prayer in a Changing Church*, ed. with Jessica Martin (London: Canterbury Press, 2017). The second volume of her systematic theology project is due to be published as *Knowing Darkly: An Essay 'On the Contemplative Life'*. A foretaste of what is to come in future volumes of her systematic project, delivered as the Annie Kinkead Warfield lectures in March 2015 at Princeton Theological Seminary, can be found in 'Knowing in the Dark: Sin, Race and the Quest for Salvation, Part I: Transforming Theological Anthropology in a *Theologie Totale*', *Princeton Seminary Bulletin*, 32 (2015), 108–22. More recently and from a postmodern perspective, Andrew Prevot has reclaimed the practice of prayer as the chief response to the 'violence of modernity'. His important manifesto *Thinking Prayer: Theology and Spirituality amid the Crisis of Modernity* (Notre Dame: University of Notre Dame Press, 2015) dialogues with Martin Heidegger, Hans Urs von Balthasar, Jean-Louis Chrétien, Johann Baptist Metz, Ignacio Ellacuría and James Cone and displays in scholarly depth the kind of possibilities offered by prayer. Rowan Williams' writings sit on the exact intersection of prayer and theology that this book is attempting to articulate. See the very accessible chapter on prayer (that draws from Origen, Cassian and Gregory of Nyssa) in *Being Christian: Baptism, Bible, Eucharist, Prayer* (London: SPCK, 2014). For a more scholarly engagement around the theme of prayer, see Rowan Williams, *On Christian Theology* (Oxford: Blackwell, 2000) and for something more historical, see *The Wound of Knowledge: Christian Spirituality from the New Testament to St John of the Cross* (London: Darton, Longman and Todd, 1990; 2nd edn). Daniel Hardy and David F. Ford's, *Jubilate: Theology in Praise* (London: Darton, Longman and Todd, 1984) is less concerned with the methodological issues around the relation between theology and prayer than with the doing of theology *as* prayer, as a work of praise. Finally, *Doxology: The Praise of God in Worship, Doctrine and Life* (London: Epworth Press, 1980) by the Methodist theologian Geoffrey Wainwright is another fine, well-researched study that attemps to reorient the task of theology towards its doxlogoical end. Wainwright interacts with the liturgical movement of the second half of the twentieth century. Two key studies in this area include Aidan Kavanagh, *On Liturgical Theology* (Collegeville: Liturgical Press, 1984) and Alexander Schmemann, *Introduction to Liturgical Theology* (Leighton Buzzard: The Faith Press, 1966). For an investigation into the relation between prayer and the formation of doctrine in the early church (especially the doctrines of grace, Christology, Trinity and mariology), see Maxwell E. Johnson, *Praying and Believing in Early Christianity: The Interplay between Christian Worship and Doctrine* (Collegeville: Liturgical Press, 2013).

APPENDIX

Prayer and the Trinity

Some of the best contemporary scholarship exploring the relation between the doctrine of the Trinity and the practice of prayer include: Coakley, *God, Sexuality, and the Self*, see the third chapter for her rendition of the 'prayer-based' model of the Trinity, which draws on previously published material: Sarah Coakley, 'Why Three? Some Further Reflections on the Doctrine of the Trinity', in *The Making and Remaking of Christian Doctrine: Essays in Honour of Maurice Wiles*, ed. by Sarah Coakley and David Pailin (Oxford: Clarendon Press, 1993), 29–56 and 'God as Trinity: An Approach through Prayer', in Doctrine Commission of the General Synod of the Church of England, *We Believe in God* (London: Church House Publishing, 1987), 104–21. Coakley interacts critically with Maurice Wiles's influential work on the *lex orandi*, see Maurice F. Wiles, 'Some Reflections on the Origins of the Doctrine of the Trinity', *Journal of Theological Studies*, 8 (1957), 92–106 and *The Making of Christian Doctrine: A Study in the Early Development of Christian Doctrine* (Cambridge: Cambridge University Press, 1967), 62–93. The 'doxological trinitarian tradition', as mentioned in Chapter 3, is differently represented in the following: Jürgen Moltmann, *The Trinity and the Kingdom of God: The Doctrine of God* (London: SCM Press, 1981), 151–61; Catherine Mowry LaCugna, *God for Us: The Trinity and Christian Life* (New York: Harper Collins, 1991), 319–75; and Alan J. Torrance, *Persons in Communion: An Essay on Trinitarian Description and Human Participation* (London: T&T Clark, 1996), 307–71. Nicola Slee, 'The Holy Spirit and Spirituality', in *The Cambridge Companion to Feminist Theology*, ed. by Susan Frank Parsons (Cambridge: Cambridge University, 2003), 171–89 provides a helpful discussion of the rich potential of feminist theology to reinvigorate the doctrine of the Spirit via prayer. A. N. Williams, 'Contemplation: Knowledge of God in Augustine's De Trinitate', in *Knowing the Triune God: The Work of the Spirit in the Practices of the Church*, ed. by James J. Buckley and David S. Yeago (Grand Rapids: William B. Eerdmans, 2001), 121–46, draws out the fascinating interrelation between prayer and the Trinity in Augustine's seminal work. Christopher J. Cocksworth, *Holy, Holy, Holy: Worshipping the Trinitarian God* (London: Darton, Longman and Todd, 1997), presents a helpful articulation of the trinitarian character of worship and prayer. Francesca Aran Murphy's chapter on 'The Trinity and Prayer' in *The Oxford Handbook of The Trinity*, ed. by Gilles Emery and Matthew Levering (Oxford University Press, 2011), 505–18 explicates some of the trinitarian opportunities prayer presents in the writings of Basil of

Caesarea, Augustine, Thomas Aquinas, John Henry Newman and Hans Urs von Balthasar.

Prayer and providence

As we saw in Chapter 5, one of the most controversial aspects of the theology of prayer concerns its relation to the doctrine of providence. A classic article exploring the philosophical complexities petitionary prayer presents is Eleonore Stump, 'Petitionary Prayer', *American Philosophical Quarterly*, 16.2 (1979), 81–91. A recent contribution to the debate, again from a theistic perspective, covering metaphysical, ethical and epistemological issues is Scott A. Davison, *Petitionary Prayer: A Philosophical Investigation* (Oxford: Oxford University Press, 2017). For a more evangelical treatment, which provides a survey of ten views of providence and prayer, see Terrance L. Tiessen, *Providence and Prayer: How Does God Act in the World?* (Downers Grove: InterVarsity Press, 2000). Stanley J. Grenz, *Prayer: The Cry for the Kingdom* (Grand Rapids: William B. Eerdmans, 2005; revised edn) is a reliable guide through the thorny territory of petitionary prayer. David Crump, *Knocking on Heaven's Door: A New Testament Theology of Petitionary Prayer* (Grand Rapids: Baker Academic, 2006) offers exegeses of the relevant New Testament texts that have a bearing on the problem of petitionary prayer. For a historical study that helpfully charts the shifts in the practice of petitionary prayer in the context of American modern Protestant theology, particularly as it relates to scientific revolutions, see Rick Ostrander, *The Life of Prayer in a World of Science: Protestants, Prayer, and American Culture 1870-1930* (New York: Oxford University Press, 2000). Peter R. Baelz's two books on the topic are important contributions to the debate, if now somewhat dated: his Hulsean lectures of 1966 published as *Prayer and Providence: A Background Study* (London: SCM Press, 1968) and his more popular work *Does God Answer Prayer?* (London: Darton, Longman and Todd, 1982). See also the influential work of H. H. Farmer, *The World and God: A Study of Prayer, Providence and Miracle in Christian Experience* (London: Nisbet, 1936). The chapter on prayer in Tim Gorringe's *God's Theatre: A Theology of Providence* (London: SCM Press, 1991) is reliable and clear. Vincent Brümmer's investigation of the topic, now in its second edition, deals with a large number of the thorny issues around the relation between prayer and providence, *What Are We Doing When We Pray? On Prayer and the Nature of Faith* (Aldershot:

Ashgate, 2008; revised edn). From a more scientific perspective, see David Wilkinson, *When I Pray, What Does God Do?* (Oxford: Monarch Books, 2015). For the set-text relating to prayer in open theism, see John Sanders, *The God Who Risks: A Theology of Divine Providence* (Downers Grove: IVP Academic, 2007), 277–84. The following sources tackle the question of the relation between providence and prayer in dialogue with Aquinas: Brian Davies, *Thinking about God* (London: Geoffrey Chapman, 1985), 307–34, *The Thought of Thomas Aquinas* (Oxford: Clarendon Press, 1992), 158–84 and 'Prayer', in *The Oxford Handbook of Aquinas*, ed. by Brian Davies and Eleonore Stump (Oxford: Oxford University Press, 2012), 467–74; the essays on prayer in Herbert McCabe's *God Matters* (London: Geoffrey Chapman, 1987), 215–25 and *God Still Matters* (London: Continuum, 2002), 54–63, 64–75 and 215–18; and Paul Murray, OP, *Praying with Confidence: Aquinas on the Lord's Prayer* (London: Burns and Oaks, 2010) and *Aquinas at Prayer: The Bible, Mysticism and Poetry* (London: Bloomsbury, 2013).

On practising prayer

The Dominican theologian Simon Tugwell offers a deep set of reflections on several practices of prayer, such as petition, thanksgiving, liturgical, tongues in two short and very readable volumes on prayer, *Prayer: Keeping Company with God: Volume 1 – Living with God* and *Prayer: Keeping Company with God: Volume 2 – Prayer in Practice* (Dublin: Veritas, 1974). For a similarly rich sample of material on the practice of contemplative prayer, see the Augustinian priest Martin Laird's two books: *Into the Silent Land: The Practice of Contemplation* (London: Darton, Longman and Todd, 2006) and *A Sunlit Absence: Silence, Awareness, and Contemplation* (Oxford: Oxford University Press, 2011). The Benedictine scholar David Foster has also written an important work on contemplation, which focuses on the apophatic dimensions of the practice, published as *Contemplative Prayer: A New Framework* (London: Bloomsbury, 2015). The Franciscan spiritual author and founder of the Centre for Action and Contemplation in Albuquerque, New Mexico, Richard Rohr has written extensively on the practice of contemplation and most recently, *Silent Compassion: Finding God in Contemplation* (Cincinnati: St Anthony Messenger Press, 2014). Sarah Coakley's chapter on contemplation, 'Traditions of Spiritual Guidance: Dom John Chapman OSB (1865–1933) on the Meaning of "Contemplation"', in *Powers and Submission*, 40–54 is also worth citing as an example of a more scholarly approach to the practice of contemplative prayer. Mattá al-Miskīn has explored the practice of contemplation in the Eastern Orthodox tradition in *Orthodox Prayer Life: The Interior Way* (Crestwood: St Vladimir's Seminar Press, 2003), and for an account of contemplation from a more evangelical perspective, see Richard Foster, *Meditative Prayer* (Downers Grove: InterVarsity Press, 1999). On the popular method of meditation known as 'centering prayer', see Thomas Keating, *The Foundations for Centering Prayer and the Christian Contemplative Life* (London: Continuum, 2006) and Cynthia Bourgeault, *Centering Prayer and Inner Awakening* (Lanham: Cowley Publications, 2004). Turning from the contemplative to the active, for explorations of the political dimensions of prayer, see Karl Rahner and Johann B. Metz, *The Courage to Pray* (New York: Crossroad, 1981) and Gordon Mursell, *Out of the Deep: Prayer as Protest* (London: Darton, Longman and Todd, 1989), and for more scholarly studies, see Andrew Prevot, 'Reversèd Thunder: The Significance of Prayer for Political Theology', in *The Other Journal: Prayer* (Eugene: Cascade, 2013), 43–51 and Matthew John Paul Tan, 'Christian Prayer as Political Theory', *Politics, Religion and Ideology*, 15.3 (2014), 1–14. The writings by Thomas Merton (details listed above, under 'Modern') are also relevant in exploring the relationship between contemplation and action. For resources on praying the Jesus Prayer, see Kallistos Ware, *The Jesus Prayer* (London: Catholic Truth Society, 2014) and from an Anglican evangelical perspective, see Simon Barrington-Ward, *The Jesus Prayer* (Oxford: Bible Reading Fellowship, 2007; 2nd edn). On the practice of writing and praying intercessions, see Samuel Wells and Abigail Kocher, *Shaping the Prayers of the People: The Art of Intercession* (Grand Rapids: William B. Eerdmans, 2014). For a more scholarly treatment of the theology of intercession, see Philip Clements-Jewery, *Intercessory Prayer: Modern Theology, Biblical Teaching and Philosophical Thought* (Abingdon: Ashgate, 2005). For theological treatments of the practice of lament, see Eva Harasta and Brian Brock (eds), *Evoking Lament: A Theological Discussion* (London: Bloomsbury, 2009); Miriam J. Bier and Tim Bulkeley (eds), *Spiritual Complaint: The Theology and Practice of Lament* (Cambridge: James Clark and Co, 2014); Kathleen D. Billman and Daniel L. Migliore, *Rachel's Cry: Prayer of Lament and Rebirth of Hope* (Cleveland: United Church Press, 1999); Sally Ann Brown and Patrick D. Miller (eds), *Lament: Reclaiming Practices in Pulpit, Pew, and Public Square* (Louisville: Westminster John Knox Press, 2005); Walter Brueggemann, 'The Costly Loss of Lament', *Journal for the Study of the Old Testament*, 36 (1986), 57–71 and Emmanuel Katongole, *Born from*

Lament: The Theology and Politics of Hope in Africa (Grand Rapids: William B. Eerdmans, 2017). The history and theology of the practice of confession is dealt with in Mark J. Boda and Gordon T. Smith (eds), *Repentance in Christian Theology* (Collegeville: Liturgical Press, 2006) and Thomas A. Kane (eds), *Healing God's People: Theological and Pastoral Approaches: A Reconciliation Reader* (New York: Paulist Press, 2013). For theological discussion on the practice of praise, see Walter Brueggemann, *Israel's Praise: Doxology against Idolatry and Ideology* (Minneapolis: Augsburg Fortress Press, 1988); Hardy and Ford, *Jubilate: Theology in Praise* – referenced above; and David J. Cohen and Michael Parsons (eds), *In Praise of Worship: An Exploration of Text and Practice* (Eugene: Pickwick Publications, 2010).

Prayer in perspectives

Prayer from the perspective of the historical desert traditions has been well surveyed by Roberta Bondi, *To Pray and to Love: Conversations on Prayer with the Desert Fathers* (London: Burns & Oates, 1991); Benedicta Ward (ed.), *The Sayings of the Desert Fathers* (Oxford: Mowbray, 1984); and Rowan Williams, *Silence and Honey Cakes: The Wisdom of the Desert* (Oxford: Lion, 2003). From the Scottish Congregational tradition, see P. T. Forsyth, *The Soul of Prayer* (London: Independent Press, 1949); from the Reformed tradition, see Richard Foster, *Prayer: Finding the Heart's True Home* (London: Hodder & Stoughton, 1992); from the broadly Ignatian tradition, see Gerard W. Hughes, *God of Surprises* (London: Darton, Longman and Todd, 1985); from the Anglican tradition, see Kenneth Leech, *True Prayer: An Invitation to Christian Spirituality* (Harrisburg: Morehouse, 1980), which also explores the political dimensions of prayer discussed in Chapter 6 of this book; from the Methodist tradition, J. Neville Ward's *The Use of Praying* (Epworth: Epworth Press, 1967) is a classic as is his *Five for Sorrow Ten for Joy: Meditations on the Rosary* (New York: Seabury Books, 2005), which considers the practice of praying the rosary beyond the Roman Catholic prayer tradition; from the Benedictine tradition, see John Chapman, *Spiritual Letters* (London: Continuum, 2003) and Columba Stewart, *Prayer and Community: The Benedictine Tradition* (London: Darton, Longman and Todd, 1998); for an example from the Carmelite tradition that integrates personal narrative with reflections on Teresa of Ávila and St John of the Cross, see Ruth Burrows, *Guidelines for Mystical Prayer* (London: Burns & Oakes, 2007), see also the collection of essays complied by Keith J. Egan (ed.), *Carmelite Prayer: A Tradition for the 21st Century* (Mahwah: Paulist Press, 2002); and from the Eastern Orthodox traditions, see Brouria Bitton-Ashkelony and Derek Krueger (eds), *Prayer and Worship in Eastern Christianities, 5th to 11th Centuries* (Abingdon: Routledge, 2017); Igumen Chariton (ed.), *The Art of Prayer: An Orthodox Theology* (London: Macmillan, 1997); Tomáš Špidlík, *Prayer: The Spirituality of the Christian East – Volume 2* (Kalamazoo: Cistercian Publications, 2005) and Sonja Luehrmann, *Praying with the Senses: Contemporary Orthodox Christian Spirituality in Practice* (Bloomington: Indiana University Press, 2017).

For important contributions on the theme of prayer from the perspective of theologies of liberation, see Leonardo Boff, *Saint Francis: A Model for Human Liberation* (New York: Crossroad, 1982), *The Lord's Prayer: A Prayer of Integral Liberation* (Maryknoll: Orbis Books, 1985) and 'Spirituality and Politics', in *Liberation Theology: An Introductory Reader*, ed. by Curt Cadorette, Marie Giblin, Marilyn J. Legge and Mary H. Snyder (Maryknoll: Orbis Books, 1992), 236–43; Pedro Casaldáliga and José María Vigil, *The Spirituality of Liberation* (Maryknoll: Orbis Books, 1994); Gustavo Gutiérrez, *We Drink from Our Own Wells: The Spiritual Journey of a People* (London: SCM Press, 2005); and Jon Sobrino, *Spirituality of Liberation: Toward Political Holiness* (Maryknoll: Orbis Books, 1985). Notable feminist engagements with the theology of prayer include Marjorie Proctor-Smith, *Praying with Our Eyes Open: Engendering Feminist Liturgical Prayer* (Nashville: Abingdon Press, 1995) and Hitchcock (ed.), *The Politics of Prayer* – referenced above, which involves a feminist critique of praying 'Our Father'; and Suchocki's *In God's Presence* – also referenced above. Feminist theologies of prayer, however, are often worked out in the actual practice of prayer, examples of which include Nicola Slee, *Praying Like a Woman* (London: SPCK, 2004); Janet Morley, *All Desires Known* (London: SPCK, 2005; 3rd edn); and Margaret Rose, Jenny Te Pae, Jeanne Person and Abigail Nelson (eds), *Lifting Women's Voices: Prayers to Change the World* (New York: Morehouse, 2009).

Material exploring prayer from the perspective of postmodern theology is significant – for example, Bruce Ellis Benson and Norman Wirzba (eds), *The Phenomenology of Prayer* (New York: Fordham University Press, 2005); Theresa Sanders, 'The Gift of Prayer', in *Secular Theology: American Radical Theological Thought*, ed. by Clayton Crockett (London: Routledge, 2001), 130–40; Laurence P. Hemming, 'The Subject of Prayer: Unwilling Words in the Postmodern Access to God', in *The Blackwell Companion to Postmodern Theology*, ed. by Graham Ward (Oxford: Blackwell, 2005),

444–57; Prevot, *Thinking Prayer*; K. Jason Wardley, *Praying to a French God: The Theology of Jean-Yves Lacoste* (Abingdon: Routledge, 2016); and John D. Caputo, *The Prayers of Jacques Derrida: Religion without Religion* (Bloomington: Indiana University Press, 1997). In other discourses, see the unfinished doctoral thesis by the seminal French sociologist and anthropologist Marcel Mauss, *On Prayer: Text and Commentary* (Oxford: Berghahn, 2003), which includes ethnographic fieldwork on prayer in Australian societies. The edited collection of essays by Giuseppe Giordan and Linda Woodhead (eds), *A Sociology of Prayer* (London: Ashgate, 2015) offers wide-ranging sociological investigation of both individual prayer and the practice of prayer as it plays out in the complex conditions of late modern society. If the following publication is anything to go by, the relationship between poetry and prayer is proving especially fruitful: Francesca Bugliani Knox and John Took (eds), *Poetry and Prayer: The Power of the Word II* (London: Routledge, 2015), which is interdisciplinary, ecumenical and explores the relation on both a theoretical level and through case studies (including in Dante, R. S. Thomas and Thomas Merton). Prayer is also proving a lively dialogue partner in the field of psychology, interfaith theology, science and pastoral theology: Bernard Spilka and Kevin L. Ladd, *The Psychology of Prayer: A Scientific Approach* (London: The Guildford Press, 2013) and Leslie J. Francis and Jeff Astley, *Psychological Perspectives on Prayer: A Reader* (Leominster: Gracewing, 2001); David Marshall and Lucinda Mosher (eds), *Prayer: Christian and Muslim Perspectives* (Washington: Georgetown University Press, 2013); Fraser Watts (ed.), *Perspectives on Prayer* (London: SPCK, 2001), covers prayer and the Bible, society, science, psychology, poetry, music, sexuality and the body; and in terms of pastoral theology, see Deborah van Deusen Hunsinger, *Pray Without Ceasing: Revitalizing Pastoral Care* (Grand Rapids: William B. Eerdmans, 2006), in which she argues that prayer is 'integral to every step' of pastoral care, and Andre van Oudtshoorn, 'Prayer and Practical Theology', *International Journal of Practical Theology*, 16.2 (2012), 285–303.

INDEX

Index

Index